*Culture in the Contemporary PRC*

# Culture in the Contemporary PRC

The China Quarterly Special Issues

New Series, No. 6

*Edited by*

MICHEL HOCKX and JULIA STRAUSS

 CAMBRIDGE
UNIVERSITY PRESS

*Published by the Press Syndicate of the University of Cambridge University Press*
*The Pitt Building, Trumpington Street, Cambridge, CB2 1RP*
*40 West 20th Street, New York, NY 10011 4211, USA*
*477 Williamstown Road, Port Melbourne, VIC 3207, Australia*

*A catalogue record for this book is available*
*from the British Library*

*Library of Congress Cataloging-in-Publication Data applied for*

ISBN 0 521 681243 (paperback)

*Printed and bound in Great Britain by Infotype Ltd, Oxfordshire*

# Contents

*Cover illustration:* Performers at a ceremony announcing the slogan
for the 2008 Olympics.
Beijing, June 2005.
Photograph by Chua Chin Hon

# Notes on Contributors

MAGHIEL VAN CREVEL is professor of Chinese language and literature at Leiden University.

DEBORAH DAVIS is a professor of sociology at Yale University.

KIRK A. DENTON is associate professor of Chinese literature at The Ohio State University. He is editor of the journal *Modern Chinese Literature and Culture* and manages the MCLC Resource Center website (http://mclc.osu.edu). He is presently writing a book on the politics and ideology of museums and memorial sites in the "post" era in Greater China (postsocialist PRC, postcolonial Hong Kong, and post-martial law Taiwan).

ANTONIA FINNANE is senior lecturer in the department of history, University of Melbourne. Her most recent book is *Speaking of Yangzhou: A Chinese City, 1550–1850* (Harvard University Asia Center, 2004). She is currently working on a book called *Fashion and Modernity in China.*

RACHEL HARRIS is a lecturer in ethnomusicology at the School of Oriental and African Studies, London. She teaches undergraduate and postgraduate courses in ethnomusicology, and on the musics of Central Asia and China. Her book, *Singing the Village: Memories, Music and Ritual among the Sibe of Xinjiang* is published by Oxford University Press. Her current research focuses on the music of the Uyghurs, especially recorded music, politics, identity and change.

MICHEL HOCKX is professor of Chinese at SOAS, University of London. His research is on modern Chinese literary communities.

JEROEN DE KLOET is assistant professsor in the department of media studies at the University of Amsterdam. His research interests include Chinese popular culture and new media technologies in the context of globalization. For further details, see (http://home.tiscali.nl/jeroendekloet).

JULIA STRAUSS is the editor of *The China Quarterly* and senior lecturer in Chinese politics at the School of Oriental and African Studies, University of London.

JING WANG is S. C. Fang professor of Chinese language and culture at MIT. She is the author and editor of several books; her most recent publication is an edited volume *Locating China: Space, Place and Popular Culture* (Routledge). She is completing a book manuscript titled *Brand New China: Advertising, Media, and Commercial Culture.*

# Acknowledgements

The papers that follow were first presented at a workshop jointly sponsored by the Fairbank Center, the International Institute for Asian Studies (IIAS) and *The China Quarterly*, held at the Fairbank Center in October 2004. The aim of that workshop and of this collection was to bring together scholars working on a wide range of areas of cultural production and consumption and to present a comprehensive overview of trends in contemporary PRC culture. The material presented at the workshop sparked very lively discussion and cross fertilization of ideas, and went through several rounds of revision and review before inclusion in this special issue.

The articles in this volume include pieces on advertising, museums, poetry, fashion, music, film, the internet and consumer culture. As the list of topics illustrates, we employed a broad definition of culture, and tilted heavily, although not exclusively, towards forms of popular rather than elite culture. These articles include texts, images and objects that possess symbolic and ideological significance above and beyond their practical and monetary value, and also discuss the people and communities involved in producing, consuming and appreciating these texts, images and objects. We invited contributors whose research methods are not only empirical but also interpretative. Both in terms of substance and approach, these articles cover scholarly territory not often explored in the pages of *The China Quarterly*, yet of undeniable importance to our understanding of contemporary China.

We are very grateful to the Fairbank Center and the IIAS for their joint sponsorship of the workshop, to the Fairbank Center's Wilt Idema and Ron Suleski for being such exemplary hosts, and to our participants for being to an individual such enthusiastic and generous producers and consumers of scholarly output. We would also like to thank our external reviewer, whose constructive comments made for a much stronger volume than would otherwise have been the case.

# Introduction

## Michel Hockx and Julia Strauss

This collection offers a variety of perspectives on culture in contemporary China. We begin and end with pieces by Jing Wang and Deborah Davis on the production and consumption of culture in general, before moving on to three specific areas: visual culture, music and poetry. Jing Wang's opening piece on "bourgeois bohemians" (bobos) in China revolves around the all-important question of how taste is constructed and a multiplicity of lifestyles imagined. In China as elsewhere in the world, lifestyles are first imagined and transmitted through advertising. Wang describes how marketing campaigns propagate idealized lifestyles to different segments of China's self identified urban middle class; notably the bohemian and the *xin xin renlei*. Deborah Davis focuses on the consumption end of culture, suggesting that for all the real resentments and worries engendered by growing income inequality and job insecurity, urbanites in Shanghai experience consumer culture and the pursuit of individual taste and comfort in the home through shopping to be positive experiences, particularly when juxtaposed against the deprivations of the past. Both Wang and Davis show that the production and consumption of culture are complex phenomena that go beyond mere market manipulation. There is substantial agency involved, from urbanites joyfully participating in redecoration of their flats to the ways in which niche segments of the urban middle class separate into different "tribes."

The Braester, Denton and Finnane essays focus on different aspects of the production and consumption of visual culture: film, museums and fashion. Braester suggests that one cannot sharply differentiate commercial film from art film on the basis of content or aesthetics, as directors previously known for making art films move into commercials, and both share similar sensibilities. Braester develops the concept of cultural broker by focusing on the emerging interplay between entrepreneurial "players" (*dawan'r*) in film and their overlap with "bigshots" in other commercial realms, particularly real estate, to suggest that film, use of space and commerce in contemporary China are in a dynamic nexus between image making, market shaping and cultural identification.

The Denton piece on the evolution of contemporary museum culture probes the changes in the ways in which the state orders and legitimates its own core values through a three-dimensional form of visual culture: museums as sites of both entertainment and instruction. Here we see that a new aesthetics of space, minimalist architecture, the use of models rather than "real" historical objects and jazzy interactive sites have replaced straightforward chronologies of suffering, sacrifice and state-led development. Yet even in its replacement of heavy handed chronological narratives with lighter, thematic exhibits, the state continues to propagate a new ideology of entrepreneurship, hard work, commerce and continued economic reform.

The Finnane piece on fashion and clothing spans the realm between the visual (the catwalk and high fashion as a show) and material (everyone has to wear clothes, and what is available to wear has changed dramatically in the past 30 years in China). Here we see a range of perhaps surprising continuities from the 1920s to the present. In terms of spatial ordering, the key nodes for the production and consumption of fashion stand unchanged with the big three of Beijing, Shanghai and Guangzhou, while Chinese designers have long and only partially successfully searched to combine a form of dress both "authentically Chinese" with acclaim and recognition by the big names in international couture.

The articles on music by De Kloet and Harris include what one might consider polar opposites within contemporary music: the alternative rock scene in Beijing, and Uyghur pop in the city and countryside of Xinjiang. Yet surprising similarities crop up, despite wild differences in musical language, propagation and consumption; both are flourishing and adapting international trends in music culture in innovative ways. De Kloet argues that the alternate rock scene in Beijing has moved beyond the *liumang* hoodlum chic of the late 1980s and early 1990s to differentiate into different sub-genres: fashionable, political and nostalgic-folk. Each of these sub-genres in turn has been influenced by the wide availability of cheap *dakou* CDs supposed to have been destroyed in the West that have ended up on the Chinese market. Harris's exploration of trends in Uyghur pop music show how a variety of musical influences, from the West, Beijing, Russia, Central Asia and Pakistan, are in the process of being absorbed into Uyghur pop themes and musical practice, leading to such seemingly strange juxtapositions as Uyghur musicians as imagined Western cowboys, strumming traditional instruments to a reggae beat.

Finally, the Van Crevel and Hockx articles both consider a form of cultural production and consumption that, unlike the others considered here, normally presents itself as being almost entirely without economic benefit and independent of market "rules": poetry. While Van Crevel focuses on print media and Hockx on web-based poetry sites, both demonstrate that the contemporary poetry scene in China is thriving and adapting well to new technologies and forms of dissemination over the internet, despite the widespread perception that contemporary poetry is either totally marginal or in crisis. Van Crevel juxtaposes an "official" political lyricism with the unofficial avant-garde, starkly illustrating how different the two are, before going on to elaborate four different trends in contemporary avant-garde poetry, informed by poets' own responses through metatextual representations of themselves. Hockx compares on-line poetry communities in the United States and the People's Republic of China. Despite the obvious technological similarities between the two, he finds that there is indeed such a thing as PRC web culture. Web moderators have taken on both editorial and censorship functions, and web literature in China has a surprising set of links to print culture; unlike the United States, web-based literature often makes the leap into print, with its own specially designated section in bookstores.

*Making Sense of Contemporary Culture in the People's Republic of China: State, Market and Internationalization*

When commissioning the papers we suggested that our contributors consider three issues common to all areas involved, linking the contents of this volume to debates more commonly encountered in *The China Quarterly*: the changing role of the state, the increasing importance of the market and globalization. During the course of the conference, a fourth, even more important, theme emerged that cut across all of the articles: the role of cultural producers as gatekeepers, brokers and taste makers.

*The changing role of the state.* Throughout the Mao era, mainland Chinese cultural products were, by definition, state products. Mao-era culture is normally associated with monotony and uniformity, epitomized in the field of fashion by an actual uniform, the Mao suit. At the same time, however, the debates and power struggles within the Communist Party, leading to endless campaigns and purges among cultural workers, were anything but monotonous, and naturally occupied most of the scholarly interest in culture at this time. In Mao's China, cultural workers fortunate enough to be assigned a role in state production (and state propaganda) had advantages as well. Many had a guaranteed state income, a guaranteed audience of unprecedented size, as well as considerable social and political status. Naturally, all these advantages needed to be balanced against the constant threat of being purged, the need to pre-empt the requirements of censorship and, more generally, the psychological pressure of experiencing a lack of freedom of expression.

During the early post-Mao years cultural workers, especially avant-garde artists, poets and filmmakers, found themselves in a new and unusual position. They were granted considerably more liberties by the Deng regime, including increased access to and exchange with cultural trends outside China, yet their use of these liberties often continued to be interpreted, both by the communist regime and by foreign observers, as a political stance of dissidence. These were the days of what Jing Wang has called the "high culture fever" of the 1980s, with cultural producers, critics and theorists in all fields and genres looking for cultural answers to the question of what caused the excesses of the Cultural Revolution, enjoying unprecedented levels of independence and prominence within what was still essentially a state system. The cultural products of these "dissidents" appeared almost without exception in state-run publications or were made in state-run companies. The state and intellectuals found each other in a new, often uneasy relationship, eliminating many of the earlier disadvantages of being involved in cultural work while maintaining many of the advantages.

In the aftermath of the violent crackdown on the people's movement of 1989, the exodus of "dissidents" to the West and the radical reform of the state sector changed the cultural landscape in China almost beyond recognition, at least from a Chinese perspective. Cultural activity was marginalized in terms of social and political importance as both the state and a new generation of cultural workers lost interest in its potential for dissidence. The state adopted a much more straightforward approach to censorship, focusing more on popular culture and the mass media and no longer bothering with trying to read possibly subversive messages into obscure poems. As a result, a much more complex cultural sphere has emerged that resembles that of societies elsewhere: with the old guarantees of subsistence and captive audiences gone, the process of marketization has pushed at least some forms of high culture and indeed the very subsistence for old-style cultural workers themselves to the margin. Not surprisingly, China's cultural intellectuals, particularly those in their 50s and 60s, often perceive this situation as a form of loss: they are delighted that more freedom of expression has been gained, but sad that the prominent position of cultural intellectuals in society and politics has been eroded. Anxieties about the role of *wenren* (literati) or *zhishi fenzi* (intellectuals) in society dating back to at least the late imperial period have once again forcefully emerged, leading to a variety of responses, including, paradoxically, that of melancholy for the state-controlled system.

All articles in this collection provide evidence of the changes brought about in these different cultural sectors. Yet the authors either implicitly or explicitly caution against such crude dichotomies as a state necessarily in "retreat" before the onslaught of homogenizing market forces. As the Denton piece on museum culture clearly shows, the Chinese state is itself in a process of transformation and articulation of new ideologies such as marketization and entrepreneurialism, and retains a good deal of capacity in framing and shaping the realm of cultural production and consumption. And Rachel Harris on Uyghur popular music illustrates that direct state censorship of well-known musicians in a politically sensitive area such as Xinjiang goes far beyond what would find in other areas: what is tolerated for the avant-garde rocker in Beijing is quite another thing for the popular Uyghur crooner.

*Marketization.* As Party and state have shed their old functions of both supporting and suppressing cultural expression, many of these functions are gradually being taken over by the market. The most significant added benefit of this is of course that "suppression" by market forces does not involve political persecution. The main drawback, at least for some cultural workers, is their perception of the marginalization of high culture and its attendant loss of status. But the market has also brought about opportunities and positive changes in the cultural realm. First and foremost, the emergence of a fast-growing market economy in the PRC has led to a huge increase in consumer-oriented and profit-oriented cultural expression, such as pop music, television and advertising. Nor has the emergence of markets spelled the definitive end of all high culture: the Shanghai music conservatory fills its concert hall nearly every night, international troupes bring experimental productions of established ballets to China's major cities, and cable television maintains channels specifically designated for youth music culture and classical symphonic music. While marketization has done away with previously guaranteed state subsidies for cultural workers, it has also created increasingly segmented and specialized niches, which in turn provide a range of surprising opportunities for more traditional forms of culture to re-establish themselves in positive ways.

A good example is the publishing and book-selling industry. After the close of many of the state-run Xinhua bookshops in the early 1990s, there was a period in the mid-1990s when there were hardly any bookshops in big cities such as Beijing. By the late 1990s, an impressive number of privately owned bookshops, selling books from a wide range of state-run and private publishing houses, had been established. Moreover, these bookshops, though obviously dependent on the profits from products of popular culture in aggregate, have been offering important niches for high culture activity, involving an increasingly large number of professional, non-state-employed cultural workers who are at times referred to (and have recently come under attack) as "independent intellectuals."

It is undeniable that China's increasingly varied and diverse sectors of cultural activity are increasingly affected (some would say overwhelmed) by a combination of market principles and internationalization. Many, particularly those who either enjoyed secure livelihoods and prestige under the state sponsored cultural bureaucracy and/or deplore the materialism and "dumbing down" of cultural products, are aghast at the ongoing and seemingly unstoppable forces of commodification and globalization. Yet all the articles in this collection see a much more nuanced reality. By any standard, marketization and globalization have brought about an enormous quantity and variety of cultural material that can be produced, consumed, enjoyed and studied. The Chinese market, as pointed out by Jing Wang in the opening article, is becoming increasingly segmented and advertising strategies aimed at reaching out to the various segments of the population provide a fascinating wealth of materials to study the emergence of cultural trends and the "tribes" and targeted groups (rather than "classes") that consume them. Nor is it a zero-sum game, as lifestyle trends in first-tier cities provide models for second-tier cities to imitate, and from there to third-tier cities and county towns.

The closing article by Deborah Davis, dealing with consumer culture, holds an even more positive view towards the market reforms in China. Arguing against scholars who consider the consumer revolution in China to be on the whole disempowering, especially for those on the wrong end of the rich/poor divide, Davis uses interviews with Chinese informants to show the empowering effects of consumer culture in terms of choice and individual agency. By focusing on personal narratives *about* consumption, rather than on what is being consumed per se, Davis's paper brings us closer to the culture of those who respond to the advertising strategies studied in the opening article. Consumer culture is far from egalitarian, and individual narratives of consumption to some extent reflect the frustration and bitterness inherent to unequal access and enjoyment. But Davis's interviewees almost uniformly compare their current material circumstances and prospects for further improvements favourably with the past. The advertising and marketing schemes elaborated in the opening article may well be ploys, but the desire to create a comfortable living space is real, and marketization has created a realm of consumer choice that individuals experience as expanded autonomy, pride and empowerment.

The market also offers new opportunities to those wishing to cross over between different genres of cultural production. The article by Yomi Braester, though mainly dealing with film, employs the concept of the "cultural broker," individuals employing a variety of market strategies to increase the impact (and profits, of course) of cultural products by selling them to other segments of the market. So filmmakers increasingly make, and star in, television commercials; "realistic" and critically acclaimed filmmakers shoot promotional videos for slick real estate developments, whose owners themselves often fund new film projects. And commodification (major brand names that cannot be explicitly labelled as such) and the globalization of the film industry itself (the "Big Shot" of *Big Shot's Funeral* is, tellingly, the Western movie star Donald Sutherland) are parodied in feature commercial films for an audience whose taste is sophisticated enough to understand the parody of the cult of brand names.

A clear market principle is also at work, perhaps somewhat unexpectedly, in the socially marginalized but decidedly avant-garde world of rock music, discussed by Jeroen de Kloet. De Kloet focuses on the huge popularity of so-called *dakou* CDs, excess or "substandard" Western CDs with a hole punched in them (*da kou*) to indicate that they should be destroyed, after which they illegally end up on the Chinese market, where they are sold for (equally illegal) profit. Access to *dakou* versions of Western rock music has, as De Kloet shows, provided a group identity for an entire generation of Chinese rock musicians. This leads to significant cultural cross-fertilization, as different sub-genres of rock musicians draw on the influences circulating on the street from an assortment of *dakou* CDs "either censored from the market or deemed too marginal by China's music distributors." In contemporary rock culture we see at work some of the trends suggested by De Kloet's discussion of consumer culture: that through commodification, the *dakou* sub-culture ironically gains subversive power in contrast to dominant culture and state supported versions of marketization.

The increased variety in modes of expression, the residual presence of the state and the access to new media and new audiences are all discussed in Maghiel van Crevel's paper on contemporary poetry, which starts out by contrasting an example of the still existing official (*guanfang*) version of poetry with a work from the PRC's most outspoken poetic avant-garde, showcasing two extremes that encompass a huge spectrum of poetic activity. Despite its marginalized position, Van Crevel argues, poetry flourishes as never before in the PRC and is slowly coming to terms with, and starting to use to its own advantage, the challenge of the new (mass) media. Significantly, the avant-garde poem that opens Van Crevel's article was published, like many other works of the contemporary avant-garde, on the internet.

*Globalization: which market and whose culture?* The impact of global trends is present throughout Chinese society but perhaps nowhere as ardently debated, and directly used, as in cultural circles, and most of the articles reflect this. China's intellectual elite, like that of many other countries, appears to be increasingly anxious about the loss of national cultural identity that comes with globalization, understandably if not entirely accurately perceived most commonly as Westernization. Many of the culture debates in China are now raging on the internet, in chat rooms and on bulletin boards. The internet itself is of course the most pertinent symbol of globalization, as its technologies and protocols spread rapidly around the globe and especially rapidly around the PRC. But Michel Hockx's exploration of the recent popularity of "web literature" (*wangluo wenxue*) and online poetry communities in the PRC suggests that, despite the obvious globalization and standardization of hardware and software in running websites, the actual output of the Chinese community contains many elements that are culturally specific, indeed identifiably "Chinese," from the ways in which online poetry communities cross over into print media to the ways in which issues of censorship are not foregrounded, despite the continued tendency of Western scholarship to emphasize them.

Similar concerns are discussed in the article on fashion by Antonia Finnane, which neatly illustrates this collection's themes of marketization and globalization. The fashion industry is of course extremely close to the clothing manufacturing industry: one historically builds on the other, and both are very close to what their respective market segments "demand." Yet the Chinese fashion industry is plagued with twin anxieties: producing fashion that is both "authentically cultural" and critically well received and respected in the big Western fashion houses. Providing a very informative comparison between the current Chinese fashion industry and that of the Republican period, Finnane demonstrates how Chinese fashion designers have long struggled to find ways to express "Chineseness" – typically through the "tyranny of the *qipao*" – within a highly globalized but also highly segmented industry well policed by a small cohort of gatekeeping tastemakers outside China who on the whole have been much more responsive to Japanese than Chinese designers. While Chinese producers of ready-to-wear apparel have in aggregate "taken over the world" and done very well, the rarefied high end of design and fashion have struggled to incorporate authenticity with the international fashionista's constant demand for novelty with each year's collection.

The papers by Rachel Harris and Kirk Denton, on the Uyghur music scene in Xinjiang and on museum culture, most clearly address all three of these main themes. The practices of Uyghur musicians in Xinjiang are shown to be changing under the influence of the local music industry, the import of foreign CDs and a continued state presence. Then again, what is shown perhaps most clearly by all these papers is that there no longer are ways to speak of "Chinese culture" as confidently as was possible during periods of excessive state control and cultural as well as economic autarky. The legacy of that period, the way it is represented and how such representations change as Chinese society changes, is the topic of Denton's paper on museum culture. Focusing on museums and memorial sites dealing with modern history and the history of the communist revolution, Denton traces the recent boom in museum culture and discusses in detail the novel ways in which these often still state-run institutions continue to tell the Party's historical narrative. The state is still very much present in contemporary museum culture, but its presence is less stark and obvious. Museums and memorials are now housed in expensive new buildings, overlaid with glitzy multimedia presentations, and look increasingly like contemporary museums more or less any-where; but their content remains the product of negotiation between curators and Party officials. In this field, too, however, Denton identifies increasing segmentation and the existence of niches that allow for alternative stories to be told.

In all these articles, globalization and the way it creates new market niches and opportunities is a force to be reckoned with for cultural production (and subsequent marketing). Globalization interacts with par-ticular cultural sectors in unanticipated ways: from the *dakou* CDs dumped on the streets of Beijing to the worries expressed by wannabe high fashion designers, to the adoption of chord progressions in flamenco music among Uyghur musicians, to avant-garde rockers keen to develop rock with Chinese characteristics. This undeniably gives rise to under-standable anxieties about cultural authenticity. But the cultural products resulting from the opportunities made available by this kind of cross-fertilization are often interesting and even popular: the source of one individual's set of cultural anxieties is often that of another's enjoyment (whether through boho minimalist chic, new and vibrant forms of musical expression, or museums that are actually fun to go to).

Culture in contemporary China also shows evidence of "glocalization"; the combination of global trends with resolutely local contexts and meanings. So the new museum of Shanghai history participates in global trends of museum design and management while reifying Shanghai's particular local history, and Uyghur popular music incorporates the Gipsy Kings while preserving motifs of Uyghur nostalgia for homeland and a receding way of rural life. And the "big three" centres of fashion and design (Beijing, Shanghai and Guangzhou) all retain undeniably local flavours, even as they all aspire to global recognition and respect. Some cultural products (music, film and clothing) travel across borders much more easily than others (poetry), and this in turn has the potential to shape both markets and the rise of new gatekeeping tastemakers and cultural brokers. The internet itself can be understood as reflection of, metaphor for, and disseminator of globalization. These articles confirm quite con-clusively, though, that globalization cannot be understood as a form of either cultural or market neo-imperialism that is resulting in blandness and homogenization. Cultural producers and consumers in contemporary

China are a vibrant and innovative lot, who work creatively with new materials, seize market and cultural opportunities, and blend the traditional and the cutting edge, often in unusual and innovative ways.

In addition to our original three commissioned themes, most of the articles collected here touch upon the emergence of a new generation of Chinese cultural producers, consumers and gatekeepers, sometimes referred to as *xin xin renlei* ("Generation X"), who feel very much at home in the complicated and segmented world of culture that has emerged in the PRC. Displaying little interest in politics, little respect for high culture and sensing little distinction between what is actual and what is virtual, this generation increasingly determines what is "happening" in PRC culture. Arguably more post-socialist than post-modern, they also pose new challenges to researchers based in the West, who not only need to come to terms with the practices of new media and new genres but also have to suppress their instinctive tendency to discuss PRC culture within a framework of (resistance to) state control. For example, the capital and investment requirements for film production are enormous, so it should come as no great surprise that the networks of film producers are now increasingly intertwined with those of big real estate developers – that is where the money is. The stakes in film development are high, but so are the rewards if a popular hit is produced, particularly so if it is distributed internationally. At the other end of the spectrum, the consumers and producers of contemporary Chinese poetry are a fairly small group, and in at least some networks, producers, consumers and gatekeepers are likely to know each other personally. Yet despite the lack of a mass audience, the avant-garde poetry scene is an incredibly vibrant one, with a small but committed group of producers, a somewhat larger but still small group of consumers, and a variety of material products ranging from the glossily luxurious for beautifully bound volumes to production costs down to nearly zero for web-based poetry.

This collection provides an initial attempt to introduce new themes, new materials and new perspectives into research on Chinese culture. While we cover a great deal of territory, we are well aware that there are many more topics in contemporary culture of equal interest that merit consideration: fine art and painting, classical music and opera (both Western and traditional), dance, forms of literature other than poetry, and dramatic performance, to name just a few. We hope that other scholars will follow where we leave off.

# Bourgeois Bohemians in China?
# Neo-Tribes and the Urban Imaginary*

## Jing Wang

ABSTRACT This article treats an understudied subject in popular culture studies: the mutual feed between lifestyle cultures and marketing through an examination of the bobo fever in urban China. How did an imaginary class of "bourgeois bohemians" emerge in a country where the bourgeois base is statistically small and where the bohemian equation is non-existent? To shed light on this pop-culture-turned-marketing-fad syndrome, the article introduces the concept of the "neo-tribes" and maps the pathways that link style cultures to consumer segmentation. A couple of critical questions arise from this exercise. First, is the separability of taste from class symptomatic of a "Chinese leap of faith"? And secondly, is the hottest market segment today – the "neo-neo-tribes" – preparing us to address the convergence of a global youth culture?

If American economist Thorstein Veblen lived in urban China today he would be very impressed. Nowhere else would he find such a large population so eager to practise his theory of "pecuniary emulation."[1] Why did Louis Vuitton, Prada, BMW and Fendi all regard China as the centre of turbo-growth? It is because their near-term investment will be paid off "in secondary cities like Dalian, Shenyang, and Chengdu, where second-tier status as a city translates into *first-tier* desires by the residents."[2] You are what you consume. That is, consumption is built on a tiered logic: for those situated lower on the hierarchy, there is no faster way of acquiring social prestige than emulating the lifestyle of those higher up. In August 2002 when I finished my internship at Ogilvy,[3] "third-tier" cities (southern county towns) had already entered the marketing lingo, conjuring up the scenario that average residents in affluent county townships will soon be catching up with second-tier desires.[4] A game of musical chairs was set in motion, with lower tiers busy making an urban imaginary that is always already a tier higher. All this, I would propose, is the social logic of consumption Veblen elucidates so well in *The Theory of the Leisure Class*.

---

* This article is an excerpt from my book project *Brand New China: Advertising, Media, and Commercial Culture*. The original book chapter was first presented at the "Urban Imaginaries" international conference at Lingnan University, Hong Kong, in May 2004.
1. Thorstein Veblen, *The Theory of the Leisure Class: An Economic Study in the Evolution of Institutions* (New York: Dover Press, 1994).
2. First-tier cities are Beijing, Shanghai and Guangzhou. Stan Stalnaker's *Hub Culture: The Next Wave of Urban Consumers* (Singapore: John Wiley & Sons (Asia) Pte.Ltd., 2002), p. 175 is extremely useful for my attempt to theorize the tiered logic of consumption.
3. I worked at Ogilvy in Beijing for two summers in 2002 and 2004 in the Department of Strategic Planning.
4. Second-tier cities are Nanjing, Chengdu, Wuhan, Hangzhou, Shenyang, Tianjin and large provincial centres. Third-tier cities are sizeable southern county towns (*zhongxin cheng*) like Changzhou.

This article deals with an understudied topic in the field of popular cultural studies: the mutual imbrication between lifestyle cultures and marketing. Marketing is often the missing link in studies of the relationship between popular culture and consumer culture. By concentrating on the Chinese bobo discourse, I wish to accomplish two goals. The first is to examine the logic of market segmentation that fuels the engine of emulative spending. More specifically, an analysis of the proliferating tribal discourses in China will map the pathways that link lifestyle cultures to consumer segmentation. The second is to treat the bobo discourse both as a pop cultural and a marketing phenomenon. I look at the contemporary mutation of the anthropological concept "tribe" into a new marketing term *zu* or *zuqun* ("neo-tribe"), and the challenge this new term poses to the old notion of "subculture." I hope to demonstrate that without delimiting and naming the target segment for a product, the engine of emulation could not get started. For emulation is made possible through the consumer's identification with a given sociocultural segment, or "tribe." To flesh out this "tribal" logic of consumerism, this article looks at the higher end of the consumption ladder in urban China. This is an imaginary space criss-crossed by various funny acronyms evolving around the concept of the "neo-tribes." The article examines the Chinese "bobos" and *xin xin renlei* (the "neo-neo-tribe") and examines the real and imaginary benchmarks for membership for each tribe.

If consumption is conceived as an upward spiral movement that progresses tier by tier, as pointed out above, what do the upper echelons do? Sit on top of the ladder waiting for those below them to close up the ranks? That is hardly the case. An upscale marketer's job is largely defined by tactics of hairsplitting those further up the social hierarchy into tiny market segments. Those niche segments serve to set themselves apart not only from mass consumers but also from each other. At first glance, the myriad "tribal" discourses now mushrooming in urban China seem nothing more than novel marketing strategies targeted at the newly affluent. However, whether marketers can create wants, as the 1960s mass culture critique would have us believe, is no simple question with a quick answer. Contemporary cultural producers themselves do not have such faith in their power of controlling the mind of consumers as their counterparts in the early 1900s did.[5] As a society grows more affluent, successful marketing depends increasingly upon unearthing consumers' own preference and desire and then selling it back to them. The tribal logic, for instance, would have no purchase if it had not tapped into the existing anxieties of the socially privileged. What are their anxieties? To be caught up by the emulative mass consumers. That is to suggest that those further up on the social ladder – neo-tribes like the bobos – play the game of differentiation as fervently as those down under. In

---

5. A typical viewpoint of the marketers can be seen in Richard Ohmann's "Knowing/ creating wants," in Richard Ohmann (ed.), *Making and Selling Culture* (Hanover & London: Wesleyan University Press, 1996), pp. 224–238.

consumerism, differentiation and emulation are two sides of the same coin. China is no exception.

*The Bobo Fever*

These are highly educated folk who have one foot in the bohemian world of creativity and another foot in the bourgeois realm of ambition and worldly success. The members of the new information age elite are bourgeois bohemians. Or, to take the first two letters of each word, they are Bobos.[6]

David Brooks's *Bobos in Paradise* is a comic sociology about the rise of America's new elite in an age of knowledge economy and its impact on American upscale culture. Who would have guessed a facetious celebration of the wedding between 1960s counterculture and the 1980s over-achievement craze would trigger a bobo fetishism in China? In September 2002, the Chinese translation of the book arrived in major cities and became an instant best seller. *Xiaozi*, "petty bourgeoisie," a term trendy only a year before, became passé overnight. "Everybody else is already a bobo, what are we waiting for?!" As 2002 drew to an end, the bobo became a Chinese poster child without a hint of irony.

A Chinese word *bobo* was coined to sound almost exactly like the English word. But many others resort to an indigenized version of the original – *"bubo"* – a combination of the first syllable of the two Chinese words, *buerqiaoya* (bourgeois) and *boximiya* (bohemia). The term advanced to the No. 3 slot on the list of top ten internet words in China in 2002, trailing "keep pace with the times" and "the Three Representatives."[7]

A small café near South-east University in Nanjing named itself Bobo Café, a perfect example of a second-tier city teeming with first-tier desires. There was at least one website *Xici hutong* (www.xici.net) that once posted a bobo page and provided advice on how bobos are supposed to act, on where to find them and how to become one. After answering some multiple choice questions (such as "are you satisfied with your life?" and "what do you think of Italian fashion?"), web surfers could assess their potential for being a bobo.[8] In the capital, businessman Zhang Luzi opened the DIY@bobo Bar to provide a home for this new social group. There was also a short-lived Bobos Club in Beijing that sponsored lectures on *fengshui* and other topics related to "spirituality." The list goes on and on. A bobo marketing craze appeared in first, second and third tier cities and an entertaining debate unfolded in the press and on the internet.

---

6. David Brooks, *Bobos in Paradise: The New Upper Class and How They Got There* (New York & London: Simon & Schuster, 2000), pp. 10–11.
7. Paul Mooney, "Bobos in Shangri-La," *Newsweek* (Atlantic Edition), 3 March 2003, http://www.pjmooney.com/bobosnwk.shtml, accessed in April 2004.
8. "Zhongguo 'bubozu': dangdai bei faxian de dushi buluo" ("Chinese bobos: an urban tribe waiting to be discovered"), www.sina.com.cn, 12 December 2002, accessed in 2004.

First, a sampler of advertising copies that cashed in on the bobo fever:

*Alcatel OT715*

Have you ever heard of "bobos"? ... a social group in search of freedom, challenges and spiritual fulfilment. They are keen on creating the genuine meaning of life for themselves. A bobo demands the best from life. They are seeking products of exquisite taste and quality, but more importantly, of products that display character and an essence of free spirit. Bobos have been looking everywhere for an ideal cell phone. Not until now did they spot the new Alcatel OT715 ... It combines the 1970s retro style of elegance and the cool attitude of the 21st century ..."[9]

*Legend Solei Notebook E100*

A well-cultivated person will not stoop to compete for the No. 1 place with average Joes and Janes. A bobo is well-cultivated. His notebook displays a style of simplicity. Bobos love country folk, a weathered fisherman, a craftsman in the remote country-side, or a short and plump artist who dances simple folk dances and sings simple folk songs. For bobos, those simple-minded country people look serene and peaceful. Although they are poor, they live a rich life ... Corresponding to the fundamental spirit of the bobos is the simple but smart looking E100. It is clothed in simple dark blue, but its keyboard and LCD screen shines in fashionable silver. A contradictory colour scheme like this matched with a daring design delivers to the bobos a jazzy sense of romance.[10]

*Bobo International, Changsha, Hunan Province*

In Bobo International, you get a perfect view of the mountains and hear the sound of the Xiang River gently stroking the banks. If you want to snack, turn on the electric burners. In a few minutes, you will be enjoying a drink with your beloved under the moonlight – over a few simple appetizers"[11]

From category to category, from copy to copy, the word "bobo" and its affinities delivered a single message: premium value. If you spot some tongue-in-cheek humour in the advertising copies above, be assured irony has no place in marketing plans in China. Chinese boboism retained none of Brooks's satirical edge. What reads like a parody to non-target segments (cultural theorists like myself) actually touched a chord in China's fad enthusiasts who are searching for a lifestyle breakthrough. Many such bobo campaigns (like the one cited below) went way over the top. You would have to wonder where the Bohemian part of the equation went.

9. " 'Bubozu' de xin chonger: Aerkate OT715" ("The new pet toy for bobos: Alcatel OT715"), http://topdigital.vip.sina.com/.../products/200208, 2002, accessed in 2004.

10. "Yidong bobo zu, Lianxiang zhaoyang E100 xuanchu xin jingying linian" ("Mobilizing the bobo tribe: Legend's zhaoyang notebook E100 promoted the concept of the new elite), www.sina.com.cn, 19 November 2003, accessed in 2004.

11. "Bobo guoji: chengshi jingying de lixiang jiayuan" ("Bobo international: the ideal abode for city elite"), http://jrnb.rednet.com.cn, 19 November 2003, accessed in 2004.

## The Guangzhou Project: Searching Online for Bobo Prospects

The corporation in question, let us call it S Real Estate, is located in Guangzhou. It singled out bobos as its target clients. To pare down advertising expenditure, the company relied on the internet for promotions. They devised an elaborate communications plan. To identify the target segment and attract their attention, several online activities were launched simultaneously: a search for bobos in Guangzhou; a contest for the ten coolest bobos in Guangzhou; a web editorial called "Bobos and their poetic lives"; an online serialized story penned by a fictional bobo living in the S apartment complex – "Love soars on the wings of poetry: the confessions of a bobo"; a FLASH animation site advertising the "happy life style of bobos" and the brand essence of the S apartments (happy life = freedom + wealth + mindfulness).

The maximum impact of this communications plan can be gauged from the questionnaires for the online bobo search:

1. Are you looking for something cool about a refrigerator rather than its cooling function when you are shopping for one?
2. Are you one of those who often wear hiking boots and ski glasses or some unconventional gear to work?
3. Will you be willing to give up your job at the drop of a hat and go to a far-off place for a month?
4. Do you feel that being single for the rest of your life is no big deal?
5. You are an atheist. But one day do you fall in love and feel that it is God's will?
6. Isn't it unbearable if your living space does not give you a poetic sense of life?
7. Is it a torture to live in a place that looks just like any other place without a personality?

If you answer "yes" to *any* of the questions above, contact the S Corporation immediately. You are a prospective bobo qualified for some incentive awards comprised of a surprise gift and a complimentary day trip to the S apartment complex. And mind you, if you are interested in running for the "ten coolest bobos" championship in Guangzhou, all you have to do is to enter a prose-writing contest by submitting the most "poetic" and "personality building" experience you have ever had. A selection panel will pass the verdict. The ten winners will be given the title of *Bubo jueshi* – Sir Bobos![12]

## The Debate: Bursting the Bubos

Not everyone, of course, was buying the trend and falling for overblown marketing ploys. After the initial fanfare waned a little, Beijing's most authoritative lifestyle magazine, *Life Weekly*, was quick to point out that there are very few bobos in China. Others, like Ye Ying, editor of "Lifestyle" at *The Economic Observer*, were reluctant to underestimate the appeal of bobo lifestyle to urban youth.[13] It is most likely,

12. Lin Jingxi, "Xiaohu xing bailing gongyu wangluo xingxiao tuiguang fang'an" ("The marketing case of a small-sized white collar apartment complex"), http:house.focus.cn/newshtml/51716.html, 23 September 2003, accessed in 2004.
13. Ye Ying,"Logo de liliang" ("The power of logo"), *Sanlian shenghuo zhoukan* (*Life Weekly*), No. 233 (23 March 2003), http://www.lifeweek.com.cn/2003–05–06/000015155.html, accessed in April 2004.

she predicted, that the fever will linger, and I add, especially at places where there is a critical mass of the nouveau riche. This observation may not be far-fetched especially in the changing social climate of the post-Jiang Zeming era. The original bobo spirit – an affluent class opposed to soulless materialism – did touch a raw nerve in China's rising social elite.

The social value of affluence in a socialist country is never stable. In 2003 and 2004, being labelled "rich" brought mixed blessings. Closer social scrutiny was but one small inconvenience the rich had to endure. It was the guilt trip that took away the pleasure of being an upstart. A new generation of Party leaders was touting the politically correct slogan "social justice" (*shehui gongzheng*), holding back, at least in theory, the ethos of mindless materialism. Media attention was lavished on the "*san nong* problems" (peasants [*nongmin*], villages [*nongcun*], and agriculture [*nongye*]). President Hu Jintao moved "poverty alleviation" and "social conscience" to the top of the national agenda. Premier Wen Jiabao made headlines in the early months of 2004 with a personal campaign helping rural migrants to collect overdue wages. The social impact of all this was a discursive backlash on the new rich and their unconscionable behaviour. Paul Mooney's report in *Newsweek* quotes a Beijing writer saying: "People look down on the nouveau riche, and that's why [the] Chinese are keen to add the bohemian title."[14] There are numerous instances emphasizing the social costs of materialism gone berserk. In 2003, a second-degree murder trial involving a rich woman running over a peasant in her BMW stirred up media furore. In 2004, the murder of four dorm mates at Yunnan University by poor peasant student Ma Jiajue triggered another round of social criticism. This time, the materialistic society at large was blamed for its indifference to a tortured student trapped in extreme poverty and driven to insanity. It is fair to say that although "wealth" will never become a stigma for the rich in the same way as "poverty" to the poor, the Chinese court of public opinion has sentenced the unconscionable rich "guilty," signalling a profound shift of the collective emotional identification away from the nouveau riche to the old and new poor. The bobo phenomenon thus provided China's new elite with the possibility that materialism can be reconciled with spirituality, elite status with egalitarian ideals.

The fever, interestingly, struck a chord with social critics as well. It rejuvenated a perennial question: just how large is China's "bourgeoisie"? China has never had bohemians, but should the bourgeois side of the equation for bobos be taken for granted? *Life Weekly* debunked both the old and new myth: "Perhaps China does not have real bobos because the Chinese 'middle class' has not been fully formed."[15] The editors went on in a satirical vein, saying that *bu* (bourgeois) is what the Chinese are really after, and *bo* (bohemian) is but sham and disposable. If we have to perform a social reading on the S Real Estate

14.  Mooney, "Bobos in Shangri-La."

15.  Miao Wei, Lu Xiaoxun *et al.*, "Bobozu yu 'xin wenhua yundong' " ("The bobos and the 'new culture movement' "), *Sanlian shenghuo zhoukan*, No. 47 (25 November 2002), http://www.lifeweek.com.cn/2003–04–08/000013313.html, accessed in April 2004.

advertising discussed above, it certainly validates such an insight. Could it be that the bobo discourse travelled well in China because it pinpointed the double lack? Rule No. 1 in the Great Book of Consumption: naming a lack is the fastest way to guarantee its quick rise in demand.

### In Search of the "Middle Class"

The bourgeoisie question predictably elevated bobo discourse to a level of discussion to which only serious sociological researchers could respond. But the transition of a lifestyle topic into a sociological one had not occurred. Nor was the challenge posed by *Life Weekly* answered by cultural critics. By spring 2004, not many follow-up discussions on the controversy had reached the public arena. One reason could be that the public's attention was diverted from the question of the "middle class" to the new benchmark for social stratification, *xiaokang* (the "comparatively well-to-do," a cut below the middle class). Clearly, although south China has a bigger stake in promoting the discourse of the "middle class," the north and the rest of the country are drawn to *xiaokang* as a policy concept that is deemed more relevant for its less affluent population.

The middle-class question, however, demands attention not least because it too often got lost in ideological clutter. The major characteristic of Chinese boboism resides precisely in its promoters' belief in the separability of class from taste. While David Brooks's American boboism is unmistakably a caste phenomenon and fundamentally a class formation, Chinese boboism as a thriving social imaginary did not correspond to the bobos as a real social class. However, the statistics of the Chinese middle class provided much fuel to those critics who debunk the bobo phenomenon. They uphold that the future of boboism hinges on whether there is a bourgeois base to begin with. Seen in that perspective, the bourgeois equation is essential for boboism to take root in China and is worthy of critical attention.

A research report published in 2004 provides statistics on the Chinese middle class.[16] Four criteria are outlined in modern sociology to assess whether one belongs to the middle class: by professional status; by income; by patterns of lifestyle consumption; and by subjective cognition. The data for the Chinese study were collected by a research team at the Chinese Academy of the Social Sciences engaged in a study called "Structural Changes of Contemporary Chinese Society." Between November and December 2001, the team collected data from people between 16 and 70 years old living in 12 provinces and special municipalities, and 73 districts and counties. At the end of the research period, they derived 6,193 valid samples.

16. Li Chunlin, "Zhongchan jieceng Zhongguo shehui zhide guanzhu de renqun" ("The middle class: a Chinese social group worthy of our attention") in Ru Xin, Lu Xueyi and Li Peilin (eds.), *2004: Zhongguo shehui xingshi fenxi yu yuce* (*2004: Analysis and Forecast on China's Social Development*) (Beijing: Sheke wenxian chuban she, 2004), pp. 51–63.

First, 15.90 per cent of those surveyed can be categorized as middle class by profession (*zhiye zhongchan*). Five professions – Party and political officials, business managerial class, private entrepreneurs, technical skilled labour, and office workers – are labelled "white collar" professions. Secondly, 24.6 per cent are middle class by income. There is no standard mean for all the regions surveyed. Income gaps are huge between different places. If the *national* income index was used as the standard for social classification there would be some very odd results: those living in the metropolis whose economic condition is inferior would be categorized as "higher income earners," and those who are relatively wealthy in underdeveloped regions might be grouped into "low income earners." It is therefore necessary that the "mean" is calculated on a regional rather than national basis. The survey areas were divided into six regions: developing cities, towns and districts; comparatively well-developed towns, cities and districts; underdeveloped cities, towns and districts; developing villages and rural areas; well-developed villages and rural areas; and underdeveloped rural areas. The research team derived the average figure of an individual's monthly income region by region. Those whose income rose above the mean in each region were counted as the "middle class," those below the mean were not.

Thirdly, 35 per cent of those surveyed are middle class by standards of consumption and lifestyle. Like the income index, a universal standard for the "middle-class lifestyle" is hard to define, let alone to achieve, in a country as culturally diverse as China. Li Chunling and her research team argue that with some exceptions seen among middle-aged and young people in metropolises, "so-called middle class culture has not appeared in China." Since a specific standard of "cultural" consumption was absent, the researchers developed an elaborate point system for measuring each household's capacity for consuming medium-range and luxury goods. "Middle-class lifestyle goods" were divided into four categories: necessity electric appliances (such as colour television, refrigerator, washing machine); medium-level consumer goods (such as telephone, mobile phone, CD player, microwave, air-conditioner); luxury goods (such as computer, camcorder, piano, motorcycle); and automobile. Each of the items listed in the first two categories is worth one point; in the third category four points; while households that own a car get 12 points. The "consumer middle class" (*xiaofei zhongchan*) resulted from the calibration and comparison of the total scores earned by each household. The 35 per cent figure, however, failed to acknowledge the wide gaps of consumption pattern between urban and rural China (50.2 per cent and 25.1 per cent respectively) and between generations (young people between 21 and 30 scored 41.8 per cent and the older generation 24.1 per cent).

The last category, "subjective cognition," yields the largest percentage. As many as 46.8 per cent of those surveyed considered themselves a member of the "middle class." Gender difference is minimal in this category. Schooling also matters little. Interestingly, 40.8 per cent of those who had not gone beyond primary school education identified themselves with the middle class, compared to 72.9 per cent of college graduates. Approximately 31.1 per cent of those who never went to school considered themselves "middle class" as well.

These are decent statistic figures. However, if the four criteria are combined to arrive at a comprehensive index for the middle class, then the percentage of Chinese bourgeoisie drops to 4.1–6.0 per cent. Even in big cities, the percentage is as low as 8.7–12.0 per cent. That is, the percentage of Chinese who are white-collar workers, whose income falls into the medium range, whose consumption level reaches the median and who at the same time identify themselves as middle class is only a little above ground-level.

### Class or Taste? A Leap of Faith

Instead of asking "where are the Chinese bobos?" one may now ponder "where are the Chinese bourgeoisie?" It seems that the country has a long way to go before a real caste with an economic power equal to that of the American yuppies-turned-hippies (American bobos) will emerge. Meanwhile, the bobo as an urban imaginary and marketing in the name of bobo seems to have paid off. That is a Chinese paradox. Nothing seemed to stop the Chinese from indulging themselves in a social imaginary that fans their dream of being part of the global, "cosmopolitan" culture.

Bobo fever was indicative of one symptom that I will call "a leap of faith in the separability of taste from 'class' " (as in *jieji*). Chinese cultural brokers sold boboism in China as a lifestyle fad rather than a product of a class culture. Does it really matter if China does not have bobos as long as upscale consumers wear the bobo lifestyle on their sleeves? Marketers couldn't care less. But it is fascinating that China's society commentators were oblivious to the real meat in *Bobos in Paradise* – the historical rise of the bobo in America as a distinct class of its own. Granted that David Brooks argues that bobos' meritocratic culture thrives on blurring class distinctions and that he debunks Marx's theory of "class conflict," a close reading of his book provides a detailed sociological profile of a new, dominant American establishment class, which, in his words, defines the "parameters of respectable opinion and taste."[17]

There is much to speculate about the characteristic of Chinese bobo fever as a discourse that decouples the bobo "class" from the bobo "taste." That phenomenon was no fluke. The popularity of *Bobos in Paradise* and other similar books about lifestyle choices points to a cultural symptom prevalent in 2000s China. Urban China was over-crowded with social trends that usually emerge in *post*-affluent societies in the West. How can Chinese consumers appreciate "one-downmanship" when they have not had enough practice of "one-upmanship"? Questions like taste, the "freedom" of lifestyle choices and "one-downmanship"

---

17. Brooks, *Bobos in Paradise*, pp. 41–46.

came to plague a country where only some 4.1 to 6 per cent were deemed middle class in 2004. Before wealth accumulates and trickles down to the masses, anxieties of abundance have already hit taste fanatics and the would-be bobos. Gaps between the post-affluent urban imaginary and the social real continued to widen as the fights between society commentators and social critics stormed on. This is probably quite a fascinating spectacle for Western trend spotters. But for the majority of Chinese for whom social classes conflict rather than blur, the urban imaginary closing in upon them seems to be spinning out of control. But then one might say, when is China *not* in crisis? And bobo fever was surely a passing trend already overtaken by other flashier neo-tribes.

## Bobos as a Market Segment

In many regards, urban China is an endless fashion race trying to beat escalating turnovers. The protagonists came and went. But the marketers stayed. From probing bobo fever as a popular cultural syndrome, this section examines it as a marketing phenomenon. In fact, some of the shrewdest observations about bobo fever were made by marketers. In April 2003, a group of 18 of them gathered at Beijing's Postmodern Tower for a brainstorming session sponsored by *Successful Marketing*, a trade magazine. The agenda was: what kind of "marketing opportunities" (*shangji*) will the bobo fever offer to Chinese marketers?

## The Bobo Symposium

There can be no better venue in Beijing than the Postmodern Tower for a marketing symposium on the bobos. Inside the Tower, everything is pared down to Rule No. 4 of the Bobo Code of Financial Correctness: "you can never have too much texture."[18] Craggy brick walls without decorations, bare unfinished wooden floor pieced together with irregularly shaped planks – the Tower exudes the bobo's spirit of calculated casualness.

Several questions were put on the table. How many bobos are there really in China? Can a minority group like that support a product line? The crowd was divided. But regardless of the size issue, they were in strong agreement about the necessity of cashing in on the trend. You don't have to believe in the leap of faith to take advantage of it. The following is a sample of quotations from the symposium participants:

"Bobos have dreams. So they are easy targets. They can be easily moved by 'concepts' and 'storytelling'."
"Sell them the bobo spirit."
"Chinese society will witness an increasingly large affluent class. Although we will probably never be sure whether X or Y is a bobo, but we will surely see them display some bobo characteristics such as a preoccupation with creativity and spiritual values."

18. *Ibid.* p. 92.

"Our marketing opportunities will rest on whether we can provide products with added values that transcend materialism. For instance, sell ambience and service at entertainment venues such as bars and restaurants."

"You can detect a new social tendency now. Business behaviour must be wedded to cultural concepts. Only when competition takes place at a certain cultural height and at a spiritual level can you make your products stand out."

"Bobos value personal experiences. They like to be adventurers. But they are not iconoclasts. Nor are they opposed to being trendy. Their main value coincides with the core value of society. That's the fundamental reason why they are so successful ... We should not associate boboism with a fad or with an act of rebellion. We should not look upon them as mere upstarts either. They don't ever rebel."[19]

*DINKs and the Neo-Tribe Co.*

The last quotation is especially revealing in its no-nonsense assessment of the bobo unconscious, in China at least. But understanding who the bobos are is one thing, motivating them to spend is another. They need a reason why they should buy. What are their desires like and how should they be captured? The answer to those million-dollar questions is simple, the marketers at the symposium argued. Give them "id" labels. Sell them distinct personalities. The symposium named such a desire "self-validation" and a burning need of China's young generation to broadcast to the world, "who I am!"[20]

This is an explanatory moment that brings to the foreground the phenomenon of proliferating "neo-tribes" in China. Barely had one tribe entered the spotlight than another emerged to upstage it, all occurring at stunningly short intervals. Other societies are plagued by neo-tribes as well (after all we live in consumer societies). But the frenzy in China, as noted above, tops them all, leading to headlines like: "The IFs[21] have come. Don't you ever mention bobos any more!" Meanwhile the International Freemen are fighting for the limelight with another tribe dubbed DINKs – Double Income, No Kids. The tiny stage is getting very crowded.

Hairsplitting stratification has indeed come in vogue since the early 2000s. Chinese marketers claim that they are merely following the social desire for stratification. And in the case of the bobo fever, they could hardly catch up. On the other hand, some symposium attendees were honest about the necessity of meticulous segmentation. Marketing follows the 2/8 principle: 80 per cent of a society's purchasing power is concentrated on the top 20 per cent consumer elites. Ironically, high income earners have grown increasingly indifferent to consumption. Old

19. "Bubo zu shangji da gonglüe zhi luntan yu dianping ("Commentaries on the symposium of 'A marketing offence targeting bobos' "), http://finance.sina.com.cn/roll/20030416, 16 April 2003, accessed in 2004.

20. Liu Wei, Wang Weiqun *et al.*, "Bubo zu shangji da gonglüe" ("A marketing offence targeting bobos"), *Chenggong yingxiao* (*Successful Marketing*). No. 4 (2003), http:/www.cmarketing.com.cn, accessed in 2004.

21. IFs are International Free(wo)men who are bi-lingual or multi-lingual, who have developed bi-cultural tastes and who travel constantly between different locales.

demographic indexes like "age" and "income" are not strong identity markers any more. Premium consumers need catchy cultural identities to distinguish themselves from the other *fellow* elites. Thus the marketing craze for fastidious positioning churns out one tribal epithet after another.

## Michel Maffesoli and the Tribal Paradigm

The previous sections should have made it fairly obvious that the situation facing China is the extreme facility with which the "neo-tribes" cast off their old identity labels and put on new ones. The Chinese have gone to an extreme, but the fever for "neo-tribes" was a "foreign" phenomenon transported from Taiwan, Hong Kong and Japan. Perhaps what is happening in China is only a hyperbole of consumer society in general. What is the connection between consumerism and the tribal discourse?

French sociologist Michel Maffesoli made a breakthrough in theorizing contemporary consumer society. We live in "the time of the tribes," he says, which witnesses the explosion of lifestyle cultures. Tribes are organized around brand names and role-playing fantasies. Old categories such as the core identity, subjectivity, autonomy and even subculture have fallen short of accounting for new forms of "sociality." He distinguishes the "social," defined in terms of the "rational association of individuals having a precise identity" from "sociality," the highly unstable space where a multiplicity of contingent tribal circles intersect and make meaning situationally. "The dramatic authenticity of the social is answered by the tragic superficiality of sociality."[22]

Maffesoli is both fascinated and repulsed by the chameleon instinct of the performing self that drives today's consumer culture. Sometimes he complains about the "conformism" of youth culture and reveals a nostalgia for a stable subject position captured in the old concept of the "individual": "what we are witnessing is the loss of the idea of the individual in favor of a much *less distinct* mass."[23] But despite a small handful of occasional epistemological slippages, Maffesoli maintains consistently, true to the Weberian spirit, that "identity is never, from the sociological point of view, anything but a simply floating and relative condition."[24] He describes the cultural moment of neo-tribalism as a multitude of fluid networks "confirmed on a daily basis."[25]

There is a flip side to this phenomenon, as Maffesoli insinuates: the guarantee of group *solidarity* of the neo-tribes became as fragile as their occasional gatherings (and dispersals). He thus raises new questions about solidarity: what happens to human fellowship in the new age of media convergence? Specifically, how is "solidarity" registered, felt and articulated when conversations are accessed on different media *simultaneously*? When karma is only a click away, what does "bonding" mean?

22. Michel Maffesoli, *The Time of the Tribes: The Decline of Individualism in Mass Society* (London, Thousand Oaks & New Delhi: Sage, 1996), p. 76.
23. *Ibid*. p. 64, italics mine.
24. *Ibid*. p. 65.
25. *Ibid*. p. 97.

*The Time of the Tribes* is littered with metaphorical moments that tease out the technological link of the tribal paradigm which, as shown below, lies at the heart of the emerging tribe of the day, *xin xin renlei.*

However Maffesoli does not provide a real-life specimen of his object of analysis, merely a theoretical skeleton. That is one of the reasons why this article consists of the social mosaic of neo-tribes *in motion.* The instantaneous rise of the bobos and other neo-tribes in China is highly instructive for the evolving critical inquiries into the tribal question at large.

A discussion of Maffesoli would be incomplete without a mention of the impact of his theories on Dick Hebdige's "subculture" couched in the tradition of the Birmingham Centre for Contemporary Cultural Studies. Or, conversely, one could say that the tribal paradigm can only make sense if it is set off against the earlier paradigm of subculture. Does the theory of "subculture," which predicates the simple dichotomy between a monolithic mainstream culture and politically conscious resistant subcultures, stand valid in the new economy where the old boundaries between "culture" and "economy," "activism" and "consumerism" can no longer be as clearly drawn as in Hebdige's time?

Perhaps the most concentrated effort to re-conceptualize Hebdige's old paradigm was seen in the Vienna symposium called "Post-Subcultural Studies" held in May 2001. A new field was said to be born, with a large contingent of European researchers of youth culture who share with each other an overriding interest in examining dance and music style cultures. Most participants in the symposium agreed on the demise of "subcultural heroism" of the 1970s and 1980s.[26] However, the allure of alternative models such as Maffesoli's is seen to have a caveat – it theorizes "politics" away too readily. If the "optimum strategy" of the neo-tribes is "to tap into a number of lifestyles, adopting whichever one best fits the situation to hand," their irreverent energy appears to be utterly purposeless.[27] How to rescue or redefine "activism" from the increasingly instantaneous tribal formations constitutes one of the central missions underlying the new critical literature that touts the arrival of the *post-subcultural* era.

One can clearly see the watershed of such a paradigmatic shift in urban China as well. Anybody familiar with the clubbing and music scene in the Chinese metropolises would be struck by the frantic tribalization of new taste cultures. Cui Jian's days are gone. So is Chinese subculture with an *angst.* Jay Chou, Faye Wong and Pu Shu, each a spokesperson for at least one major commodity product, are now the hottest pop icons. Rebellious postures are chic. It has little to do with iconoclasm. China's young generations are courting the *safe cool*, a party-going esprit unattended by the kind of soul-searching sought by the proponents of the new European post-subcultural movement bent on repoliticizing youth

26. Rupert Weinzierl and David Muggleton, "What is 'post-subcultural studies' anyway?" in David Muggleton and Rupert Weinzierl (eds.), *The Post-Subcultures Reader* (Oxford & New York: Berg, 2003), pp. 6–9.

27. David B. Clarke, Marcus A. Doel *et al., The Consumption Reader* (London & New York: Routledge, 2003), p. 137.

cultures with a carnivalesque twist. One should, of course, not preclude any examination of what is emerging in China by taking a European model as a starting point of analysis. The temptation to make such a comparison is, however, difficult to resist precisely because cool marketing and global branding has given new impetuses to the formation of the target segment called "global youth" – international urban youths aged from late teens to early 20s. It is a transnational marketer's ultimate dream: enabled by digital technology and international marketing, a global youth culture is converging from the Atlantic to the Pacific. Is it happening? It would seem that there is not such an easy equation between the West and the rest as maintained by earnest advocates of cultural globalization. "Cool" music and "alternative" youths in China hardly signal the same thing as their counterparts in Euro-America.[28] The concept of "convergence," however, has real value when applied to the East Asian equation. There is no denying that East Asian youth cultures are now converging on a new tribal sensation, *xin xin renlei*.

### *Xin Xin Renlei: The East Asian Connection*

A litmus test of Maffesoli's theory can be conducted with success in East Asia where market segmentation in tribal terms has taken on a life of its own. Maffesoli's *tribus* has splintered into tiny subdivisions, each half-a-generation apart, in places like China, Taiwan, Hong Kong and Japan. Not surprisingly, neo-tribes in China such as the bobos, DINKs and IFs are now considered rather conservative in their taste because as the established social elites, they are not as cool as their followers, the "neo-neo-tribe" – Asia's hottest market segment. Members of this emerging tribe are in their late teens and early 20s and cross gender divisions. They have a symbiotic existence with high-tech communication gadgets. Their threshold for irreverence is immeasurable. And with less money than the bobos, they are no easy prey for mainstream consumerism.

Maffesoli should be given credit for mentioning that "the feeling of tribal belonging can be reinforced by technological developments."[29] But when he penned his theory of neo-tribalism in 1988, he hardly foresaw that technology itself could create a tribe of its own complete with a system of distinction that sounds alien even to the neo-tribes. In China, the neo-neo-tribe is the first generation who grew up in the internet chat rooms. Their counterparts in Japan are participants in a vibrant cell phone youth culture which has just begun to sweep urban China.

It is not a coincidence that the Chinese term *xin xin renlei* is a transliteration of the Japanese term *shin shin jinrei* introduced to the mainland via Hong Kong and Taiwan. This word is used almost synonymously with "Generation X and Y" in Taiwan. In Japan, it refers to the post-second baby-boomers generation who are in their late teens and

---

28. Jing Wang, "Youth culture, music, and cell phone branding in China," *Global Media and Communication*, Vol. 1, No. 2 (2005), p. 85–201.
29. Maffesoli, *The Time of the Tribes*, p. 139.

early 20s. A discussion about the cross-border journey of a marketing concept is perhaps long overdue for we cannot talk about the urban imaginary in one East Asian country without crossing national boundaries. Indeed, the tribal logic in consumer culture is as much an inter-Asian phenomenon as it is Chinese. The challenge is to work out how to trace its traffic when sources are mostly hearsay and of electronic origins. It is not within the scope of this article to address the comparative question about the East Asian neo-neo-tribes at length. To raise this subject, however, serves an immediate purpose: it is a reminder of the important link of marketing to our study of East Asian youth culture and consumer culture.

### Chinese Xin Xin Renlei

What is a Chinese neo-neo-tribe like? A quick profile should confirm its parasitic existence with its counterparts in other Asian societies.

"*Xin xin renlei* don their hair in all kinds of colours. Their cool faces give an exaggerated cold blank stare. They are dressed in plastic and metal looking clothes ... They just want to look different. They are trend pursuers. They are a superficial and restless tribe ... There is another way of portraying them: if you look human, then you do not belong to the neo-neo-tribe yet."[30]

"*Xin xin renlei* is inexplicable. So far we have not yet figured out their lingo, behavioural code and life philosophy. The so-called neo-neo-tribe should not be seen as a mere signpost for a certain historical period. More important, it points to an uncertain ideology. In China, this tribe's ties with traditionalism are disappearing. Their thoughts and views on life are rapidly aligned with the international norm. Born in the late 1970s, they are distanced from 'tradition.' Their knowledge about the past was channelled indirectly through movies, novels and TV drama. Their literary sensibility is nurtured in Japanese manga. This is a generation fed by 'fast food culture' while they are growing up. Compared to the previous generation, they are much more independent, wilful and self-centred. Their way of absorbing things is DIY (do it yourself). Indoctrination and preaching find no place in their lives."[31]

"Having fun is the most important thing in life ... Acting 'cool' is the art and wisdom of a rebellion against a mediocre life."[32]

Pinning them down to a consistent profile is difficult. Real-life *xin xin renlei* can be seen at China News online, exemplified by Xiaolong (Little Dragon) and Nina.[33] This is a generation known to care about nothing but "fashion," "hair styles," "computer gadgets" and "relationships."[34] But

---

30. Longyuan huquan, "Zouchu liuxing xianxiang de xin xin renlei" ("The neo-neo-tribe that transcends fads"), http://www.54youth.com.cn/gb/paper107/zt/xyzt/hz7.htm, accessed in April 2004.

31. Guoke, "Xin xin renlei ji duo xin" ("How trendy is the neo-neo-tribe"), http://campus.etang.com/html/life/heter/daily/life-heter-daily-0192.htm, accessed in April 2004.

32. "Xin xin renlei de 'ku' shenghuo" ("The 'cool' life of a neo-neo-tribe"), http://www.xiayidai.com.cn/qczx/ssx/xxrl, accessed in April 2004.

33. Yu Ruidong, "Liuxing jujiao: wo xing wo ku, xin xin renlei" ("Trend focus: I do what is cool, neo-neo-tribe"), China News Service, 2002, http://www.chinanews.com.cn/2002–04–25/90/6.html, accessed in April 2004.

34. *Ibid.*

"fashion" here takes on a different meaning from what it means to the neo-tribes. It points to an attitude rather than glittering material objects.

We can debate to no end as to whether *xin xin renlei*'s rebellious attitude is reminiscent of Hebdige's subculture paradigm or of Maffesoli's tribal logic. But I think the question of rebellion is a red herring. "Having fun" and "doing whatever I want to do" is the key to unlocking the enigma of the neo-neo-tribe. Another point of entry is technology. A "classic visual image of the neo-neo-tribe" is "a lone figure arching over a computer like a big shrimp."[35]

## The Sammy Point of View, Hong Kong Style

This final section provides a case study of an advertising campaign for Philippine's leading brew San Miguel Light Beer sold in Hong Kong. It is a campaign about "attitude," and its target is Hong Kong's neo-neo-tribe.

How to position a light beer that is a line extension of an ageing flagship brand posed a challenge to the Ogilvy Hong Kong team. The breakthrough came when researchers started inserting San Mig Light right into the social space of young drinkers.[36] The research question was: what is going on in their fickle minds? Through a five-pronged approach, a mosaic of stories and dialogues among those youngsters and about them were sampled. Together, they reveal a pattern of consistent "attitude" as follows:

"Their conversation is disorganized, there is no subject or theme, [they] live in a blue sky conversational world ... as the conversation goes... , they start to shift to other things";
"The most difficult problem is 'what to eat' ... Simply thinking about what to eat will spend us a day";
"Who will be calling me? Who will have nothing to do now? After calling him, I'll call someone else who has nothing to do";
"I'm seduced by sensory stimulus."[37]

This is obviously a tribal group seeking instant gratification listlessly, but a deeply bonded crowd. Thinking that home is the "most boring place of all," they are driven out into the metropolis of urban Hong Kong. They are crazy for visual and sensory stimuli, "anything that hints of mischief-making, that is visually fun ... But everything is instantly disposable."[38] They move quickly on to the next "hit."

This profile is similar to that of China's neo-neo-tribe, crazier and wilder than the Japanese *shin shin jinrei*, but they all share the same C-culture – cartoons, computers, comic books and nintendo games. They all speak and consume the same visual language. Based on those field observations, the brand personality for San Mig Light took shape quickly.

35. Longyuan huquan, "The neo-neo-tribe that transcends fads."
36. "The launch of San Mig Light," power-point presentation, Ogilvy-in-Beijing.
37. *Ibid.*
38. Mark Blair, Richard Armstrong *et al.*, *The 360 Degree Brand in Asia* (Singapore: John Wiley & Sons (Asia) Pte Ltd., 2003), pp. 75–76.

He is a little guy who follows his own instinct, who does not give a damn for public opinion, a trickster guided by impulses rather than by the mind. A new mascot was born: Sammy.

When I first encountered that naughty little devil in a series of print advertisements for San Mig Light, I saw him as an obnoxious male prankster and a highly gendered invention. However, that cartoon figure, juvenile and delinquent, appeals to the target consumers regardless of their gender. He is the "ultimate spontaneous animal" that lurks in the minds and hearts of the Hong Kong neo-neo-tribe, an unstoppable phenomenon. He is everywhere. Private Sammy moments are posted in public. The Sammy "virus" was unleashed openly on television, billboards and print advertisements.[39] He pops up in shops, public lavatories, bars and restaurants, on the streets, at MTR, as tattoos and stickers, any medium you name, braving the public: "I dare, do you?" He pees whenever he can't hold it; he moons at you and dares you to spank him; he farts purposefully in a crowded elevator; he targets the urinal from a far distance; he shows love to a young girl by pushing her off a cliff. Scatological humour is his trade mark. The tag lines feature Sammy-style outbursts: "Come on, man!" "Hey man, that's fun." "Maybe we don't need to take things that seriously." He is in our face, asking, "will you be Sammy enough when you are allowed to?"

If you feel timid answering those challenges, you are simply not a Hong Kong neo-neo-tribe, but you may still qualify for its Chinese or Japanese incarnations. We can find Sammy's golden mean – "[my] only rule is to bend the rules, disruptively but not destructively" – performed by his counterparts in China, Japan and perhaps in other parts of Asia. This is, in short, the rise of a hot East Asian youth cultural phenomenon.

This article began with the bobos, an imaginary class, and ends with the neo-neo-tribe, a real-life social segment. I have yet to spot a television commercial that captures the dual traits of the Chinese bobos, namely that they have to practise both "one-upmanship" and an imaginary "one-downmanship" at the same time. Such real-life specimens are rare, to say the least. In contrast, the visual representation of *xin xin renlei* flooded the media precisely because it is a tribe rooted in reality. The arrival and popularity of both discourses, however, is a sure sign of the tribalization of the Chinese market. The theorem of tribal discourse aside, however, two other important questions were raised in this article. While no quick answers can be found, the taste versus class question and the theoretical possibility of an emerging global youth culture point to the heart of my critical concern: the importance of taking "marketing" into serious account in any study of regional and transnational popular cultural trends. As shown above, marketers only need to take a tiny step to turn a popular discourse about a tribe into a new marketing phenomenon. And one can certainly argue the reverse. Indeed, it is difficult to tell which comes first – a real-life tribe or its incarnation as a market segment. Either way, when marketing meets culture, can a new pop culture movement be far away?

39. See Ogilvy Interactive Asia for the Sammy advertising campaign: http://our-work.com/version1_2/files/web_sites/sammy_site/sammy_explan.htm, accessed in June 2005.

# Chinese Cinema in the Age of Advertisement: The Filmmaker as a Cultural Broker

Yomi Braester

ABSTRACT  The article looks at a model of filmmaking that has emerged since the rise of "cultural economy" in the mid-1990s. Directors have collaborated with real estate developers and other entrepreneurs and become cultural brokers. They use the prestige, access and popular appeal of the cinema to establish a stronger connection between film and market forces. As filmmakers become trendsetters, their films aim not only at box office success but also at shaping economic agendas and visual experience, social networks and the aesthetic environment. Filmmaking as cultural brokering has been practised by directors as disparate as the market-oriented Feng Xiaogang, the neorealist Ning Ying and the documentary producer Wu Wenguang.

In a television commercial aired in the PRC in March 2002, a master of supernatural martial arts arrives at an inn and asks for Longjing tea. As he raises his head and reveals his face, one sees that the knight is played by the film director Feng Xiaogang. The commercial is one of a series made by the Hong Kong "comedy king" Stephen Chow Sing-chi (Zhou Xingchi) to endorse the Wahaha brand bottled tea, "the Longjing tea you don't need to brew." It was the first commercial directed by Feng (together with Li Geng)[1] and his first collaboration with Chow. The commercial presents in a nutshell the characteristics of mainstream filmmaking in contemporary China. The fast-pace 15-second flick builds on a popular genre and star power. It features Feng Xiaogang as a recognizable figure on par with the Hong Kong megapopular actor, and his status is directly translated into selling power. Various media blend, blurring the lines between feature film and commercial advertisement.[2]

The junction between film – often associated in China with social and political agendas – and crass market forces may seem jarring, and many observers have come to regard commercial film as a distinct genre. Those who focus on the box office claim that in commercial film Chinese cinema has developed a strain that prioritizes revenue and pays little attention to narrative and ideology. These claims are buttressed by the increasing importance of fiscal factors affecting the film industry, such as China's entrance into the World Trade Organization (WTO) in

---

1. On Li Geng, see Zheng Xin'an, *Jingtou li de shangpin: Zhongguo youxiu guanggao daoyan quan jilu* (*Merchandize in the Lens: A Full Record of Masterful Chinese Advertisement Directors*) (Beijing: Shijie zhishi chubanshe, 2003), pp. 70–90.

2. "Zhou Xingchi + Feng Xiaogang = daxia + dian xiaoer?!" ("Stephen Chow plus Feng Xiaogang equal martial arts master and inn attendant?!"), http://ent.enorth.com.cn/system/2002/03/11/000286869.shtml (visited 17 October 2004).

2001 and the concurrent collapse of the state-owned studio system. Feng Xiaogang's films, which have targeted mass audiences, have been cited as a major instance of the commercial turn, together with Zhang Yimou's interest in crowd-pleasing genre films, from the urban comedy *Xingfu shiguang* (*Happy Times*, 2000) to the martial arts films *Yingxiong* (*Hero*, 2000) and *Shimian maifu* (English title *House of Flying Daggers*, 2004). Even the *enfant terrible* of Chinese cinema, Zhang Yuan, has turned away from the hard-hitting social criticism of films such as *Erzi* (*Sons*, 1996) to slick flicks such as *Lücha* (*Green Tea*, 2003) and television commercials.

And yet I argue that critics have overstated the case for defining commercial films as a separate trend that breaks away from earlier models of literary sensibility and social engagement. Whether state-subsidized or not, filmmaking remains motivated largely by the desire to communicate with a large audience. Literary sensibilities have not disappeared, though their sources of inspiration have shifted from Lu Xun and Zhang Xianliang to Wang Shuo and Gu Long. One should not put down too quickly the statements of successful directors such as Feng Xiaogang and Zhang Yimou, who claim to be making art films. So-called commercial movies show practical sense in appealing to a wide spectatorship, yet they retain a keen concern with current issues, including the illnesses of the rapid transformation to a consumerist society. I discuss elsewhere how Chinese films, across purported genres, have addressed unregulated urbanization and the concomitant demolition-and-relocation projects.[3] This article touches on the related topic of filmmakers' response to brand-name consumption and the rampant commercialization of emblems of cultural heritage.

Commercial filmmaking opens new possibilities not, as has been proposed, through distinct content or cinematic form, but rather because the director's entrepreneurial engagement redefines the social forces with which the cinema interacts and determines anew how films ally themselves with other media. In a system where filmmakers no longer identify with a sponsoring state apparatus, they may emulate the operation methods of commercial sponsors, to the point of becoming one with the entrepreneurial system at large. Whereas Maoist thought required artists to "unite with the masses," directors now merge with the commercial production and distribution units. Filmmakers take over not only directing but also advertising and promotion, and their work expands far beyond the artifact screened in theatres. A new model of filmmaking is in the process of emerging, which is akin to other forms of entrepreneurial use of culture. A certain symbolism may be found in that both masterful artists and real estate moguls are referred to as *dawan'r*, a term reserved for large-scale market manipulators.

3. Yomi Braester, "Tracing the city's scars: demolition and the documentary impulse in New Urban Cinema," in Zhen Zhang (ed.), *The Urban Generation* (Durham: Duke University Press, 2006).

The term *dawan'r* originated in the circles of vernacular performers and referred to skilled artists of great reputation.[4] In contemporary parlance, it designates high-level managers who create and mould markets. Jing Wang notes that the new *dawan'r* mediate between various strata of culture, contradicting the artificial distinction between high and low culture, or, for that matter, between Marxism and capitalism as opposed market forces. With the rise of "cultural economy" (*wenhua jingji*) in the mid-1990s, cultural capital and economic capital became exchangeable. Cultural references could be cashed in to enhance the monetary value of a commercial project, and the brokers of culture became a powerful elite.[5] Under these circumstances, filmmakers – like their counterparts in music distribution, art exhibition and literary promotion – could benefit from their skills as producers of artifacts of wide appeal and their proximity to intellectual circles to become influential middlemen. In this article I examine the recent respositioning of filmmaking in the PRC's cultural matrix and focus in particular on Feng Xiaogang's *Dawan'r*, known in English as *Big Shot's Funeral* (2001). I argue that the film both signals the turn to cultural brokering and provides a wry commentary on the limits of commercial enterprise.

The filmmaker's role as a cultural broker erases the distinction between ideological and commercial cinema as well as between art film and market-driven media. Cultural brokering is practised by box office-oriented directors as well as more independent filmmakers. A more sober examination of cinema as cultural capital may also demystify independent film. The talent of "six-generation" directors notwithstanding, such directors have enjoyed an aura created by skilful brokers. Labelling films as alternative, avant-garde and dissident has become a profitable marketing ploy that has sustained beyond its usefulness the distinction between commercial and independent cinema.

Acknowledging the commodity value of films entails, paradoxically, a disregard of their cost. Films cannot be judged by their box office success. Hollywood-trained media and scholarship has used revenue figures to claim "the blockbuster" as a genre. Yet Jonathan Rosenbaum points to the fact that bestseller lists evidence only the marketing skills of specific distributors.[6] The box office standard works to the advantage of marketing experts – in Hollywood as well as in Beijing's central business district and even in the official compound in Zhongnanhai – who can, and

4. "He wei 'dawan,' 'dakuan'" ("What are 'dawan' and 'dakuan'"), *Zhongguo gonghui caihui* (*Trade Union Financial Affairs of China*), No. 1 (1994), n.p.

5. Wang Jing, " 'Culture' as leisure and 'culture' as capital: the state question and Chinese popular culture," *Positions*: East Asia Cultures Critique, Vol. 9, No. 1 (Spring 2001), pp. 69–70. For the term "cultural broker," referring to a person who mediates between groups of differing cultural backgrounds, see for example Clifford Geertz, "The Javanese Kijai: the changing role of a cultural broker," *Comparative Study of Society and History*, Vol. 2 (1960), pp. 228–249.

6. Jonathan Rosenbaum, *Movie Wars: How Hollywood and the Media Limit What Movies We Can See* (Chicago: A Capella, 2000).

often do, rig the numbers to promote specific films.[7] The attention to so-called commercial cinema has privileged reception statistics and industrial bottom lines, at the expense of inquiring into the form of cinema in the age of commercial advertisement. As filmmakers start regarding themselves as trendsetters, their films aim not only at box office success but also at shaping economic agendas and visual experience, social networks and aesthetic environment. The new playing field expands the definition of the cinema and necessitates a closer attention to the role of filmmakers as cultural brokers.

### The Rise of the Cultural Broker

The current paragon of cultural brokering may be found in China's booming real estate business. The most visible company is SOHO China, owned and managed by Pan Shiyi and Zhang Xin. The ascendance of the husband-and-wife team has become a rags-to-riches legend. Starting in 1998 with a profitable double-use project (Small Office, Home Office, hence SOHO), they launched in February 2001 a complex of eleven villas and a clubhouse, known as Commune by the Great Wall. The project was originally planned to comprise up to 50 villas to be sold at US$500,000 each, but it was not a commercial success and the villas are now rented out as a "boutique hotel." Yet it was essential to establishing the company's name recognition and prestige. The buildings were designed by 12 Asian architects of modest fame, and the result was a modernist, experimental complex. SOHO China submitted the Commune by the Great Wall to the Eighth International Architecture Exhibition of the Venice Biennale (2002), and Zhang Xin won an unprecedented special prize for an individual patron of architectural works. The shortcomings of the project and its commercial unviability were dwarfed and forgotten in light of this critical acclaim and international fame.

The case of Zhang Xin and Pan Shiyi illustrates how players in the financial field make use of culture. Even Pan, seemingly the more practical of the two, expatiates in a recent interview for *Culture* magazine on a cultural comparison between Russia, China and Japan.[8] Pan's name recognition has even made him a movie celebrity, as the male lead in *Asipilin* (*Aspirin*, 2005). SOHO China owes much of its success not only to marketing its individual products but also to promoting the company's image as a leader in setting cultural trends. Its projects – including currently the SOHO Shang Du building by Lab Architecture Studio of Melbourne and a residential subdivision by Zaha Hadid – are wrapped in

---

7. Some filmmakers who have access to industry records doubt, off the record, the commercial success of some of Feng Xiaogang's films; in other cases, such as Zhang Yimou's *House of Flying Daggers*, the numbers tell little, since no other films were allowed to be screened during the first weeks of the film's theatrical release.

8. Fang Zhenming, "Zhongguo haishi yao kaifang: Fang SOHO Zhongguo dongshizhang Pan Shiyi" ("China still has to open up: an interview with Pan Shiyi, general manager of SOHO China"), *Wenhua*, September 2004.

the glory of foreign designers and recognition by the international art world.

Zhang Xin and Pan Shiyi are not only exemplary of the real estate *dawan'r* and an inspiration to the PRC's business elite; their activities implicate also the new role of filmmakers. The Commune by the Great Wall was presented in Venice through a video made by the film director Ning Ying, who also shot other promotional pieces for SOHO China. The slick 12-minute video (available on DVD upon request and downloadable at SOHO China's website) associated the company's products with Ning's reputation as an art film director and contributed to the project's success in Venice, and hence also to the company's market value. SOHO China's slightly provocative yet ultimately non-contentious aesthetics – introducing, for example, Beijing's first brightly-coloured buildings – has become one of its most important financial assets. In expanding real estate development to novel ways of visualizing the urban environment, Zhang Xin and Pan Shiyi have relied not only on architectural design but also on filmic presentation.

Ning Ying's involvement with SOHO China is far from self-evident. The director is known for her Beijing trilogy (*Zhao le /For Fun*, 1992; *Minjing gushi /On the Beat*, 1995; *Xiari nuanyangyang /I Love Beijing*, 2001), which looks critically at urban change of the kind promoted by land speculators. Her works draw close to documentary cinema and preserve the course grain of everyday life. Ning's video of the Commune by the Great Wall, on the other hand, comports well with the commercial expectations. Smooth camera movement and a sound track comprised mostly of electronic music accompany a cursory introduction to each villa, an on-site fashion show and a dramatic overview of the Commune during a stormy night. Ning Ying maintains a distinction between her commercial exploits and personally-motivated filmmaking. She does not use her image to promote sales – unlike, for example, Feng Xiaogang, who collapses his personal and filmic personae in the Longjing tea commercial. Nevertheless, Ning's collaboration with SOHO points to ways of expanding filmmakers' cultural playing field.

A wide spectrum of entrepreneuring filmmakers use their media knowledge and cultural status to add prestige and monetary value to commercial products. Perhaps the most unlikely example involves the pioneer documentary filmmaker Wu Wenguang. In June 2001, Sino-Ocean Real Estate Development Co. launched its Ocean Paradise (Yuanyang tiandi) project. This housing complex for Beijing's "yuppies" was promoted through the added value of culture, in this case, the Eastern Modern Art Centre (Yuanyang yishu zhongxin), touted as a centre for alternative art. The project was chosen by *Beijing wanbao (Beijing Evening News)* as one of the ten "star developments" of 2001.[9] Two months into the presales, the art centre sponsored a much-publicized avant-garde performance, Wen Hui's "Dancing with migrant workers" ("Yu mingong yiqi wudao"). The entire rehearsal process and the single

9. http://www.cosred.com/cosred/index.php (visited 10 October 2004).

public performance were recorded by Wen's husband, Wu Wenguang, in a documentary bearing the same title.[10] The symbiosis between Wu, a vocal proponent of using digital video to circumvent the film industry establishment on the one hand, and a commercial development on the other, shows how entrepreneurship is not alien even to independent filmmakers.

The more blatantly commercial directors are especially adept exponents of the new cultural economy. Zhang Yimou, for example, has closely interlinked cinema and image design. Zhang provided the filmic promotion for Beijing's bid for the 2008 Olympics, in a short that boasts the capital as place where old and new meet, a business hub, a cultural centre and an architectural marvel. Zhang has applied the same zeal to advancing his films. He pioneered the extensive use of "making of" documentaries, released in advance of his feature films – the most recent of which, *House of Flying Daggers*, was launched in a televised ceremony. It should come as no surprise that Zhang also collaborates with real estate moghuls. One of his main funders has been the developer Zhang Weiping, and recent reports indicate that Zhang has become a property speculator in his own right.[11]

In this environment, where filmmakers not only rely on cultural brokering but also promote their image as *dawan'r*, it would only be appropriate that Feng Xiaogang would make the self-referential film *Big Shot's Funeral*, or as its Chinese title literally goes, *The dawan'r*.

### The Cultural Broker: A Filmic History

Feng Xiaogang presents a loving if parodic portrait of the *dawan'r*. *Big Shot's Funeral* starts as a famous Hollywood director, Donald Tyler (Donald Sutherland), arrives in Beijing to shoot an updated version of *The Last Emperor* and falls into a coma. The cinematographer Yoyo (Ge You) takes to heart Tyler's request for a "comedy funeral" and plans an uplifting spectacle worthy of the director's reputation, to take place in the Forbidden City. To cover the costs, the cinematographer takes every opportunity for direct advertising and product placement. The body of the deceased is to be placed on sponsored furniture, surrounded by large product mockups and dressed in sponsor brands. The event, attended by cultural luminaries and featuring various performances, ends up in the cinematographer's imagination as the shell for an elaborate lucrative enterprise. With his friend Louis Wang (Ying Da) he envisages the funeral as replete with opera and rock performances, the appearance of cultural luminaries, and a specially-produced movie on Tyler. They launch their enterprise with an extravagant multimedia press conference, making full use of what is called in advertisement parlance "eventizing"

10. My thanks to Sasha Welland for drawing my attention to the connection between Wu's film and the real estate project.

11. Tang Yuankai, "Movie makers at crossroad," http://www.bjreview.com.cn/200435/Nation-200435(B).htm (visited 7 January 2005); Geoffrey Macnab, "I'm not interested in politics," http://www.guardian.co.uk/arts/fridayreview/story/0,,1374950,00.html [*The Guardian*, 17 December 2004] (visited 7 January 2005).

a product release. In a delirium, the producers later calculate DVD sales from the event and plan to launch their enterprise on the American stock market. Yoyo makes use of Beijing's cultural heritage both to lend elegance to Tyler's funeral and to make it profitable.

Pulling off the implausible scheme distinguishes Yoyo as a cultural broker. At first, the eponymous *dawan'r* in Feng's film appears to be Tyler. "What is a *dawan'r*?" Yoyo is asked, and he answers, in line with the older lexical definition, "a famous star." Yet Tyler is no more than a celebrity, even though his reputation enables Yoyo's scheme for the funeral. Yoyo, on the other hand, is little known but becomes a *dawan'r* in the 1990s sense of the term, and the storyline follows his rise to a cultural broker. Originally hired to shoot the "making-of" documentary (a mark of strategic DVD marketing) and explicitly given no decision-making power, Yoyo negotiates an increasingly complicated deal.

The protagonist in *Big Shot's Funeral* is immediately recognizable as an updated version of the entrepreneurial fantasy providers in two earlier films, both played, like Yoyo, by Ge You. *Wanzhu* (*The Troubleshooters*, 1988, directed by Mi Jiashan) was among the most prominent new urban films made in the late 1980s. The first movie based on a text by Wang Shuo, it exhibits the street wisdom that has earned Wang's works the description "hoodlum literature" (*pizi wenxue*). The plot revolves around three young men, under the leadership of Yang Zhong (Ge You) who, in the spirit of the economic reforms, start their own enterprise, 3T. The company name alludes to its Chinese slogan, centred on three services: removing worries, solving difficult situations and covering up for mistakes. In the most elaborate episode, 3T arranges for a pulp fiction writer to receive a literary prize. With the money paid by the author who craves for public recognition, they stage a free fashion show at the World Expo Centre, at the end of which they assume the roles of scholarly judges and give the writer his long-awaited award. As soon as the cultural economy appeared in the late 1980s, cinema was there to spoof it.

The smooth operators in *The Troubleshooters* signal the coming of the cultural broker. The literary prize episode mediates between high and low culture by acknowledging in mock-scholarly fashion the works of an author presumably rejected for his lowbrow writings. The author is unashamed of his popular publications yet yearns for recognition from the establishment, and the three entrepreneurs step in (the contrast between the author's practice and aspirations is highlighted by his pen name, Zhiqing, which alludes to the sent-down youth whose "root-seeking literature" – *xungen wenxue* – dominated the literary scene at the time). The 3T hoodlums further blur the line between low- and high-brow by including in the literary award ceremony a fashion show – a novel consumerist spectacle at the time – and crowd the catwalk with Beijing opera and modern drama characters, alluding to the declining status of traditional and socialist theatrical forms. The make-believe exploits of 3T soon branch into cinema as well. Yu Guan (Zhang Guoli) takes on a stuntman's job, willing to risk his life in the name of making a Chinese film as good as Hong Kong action movies. The cultural broker's next stop, it is implied, would be commercial filmmaking.

Yet the three entrepreneurs fail to translate cultural capital to economic benefits; they are sued out of business and end up in the unemployment queue. In portraying the enterprise as a failure, the director Mi Jiashan sides with social norms. In an essay about the film, Mi describes the three as "abnormal human characters and disturbing social phenomena."[12] The resistance to changing lifestyles is also made evident in the title song, by rock'n'roll singer (and later music producer) Wang Di: "I used to dream of modern urban life/But I don't know how to say what I feel now/There are more high rises by the day/It's not easy to live here." The song continues after the protagonists' downfall: "TV commercial time is increasing/It's as though you can't hold on to that golden moment/You can't do what you want/What you don't want comes in droves." The lyrics single out rapid urban development and television commercials as symptoms of unwanted change. Mi Jiashan takes from Wang Shuo the urban youngsters' glib tongue, cynicism and sense of rebellion, but not the novelist's sympathy for such characters.

*The Troubleshooters* laid the ground for later movies on entrepreneur cultural brokers and catapulted Ge You to star status. He appeared in Zhang Yimou's and Chen Kaige's epic films, but was more often typecast as a cool-mannered Beijinger, similar to the character developed in *The Troubleshooters*. When Feng Xiaogang ventured from TV into film, in *Jiafang yifang* (English title *Dream Factory*, 1997), he made Ge You the lead, and the actor has played in almost all of Feng's films since. *Dream Factory* reworks, in many respects, Mi Jiashan's plot. Four unemployed film workers (among them the actor Yao Yuan, played by Ge You, and the scriptwriter Qian Kang, played by Feng Xiaogang) form a business called "The day trip of your dreams" (*Hao meng yiri you*), designed "to let the consumers have their dreams come true for one day." The Chinese title for the film, literally "Party A, Party B," refers to the contract drawn between the company and its customers, emphasizing how free play is moulded into commercial transaction. The customers' fantasies are more varied than those in *The Troubleshooters*, from a General Patton wannabe to a famous actress who craves for anonymity (or so she fancies at first). The entrepreneurs give the lie to high culture, as they conjure one film genre after the other as part of their schemes: a book seller stars in his own war movie modelled after Hollywood's *Patton*, and a cook is made the protagonist of a Qing-period costume drama. The four clearly draw inspiration from their experience in the film industry, creating movie-like settings and quoting well-known quips (and in doing so blurring the line between the fictional characters and the celebrities who play the parts). Whereas the 3T trio fails to get into the movie business, the *Dream Factory* quartet are industry veterans who find even more lucrative venues for their filmmaking experience and talent.

---

12. Mi Jiashan, "Discussing the troubleshooters," *Chinese Education and Society*, Vol. 31, No 1 (Fall 1998), pp. 8–14.

Most significant for the developing filmic portrayal of the cultural broker, the entrepreneurs in *Dream Factory* are presented in a favourable light. They are considerate of their clients, to the point where the customers' changing whims cause comic role reversals with the benevolent service providers. They volunteer to help the unfortunate, and even when they tell white lies they worry about the ethical consequences. They adhere to the Maoist maxim of "serving the people" and sacrifice their comfort (even giving up their apartment) to address social wrongs. They foreshadow the characters in Feng Xiaogang's *Tianxia wuzei* (*A World Without Thieves*, 2004) as the post-socialist version of model workers.

Such positive characters were required for the setting in which Feng's film was screened, namely as an upbeat production to celebrate the Chinese New Year.[13] In fact, Feng's unparalleled success and ascendance to cultural broker status may be attributed to adapting the model of the New Year's film (*hesuipian*). The marketing ploy of releasing a comic film tagged for the Chinese New Year had become standard practice in Hong Kong since *Xiyouji di yibailingyi hui zhi yueguang baohe* (English title *A Chinese Odyssey*, 1994), starring Stephen Chow. The Film Bureau introduced the term in the PRC when distributing Jackie Chan's *Rumble in the Bronx* under this rubric in 1995.[14] *Dream Factory* was the first made-in-the-PRC New Year's film, and following its success Feng has released increasingly popular movies every January, including the 2001 production *Big Shot's Funeral*. The trajectory from *The Troubleshooters* to *Big Shot's Funeral* may be symbolized in the differences between the 3T Company and Louis Wang's 3W.com.

Considering its lineage of make-believe protagonists, comic star power and New Year's films, *Big Shot's Funeral*'s plot stands as a metaphorical celebration of Feng's accomplishment in becoming not only a successful director but also a cultural celebrity. Yoyo starts as a streetwise guy akin to Ge You's character in the earlier movies and ends in a Feng Xiaogang-like role, a committed filmmaker who explicitly seeks economic profit and creates his market niche. Like real estate *dawan'r*, Feng has risen to cultural broker status by reaching beyond selling specific products. He relies not only on direct revenue from his films but uses also the interest in his work to sell his image at a profit and promote his vision of culture at large.

## The Culture of Capital

Feng Xiaogang, like his cinematic reflection in Yoyo, makes use of his position as a mediator between culture and capital. Yet the task becomes

---

13. For the same reason, the original Chinese title, *Dawan'r de zangli* (*Big Shot's Funeral*), was shortened to *Dawan'r*, since it was deemed inauspicious to mention a funeral on New Year's Eve. According to Feng, he omitted reference to death after being hospitalized in the middle of the shoot: Feng Xiaogang, *Wo ba qingchun xiangei ni* (*I Gave You My Youth*) (Wuhan: Changjiang wenyi chubanshe, 2003), p. 184.

14. My thanks Lihong Tang for clarifying Feng Xiaogang's use of Stephen Chow's New Year film formula.

more complex when it involves not only the translation of culture into capital but also the translation of one culture into another. In the beginning of the 21st century, in a business environment that relies on foreign investment and transnational film production, the cultural broker faces new challenges. *Big Shot's Funeral* addresses this situation and alludes to the limitations of the *dawan'r*.

Critics were quick to observe that *Big Shot's Funeral* was an index for the state of Chinese cinema as the PRC joined WTO on 11 December 2001, ten days before the film's release.[15] The plot features an international team-up, mirrored in the transnational collaboration, unprecedented under a PRC director. Produced jointly by the local Huayi Brothers & Taihe Film and by Columbia Pictures Film Production Asia, *Big Shot's Funeral* features a mostly PRC-based cast alongside the Hong Kong and American actors. Shujen Wang notes that the point-of-view shots in the opening sequence serve as a metaphor for the inversion of power relations between PRC filmmakers and Hollywood. The initial American dominance gives way to collaboration with the Chinese industry, with the initiative placed firmly in the latter's hand. Citing the movie's unprecedented box office record of ten million RMB, Wang sees both the plot and the film itself as a response to anxieties about the predatory businesses granted access by WTO.[16] Wang focuses on the film's ambivalence towards invading commercial practices, especially in regards to copyright regulation. Both the pattern of production and the narrative reflect recent and anticipated changes in the way film business is conducted in China, and the movie lends itself to be read as an allegory on Feng Xiaogang's role as a director in an increasingly commercialized market.

Yoyo's skilful product placement (called in Chinese *ruanxing guanggao*, or "soft advertisement") reflects Feng Xiaogang's mode of operation, which would become explicit in bundling his *Shouji* (*Cell Phone*, 2003) with Motorola and China Mobile campaigns.[17] When Feng hit upon the idea of the "comedy funeral," he thought, "isn't it the same as making a movie? Finding a theme, a sponsor … that's thinking playfully about our life."[18] This insight into the director's view of filmmaking notwithstanding, the film's portrayal of advertisement also shows the difficulty in negotiating with commercial interests.

Although the storyline features large, well-known companies sponsoring Yoyo's scheme, Feng was unable to use genuine brand names. Even the few exceptions, such as BMW and Outback, would not be associated with the funeral. The solution was a humorous parody on well-known names: instead of Coca Cola (Kekou kele), Crazy Cola (Kexiao kele); sohu.com (literally, "retrieving fox") is substituted by sodog.com. Yoyo

15. "Galaxy of stars come out for film awards in China," http://english.people.com.cn/200210/23/print20021023_105536.html (visited 20 December 2004).

16. Shujen Wang, "*Big Shot's Funeral*: China, Sony, and the WTO," *Asian Cinema*, Vol. 14, No. 2 (Fall/Winter 2003), pp. 145–154.

17. The combined campaign is described in detail in a forthcoming essay by Jing Wang.

18. Feng Xiaogang, personal interview with the author (Beijing, 19 July 2002).

has his arm twisted by a mobster who wants to promote his brand of bottled water, Lehaha – spoofing on the brand name Wahaha and alluding to the shady business of rebottling. On the one hand, Feng's playful use of names may be understood as mimicry, which Homi Bhabha regards as a form of resistance to cultural imperialism.[19] On the other hand, Feng admits that he resorted to paraphrasis only after Columbia Pictures had vetoed his original ideas on legal grounds. Feng found that his latitude diminished radically once he collaborated with foreign investors.[20]

The transnational cinema mode of operation delimited Feng's famous wit, allowing for insider jokes on Chinese cultural icons but showing only reverence towards Hollywood's mode of operation. The funeral plans parody Chinese media celebrities, mentioning Zhang Yimou's relationships with the actresses Gong Li and Zhang Ziyi and dropping names such as the comedians Feng Gong and Niu Qun and the rock star Zang Tianshuo. Yoyo is complimented, tongue in cheek, and told that he should run the Olympic Games – a jab at Zhang Yimou's over-the-top promotion of the 2008 events. The "comedy funeral" is first mentioned after Yoyo's friend, Louis, brags that he could stage the funeral of the sailors aboard the drowned Russian submarine Kursk. By implication, the commercialized funeral is regarded as an updated equivalent to ceremonies for national martyrs. The correspondence between the dead director, lying in state inside the Forbidden City, and the PRC's former leader, lying embalmed just outside Tiananmen Gate, follows the conventions of post-socialist quips ridiculing Maoist pomp. The American director, on the other hand, is portrayed as an undisputable authority. Insofar as the plot relies on Yoyo's abrogation of Tyler's prerogatives, planning the funeral while the director lies in a coma, the Chinese photographer is vindicated by the fact that Tyler has woken up and consented to the young man's entrepreneurial exploits. Even though Tyler hands over film direction to Yoyo, explaining that the young upstart possesses the inspiration that the Hollywood director has lost, Yoyo's dexterity as a cultural broker must meet with Tyler's stamp of approval.

The premise of an American "big shot" as the model of imitation for the local *dawan'r* seems especially out of place in view of the first draft for the plot. The idea for the film originated during Feng Xiaogang's regular drinking and bantering get-togethers with his friend, the director Chen Kaige. Chen told Feng of Akira Kurosawa's funeral in 1998, which he attended – the roads were blocked with people coming to pay a last tribute to the legendary director. Feng began fantasizing in jest about Chen's funeral and told his friend, "leave it to me and I'll give you an even more spectacular funeral!" During the next two months, whenever the two directors met, they would take up the joke and expand on it. Feng said that he could direct the funeral as either a tragedy or a comedy, and gradually came up with an entire scenario: the funeral would be treated as a commercial product and broadcast worldwide; Chen's fame would be

19. Homi K. Bhabha, *The Location of Culture* (New York: Routledge, 1994), pp. 85–92.
20. Feng Xiaogang, personal interview.

used to attract celebrities and advertisers and "make a pile of money." At first Feng thought about the hearse and the flowers, but as the running joke became more elaborate, Feng parodied advertising practices by adding products unrelated to the funeral. The friendly exchange between the two directors produced details remarkably similar to the final storyline of the *Big Shot's Funeral*: the dead Chen Kaige would lie on an Italian bed, bedecked with brand-name clothes; half his hair would be strewn with dandruff, the other half cleaned with an advertised shampoo.[21] Just as Yoyo's character reflects Feng's cultural brokering, the "big shot" was created in the image of a Chinese filmmaker.

Negotiating with foreign investors ended up, however, in a casting that erased the references to the PRC cinema scene. Columbia Pictures expressed interest in Feng's proposed storyline, but whereas the original draft featured a Chinese director for the title role, the American producers looked for international stars. They chose Donald Sutherland and contracted the Hong Kong actress Rosalind Kwan, known mainly for acting alongside Jet Li in the *Once Upon a Time in China* series, to ensure exposure in the Hong Kong and Taiwan markets. Such modifications should not be regarded simply as impositions – Feng acknowledges that Chinese audiences would find a foreign "big shot" more plausible. Moreover, Columbia was following a pattern of reinvigorating Asian film markets and had just funded Tsui Hark's *Time and Tide*, helping the Hong Kong director to rebound from an unprecedented two-year lull. *Big Shot's Funeral* can also be seen as an acknowledgement of Feng's talent. In addition to Sutherland, Feng also recruited Paul Mazursky, based on his impression of Mazursky's extroverted Italianate character.[22] And yet, even though Feng has claimed that the collaboration allows "the foxes to get the strength of the wolves, the wolves the cunning of the foxes; a win-win deal,"[23] and although *Big Shot's Funeral* paints a rosy picture of Chinese filmmakers' ability to operate in a global market, the production process indicates that China's cultural economy cannot be translated without compromising its vitality.[24] Yoyo achieves the ultimate success for a Chinese director, namely receiving the blessing of Hollywood producers and heading an international production, yet the film leaves a doubt about the legitimacy of Yoyo's advertisement gig and his unabashed use of cultural relics to promote global commerce.

Tyler's assistant, Lucy, stands for the rewards and dangers awaiting the successful cultural broker. Lucy (Rosalind Kwan) is an overseas Chinese, adept at literal translation but unfamiliar with local customs and idioms. She falls in love with Yoyo, and the film ends with their off-screen kiss. Yoyo, on the other hand, manages to communicate with Tyler without

21. *Ibid.*
22. *Ibid.*
23. Feng Xiaogang, *I Gave You My Youth*, p. 186.
24. As Ying Zhu notes, PRC cinema in the 1990s has become not only more commercial but also more local, relying on the domestic market: Ying Zhu, "From New Wave to Post New Wave: Chinese fifth generation cinematic transition, *Asian Culture Quarterly*, Vol. 27, No. 2 (summer 2000), pp. 13–47.

Lucy and even against her will. Yoyo and Tyler bond and reaffirm their collaboration by sharing Lucy. Questionable gender politics aside, the character of a translator who acts as Tyler's confidante and as Yoyo's minder also conveys the limitations of Yoyo's autonomy. The film's last part, in which Yoyo is committed to an insane asylum and communicates with the outside world only through Lucy, turns out to be part of Yoyo's new film. The quick reversal of alternative realities through the play-within-a-play not only alludes to the failure of narrative but also leaves a lingering impression that unless Yoyo chooses to remain confined within his solipsistic fantasies, he needs Lucy as his enabler. To turn his "troubleshooter savvy" and Beijing-style self-effacing wit into an international success, the cultural broker must in turn be brokered by Hollywood's agents of so-called global film culture.

In China's media environment, where filmgoers have followed Feng's New Year's productions and the director has made a spectacle out of his success, the analogy between Yoyo's entrepreneurship and Feng's ascendance to *dawan'r* status would not be lost on the audience – and neither would the ambiguity of his position vis-à-vis the Hollywood producers. Insofar as the film fits neatly into the mediascape of post-WTO China, it is also because it marks a perceived crisis in filmmaking and calls for resourceful manipulation of the new cultural economy, introducing changes not only into film viewing and production patterns but also into brand-name consumption and even spatial practices.

## Space as Cultural Capital

The frequent association between entrepreneurial filmmakers and commercial uses of space raises the question of why directors and real estate developers share similar modes of operation as cultural brokers. What prompted Ning Ying and Wu Wenguang to team up with the builders of extravagant architecture and yuppie residences? To what effect does *Big Shot's Funeral* link Yoyo's ambition of going on the stock market with fantasies of designing a residential project? Why does Feng's self-referential allegory on filmmaking revolve around the irreverent use of a space emblematic of Beijing's culture? The concurrence may be explained by the explosion of land value and the building boom of the past decade, which has had a major impact on many aspects of the PRC's economy and culture. The idioms and practices of real estate have taken over other areas. Moreover, cinema is largely spatial, and the filmic allure of places such as the Commune by the Great Wall and the Forbidden City is self-evident. Yet I argue that beyond these general motives, the collaboration between real estate developers and filmmakers results from a growing understanding of space as cultural capital and from the increasing involvement of movies in shaping the cultural value of space in the past decade.

Since the early 1990s, a large number of films have focused on Beijing's changing cityscape, depicting urban malaise and engaging in nostalgia. In a forthcoming study I show how the New Urban Cinema (*xin chengshi dianying*) has negotiated with the city's perceptual matrices, as laid out by artists, political decision makers, professional planners and developers. In the context of *Big Shot's Funeral* and the linkage between film and advertisement as forms that capitalize on cultural cachet, special attention should be given to the import of the Forbidden City.

The process of turning the Forbidden City into a film location is emblematic of the transformation of the ideological, economic and cinematic significance of Beijing spaces. The palace complex was first used as a film location in 1987, for Bernardo Bertolucci's *The Last Emperor*. Bertolucci realized the Forbidden City's marketing value and convinced the authorities to grant him permission to shoot on location, which greatly enhanced the film's appeal. A decade later, the Forbidden City opened for filmed cultural events, beginning with Yanni's concert in May 1997 (following his performance at the Taj Mahal); Puccini's *Turandot*, conducted by Zubin Mehta and staged by Zhang Yimou in September 1998; and a concert by Luciano Pavarotti, Placido Domingo and Jose Carreras on 23 June 2001. These events promoted Beijing's international image as a cultural centre, and in the case of the three tenors, the event aimed specifically to promote Beijing's bid for the 2008 Olympics. These occasions, condoned by the Beijing Cultural Relics Bureau, generated filmic images that would be exploited for economic and political purposes.

The imagined funeral inside the Forbidden City stretches the existing practices by almost-credible margins. *Big Shot's Funeral* brings to the absurd the relations between power, urban space, commercial advertisement and filmmaking. The film exploits the comic effect of portraying improbable situations that nevertheless comport with reality. It offers the sum total of previous events: Tyler reshoots *The Last Emperor*, Zhang Yimou would stage *Turandot* and Louis Wang would produce entertainment shows in the vein of televised New Year extravaganzas. Nor is the commercial use of the space implausible: advertisers had already gained access to the palace in 1996, when Land Rover launched its campaign on the premises. In fact, the Forbidden City has since become such a popular location for advertisement and movie shooting that officials have recently expressed the need for stricter regulation.[25] In addition, the 1999 ban on commercial billboards at Tiananmen Square was expanded on 1 October 2004 to various cultural relics in the capital and even to vehicles entering Tiananmen Square.[26] The need for legislation indicates how far the advertising industry had been encroaching on cultural relics and state emblems. Evidently, promoters found it tempting to publicize their

25. "Beijing gets tough on relics protection," http://www.china.org.cn/english/2004/Jul/102624.htm (visited 7 January 2005).

26. "Outdoor ads banned in Beijing's special areas," http://www.beijingportal.com.cn/7838/2004/09/14/207@2275512.htm [Beijing Portal, 14 September 2004] (visited 7 January 2005); Liu Li, "Beijing to continue ban on ads in Tian'anmen," http://www.chinadaily.com.cn/english/doc/2004–04/13/content_322739.htm (visited 7 January 2005).

products in the vicinity of emblems of tradition and power. Yet leaders must have found it equally inconvenient that the association between cultural prestige, buying power and political authority was flaunted precisely in the locations where cultural symbols were reappropriated by the state. As befits a *dawan'r*, Feng Xiaogang not only comments on cultural phenomena but also predicts them and determines their significance in advance.

Feng Xiaogang's film, like Yoyo's enterprise, relies on the cultural prestige and cinematic renown of the Forbidden City. Tyler plans a remake of Bertolucci's *The Last Emperor*, looking for inspiration after experiencing a crisis. Similarly, Feng Xiaogang revisits *The Last Emperor* and returns to the Forbidden City as a way of introducing a fresh look to Chinese filmmaking. Like Yoyo, who does not settle for a "comedy funeral" in a film studio, Feng Xiaogang seeks out the palace compound as a mark of authenticity. In "using the plot to break away from Bertolucci's images and present the Forbidden City in a novel way"[27] and suggesting even more daring commercial uses of the familiar place, Feng raises the economic stakes in cultural productions and enhances his standing as a broker.

*Big Shot's Funeral* sums up the various cinematic and advertisement practices that have made use of Beijing's spaces, as well as the ways in which cultural brokering relies on manipulating space. The film diverges from many New Urban Cinema pieces that depict locations in the process of being built, sold and demolished, yet the focus on the touristy Forbidden City, seemingly disconnected from city life, makes the urban change even more poignant. As a recognized cultural relic, the palace is preserved in almost pristine form (with additions such as the Starbucks franchise); nevertheless, it is put up for rent as any real estate, for film locations and advertisement campaigns. *Big Shot's Funeral* describes the Forbidden City as "the most expensive location in the world." Its cultural cachet raises its price and turns it into a chip in high-stakes games that involve capital, social connections and political clout. Yoyo – and Feng Xiaogang himself – distinguish themselves from advertisers and film directors who use readily-available locations and flaunt their ability to subject even the most inaccessible spaces to market economy.

In his position as a cultural broker, Feng leverages the prestige of his ground-breaking venture and renders filmmaking itself into a metaphor for his vision of Beijing's cultural heritage. The striking image of the last emperor – or rather, the child who plays the role in Tyler's production – drinking Coke is, on its face, amusing. Yet it also evidences Feng's skill in turning on its head the authenticity of *The Last Emperor* and, even more important, assert that his authority – like Zhang Yimou's in staging *Turandot* – lies in publicizing the city's hybrid image as representative of the new Beijing.

Feng Xiaogang's case demonstrates the futility of pigeonholing, in early 21st-century China, cultural productions as either complacently

---

27. Feng Xiaogang, personal interview.

commercial or hard-edged dissident. The celebration of consumerism does not simply play into the hands of the Dengist policy of "to get rich is glorious." When the TV, MTV and commercials director Wu Ershan claims that "shooting commercials is serving the people," he does not simply parody the Maoist adage but rather alludes to the new contract between filmmakers and their audience. Cinema, space and commerce in contemporary China have combined to form an innovative nexus between image making, market shaping and cultural identification.

# Museums, Memorial Sites and Exhibitionary Culture in the People's Republic of China*

## Kirk A. Denton

ABSTRACT This article presents an overview of post-Mao museum representations of modern Chinese history. The focus is on changing exhibitionary practices and historical narratives in PRC history museums in the period of market reforms and globalization. It shows how new museum architecture, the place of museum buildings in the cityscape and new exhibitionary technologies (such as multimedia displays, dioramas, miniatures) are tied to new narratives of history that serve the interests of the ideology of market reform. Conventional socialist narratives of martyrdom and revolutionary liberation have not disappeared by any means, but they are being reshaped to downplay class issues and to legitimize commercial interests, a work ethic ideology and nationalism.

Overviews of contemporary Chinese culture, such as that envisaged for this volume, rarely consider museums and exhibitions as part of their purview. Yet, annually, 150 million visitors attend some 8,000 exhibitions held in China's 2,000 museums.[1] Museums and exhibitions constitute an important cultural form through which art, history and politics are presented to and experienced by many Chinese. Originating in Europe with the Enlightenment and its scientific project of categorizing knowledge and developing in service to the 19th-century nation state, the public pedagogical display of cultural and historical objects – what Tony Bennett has called an "exhibitionary complex"[2] – is a quintessentially modern phenomenon, and China is certainly not alone in placing a high priority on this practice.

In the past few decades museums have proliferated worldwide in unprecedented numbers. According to one account, three-quarters of all active museums in the world today were established after 1945,[3] and in China the percentage would be higher still. Among the reasons for this global flourishing of museums are the increase in consumer markets for culture, perhaps especially with the development of global tourism; the emergence of new forms of memory and memorialization that compete

*Many thanks to Michel Hockx and Julia Strauss for inviting me to the conference that led to this special issue. Thanks also to Eliza Ho for first alerting me to Luzhen. Grants from the Ohio State University helped support research for this article.

1. Jianzhu chuangzuo (ed.), *Zhongguo bowuguan jianzhu yu wenhua* (*The Architecture and Culture of Chinese Museums*) (Beijing: Jixie gongye, 2003), p. ii. The 2003 edition of the *Zhongguo tongji nianjian* (*China Statistics Yearbook*) (Beijing: Zhongguo tongji, 2003) gives the figure of 80 million visitors for the year 2002 (p. 787). To put this in some comparative perspective, about 100 feature films (officially-approved) were produced in 2002; and 170,000 books were published (with sales amounting to some 43 billion *yuan*). See *China Statistics Yearbook*, pp. 783–795.

2. Tony Bennett, *The Birth of the Museum: History, Theory, Politics* (London: Routledge, 1995).

3. See Stephen E. Weil, *Making Museums Matter* (Washington: Smithsonian Institution, 2002), p. 31.

with those of older, more established national museums; and a nostalgic reaction to the sense of disconnect from the past that is the product of modernization and globalization.

This article focuses on the explosive rise in museums in China's post-Mao period and their changing exhibitionary practices and historical narratives.[4] Despite competition from new media such as the internet and the continuing popularity of television, museums continue to be built and exhibitions put on in record numbers in China, and established museums are undergoing expensive renovations, both to their buildings and to their exhibitions. During this period, Chinese society has experienced radical changes, including the emergence of a market economy, globalization, the rise of a vibrant commercial popular culture and unparalleled social mobility. Whereas urban popular culture tends to stress the importance of self, self-fulfilment and personal consumption,[5] museums of modern history – the focus of the present article – emphasize the centrality of self-sacrifice to the grand narratives of nation and the communist revolution. In contrast to China's vibrant popular culture, such museums and their exhibitions often appear staid and stodgy, as if defying the changing world beyond their walls. That museums have been slow to respond to this changing world is not surprising given the fact that they are primarily state funded and thus more closely associated with the state cultural bureaucracy than other cultural forms and institutions.[6]

The central issue addressed in this article is how museums have responded to these social, economic and cultural transformations. Is museum practice really changing from the norms of the 1980s and earlier, or is it merely repackaging old messages in fancy new buildings and through sophisticated display techniques? In what follows, I describe some recent trends in museum development in China and filter this description through the question of how museums are being made

4. To put museum growth in China in perspective, it should be pointed out that in 1949 China had around 20 museums. By the beginning of the Cultural Revolution there were 160. From 1980 to 1999, the number rose from 365 to 1,357. For figures, see Wang Hongjun (ed.), *Zhongguo bowuguanxue jichu* (*Foundation of Chinese Museum Studies*) (Shanghai: Shanghai guji, 2001), p. 114. The PRC ranks seventh in the world in number of museums, well below the top three, the US (over 8,000), Germany (over 4,500) and Italy (just under 3,500). *Ibid.* pp. 129–130. Museum construction and renovation is continuing at a fast pace. In Beijing alone, in the next few years, the number of museums will increase from 118 to 130, through an investment of some RMB 7 billion. According to Su Donghai (in *ibid.*), China is entering a new "peak" in museum construction. Some project that by 2015, China will have half again as many museums as it does today.

5. I am thinking of such cultural forms as television soap operas centred around teenage love, pop music concerts, "campus fiction" about young love, internet novels (and, more recently, a text messaging novel), pornographic internet sites, fashion and design magazines.

6. There are an increasing number of privately-owned and funded museums in China, but the vast majority continue to be funded primarily by different levels of government. It is also true, however, that some state-run museums are able to rely increasingly on non-state funding (donations from outside sources and revenue from visitors). James Flath argues that this frees them from the imposition of official "stateist" narratives of history, but as I argue below I don't think this is necessarily the case. See James Flath, "Managing historical capital in Shandong: museum, monument, and memory in provincial China." *The Public Historian* Vol. 24, No. 2 (Spring 2002), p. 54. As it is for museums in the West, funding is clearly a concern for Chinese museologists today (see Wang Hongjun, *Foundation of Chinese Museum Studies*, pp. 398–414).

relevant to a radically changing society. My particular focus is museums and memorial sites related to the history of modern China: revolutionary history museums, military museums, memorial halls for martyrs, ethnographic museums, modern literature museums and the like. Since the founding of the PRC, such places have been used as tools by the state to propound officially sanctioned views of modern history. These kinds of museums have been – and many continue to be – pedagogical tools for the teaching of Party history to the masses. They embody state power, and this power is expressed at a variety of levels: the architectural style of museum buildings, the location of museums in the cityscape, the "authenticity" of concrete artifacts, and the display of those objects and their arrangement into narratives. Of course, "official" Party history has changed in substantial ways in state museums from the 1950s to the present,[7] but there have also been many constants, including the central role of the CCP, the grand narrative of historical development, the importance of martyrdom and the theme of national humiliation.

With the post-Mao relaxation of control over the cultural sphere, and the orientation towards the cultural market in the past decade and a half, has the "official" representation of modern Chinese history undergone substantial changes? How have museums sought to make the message of revolutionary history relevant to an audience whose lives are so radically removed from that history? How have new aesthetics, new technologies and new forms of popular culture affected museums and their representations of the modern past? As China moved boldly into a market economy in the 1980s and 1990s, I argue, museums of modern history edged slowly away from standard narratives of class oppression and revolutionary struggle towards representations of the past that legitimize the contemporary ideology of commerce, entrepreneurship and market reform. This new ideology is brought out through new modes of representing the modern past (addressed at the end of the article) but it also gets expressed more obliquely through new architectural design and exhibitionary styles.

*Museum Development in Post-Mao China*

The post-Mao flourishing of museums occurred in two waves: in the early to mid 1980s and then from the 1990s into the present century. The first wave was clearly a response to the Cultural Revolution and its degradation of cultural institutions. Building new museums and memorial sites or reopening established museums and revising their exhibitions marked what could be called a "reinstitutionalization" of memory of the past after the uncertainty of the Cultural Revolution period. For Su Donghai, a curator at the former Museum of the Chinese Revolution and a leading figure in the Chinese museum world, among the important

---

7. See Kirk A. Denton, "Visual memory and the construction of a revolutionary past: paintings from the Museum of the Chinese Revolution," *Modern Chinese Literature and Culture*, Vol. 12, No. 2 (Fall 2000), pp. 203–235.

values for museums in the post-Mao period are to "verify" history and to extol such moral virtues as patriotism and self-sacrifice.[8] Consistent with the ideological values of the Deng regime, museums sought to "seek truth through facts" and restore a "scientific" representation of the past, in contrast to the distortions and misrepresentations of the Cultural Revolution. Just as museums in the early post-revolutionary period of the 1950s were established to help legitimize the new regime, the restoration of old exhibitions and the establishment of new revolutionary history museums in the post-Mao period served to restore the Party's image in the wake of the Cultural Revolution and to legitimize the authority of the Deng regime.[9] Wang Hongjun writes that the state and the Party placed more importance on museums in the 1980s than ever before.[10] Museums were even mentioned in the 1982 constitution, where their service role was emphasized. The role of museums in fostering "spiritual civilization" was promoted, and laws were passed enhancing the protection of cultural artifacts and regulating museums.[11]

A second wave of new museum construction and revamping of old museums and their exhibits occurred in the wake of the Tian'anmen movement and the collapse of communist states in Eastern Europe.[12] Many new museums and memorials sites were built to restore waning socialist values and increase patriotism and nationalism. With a general loss of faith in socialism among the populace and the rise of competing forms of identity with the influx of foreign cultural products and the emergence of a thriving indigenous pop culture, the state was clearly concerned that Chinese "not forget" the humiliations and heroism of China's revolutionary past.[13] The CCP remains invested in a representation of the modern past that makes the rise of the Party "inevitable" and justifies its continued place in power. A 1991 circular issued by several state bureaus involved in propaganda work emphasizes the importance of cultural artifacts and museums and memorial sites in stimulating patriotism among the young and of using fresh techniques to increase the "attractiveness" (*xiyinli*) and "influence" (*ganranli*) of exhibits so that history can be perceived "directly through the senses" (*zhiguanxing*) and

---

8. Su Donghai, "Museums and museum philosophy in China," *Nordisk Museologi*, No. 2 (1995), pp. 61–80.

9. Lü Jimin (ed.), *Dangdai Zhongguo de bowuguan shiye 1998* (*The Enterprise of Contemporary Chinese Museums, 1998*) (Beijing: Dangdai Zhongguo 1998), pp. 101–103.

10. Wang Hongjun, *Foundation of Chinese Museum Studies*, p. 109.

11. For a collection of state laws and official proclamations regarding cultural heritage, see *ibid.* pp. 493–559. For the reference to "spiritual civilization," see *ibid.* p. 511.

12. For a general discussion of the rise of patriotic education (*aiguo jiaoyu*) in the 1990s, see Baogang He and Yingjie Guo, *Nationalism, National Identity and Democratization in China* (Aldershot: Ashgate Publishing, 2000).

13. As Paul Cohen has shown, nationalism and patriotism were not just a product of state intervention, they constituted a general ethos in the cultural field as a whole. The 1990s saw the appearance of numerous texts in the "national humiliation" (*guochi*) mode, works that sought to recall China's history of national humiliations at the hands of Western and Japanese imperialists, the *Zhongguo keyi shuo bu* (China can say no) books being only the most obvious examples. See Paul A. Cohen, "Remembering and forgetting: national humiliation in 20th-century China," *Twentieth-Century China*, Vol. 27, No. 2 (April 2002), pp. 1–39.

has a greater "sense of reality" (*zhenshigan*).[14] Despite a lot of rhetoric about "globalization" and "pluralism" from museum curators and museologists, museums in China, it seems, continue to be used by the state for legitimizing purposes or are at least closely aligned with state interests. This is not to suggest that Chinese museums are not changing – they clearly are – but I do want to emphasize that their propaganda role continues to be strong in the era of the market economy. The messages propagated by museums are certainly changing, but so too is the ideology of the state. Museums in China have not gone postmodern, in the sense of tackling the past from multiple perspectives and highlighting the very notion of representation.

Revolutionary history museums and memorial sites were an important part of this state-sponsored nationalism of the post-Mao era. Among the more significant museums constructed during these two waves of growth are the Longhua Martyrs Memorial Park, Yuhuatai Memorial Park, Memorial Museum of the People' Resistance to Japan, the Hongyan Memorial Hall, Museum of Modern Chinese Literature and the Nanjing Massacre Memorial Hall. In one of the more manifest indications of the importance the state places on the educational value of museums and memorial sites, in 1995 the Ministry of Propaganda approved the Hundred Patriotic Model Sites to promote patriotism and knowledge of China's past.[15] Although sites of ancient culture and premodern history – such as the Yellow Emperor's tomb, the Great Wall and the Dunhuang caves – are on the list, the large majority are revolutionary history sites. In the present century, the state continues to envisage a nationalist and ideological role for museums. Museums and new exhibits are given lots of coverage in the mass media. For example, when the special exhibits on Xibaipo (National Museum of China), the Yan'an Spirit (Military History Museum) and Deng Xiaoping (National Museum of China) were put on in the summer of 2004, the print and television media lavished attention on them, so as both to increase attendance and help propagandize the official interpretation of the exhibits.

To conclude this overview of museum development in post-Mao China, I look briefly at the exhibition associated with the 28th Session of the World Heritage Committee, convened in Suzhou in June 2004. The exhibition demonstrates perfectly the value the state continues to place on cultural heritage and its primary role in regulating and shaping it. Discussion about the meeting and its accompanying exhibition was all over the Chinese media throughout the summer of 2004, revealing a clear collusion between the state and the media in this discourse of "cultural

---

14. See Wang Hongjun, *Foundation of Chinese Museum Studies*, pp. 522–25. The language of this state document reveals, to my mind, a strong self-consciousness in officialdom about the appeal of popular culture forms.

15. For a complete listing of the sites, as well as a detailed description of each, see *Aiguozhuyi jiaoyu shifan jidi da bolan* (*Great Overview of Patriotic Model Sites*) (Beijing: Hongqi and Guangdong renmin, 1998).

heritage."[16] Cultural heritage, and the museums and exhibitions that preserve and interpret it, represent many things in China today, but national pride, tourism profits and ideological legitimacy are among the more prominent. It is one way for China both to "enter into the world" (to become global) and to express nationalism. It should be remembered that world heritage sites are of two kinds – cultural and natural – so world heritage serves to invest Chinese citizens more deeply in the history (cultural) and territory (natural) that makes China a powerfully-imagined community.

The first part of the exhibit was devoted to world heritage sites (apart from those in China). Organized by continent and nation, it presented small displays consisting of photographs, maps and textual explanations in Chinese and English. The second part was devoted to the roles of various state ministries and bureaus in the PRC – the Ministry of Construction, the National Commission on Cultural Heritage and the Cultural Relics Bureau – in promoting the preservation of cultural heritage sites. The third and final part offered displays of all 29 of China's world heritage sites. The exhibition proceeds from the global to the local, but it does so only through the filter of the state. The middle exhibit on the state cultural heritage agencies, which visitors see before the final exhibit of China's world heritage sites, suggests the state's primary role in defining China's history and its territory, in controlling China's time and space, so to speak. As a whole, the world heritage exhibition reveals the importance the state places on cultural heritage as a way of fostering national pride and as means for China to assert itself in the world arena. Of course, this is not just about political power and cultural prestige. Clearly, tourism and the money it generates are key factors in world heritage designation, as well as in the cultural heritage field more generally, but the ideological and political are never far removed. In some cases, as discussed below, this rise of commercialism in museum practice and exhibitions works to undermine more conventional narratives of modern Chinese history. But this commercialism also bears the imprints of ideology, an ideology that is often consistent with the market reforms and entrepreneurship favoured by the present Party leadership.

*Museum Design and Exhibition Aesthetics*

I begin my examination of contemporary museum practice with architecture and urban design because changes in museum design and the symbolic meaning of museum buildings in the cityscape are ultimately tied to new forms of exhibitionary practice and new historical narratives. Not surprisingly, the past two decades have seen dramatic changes in museum architecture. There has been a gradual shift away from the socialist realist aesthetic of museum buildings constructed in the 1950s

---

16. When I visited the exhibition, the hall was packed with visitors. Though the free admission and the fact that it was a Saturday no doubt accounted for the large turnout, the national media attention contributed to it.

and 1960s towards a more modernist or even postmodern aesthetic that is at once global and draws from local inspiration.[17] Chinese cities are increasingly using powerful and arresting design in museum buildings to forge modern and sophisticated self-images as they seek to "join the world" economically and culturally.

As elsewhere, museums in China have important symbolic roles in the larger context of the urban environments in which they are located.[18] The Shanghai Museum, for instance, has emerged as something of a visual symbol of the new Shanghai.[19] Completed in 1996, the museum is a centrepiece in the newly-fashioned People's Square, which like Tiananmen Square for Beijing is the political, cultural and symbolic heart of Shanghai. People's Square, radically transformed from its socialist legacy (which was itself a radical transformation of the site during its colonial days), is also framed by the Grand Theatre, the headquarters of the Shanghai city government and the Shanghai Municipal Urban Planning Exhibition Centre. Taken together these represent the official face of Shanghai: the government headquarters is the political and economic present; the Urban Planning Exhibition Centre embodies, both in its exterior and in its exhibitions, a progressive commercial future; and the Shanghai Museum conveys a glorious past. The museum and the Grand Theatre present to the world a cultured image of the city that is crucial to its larger image as a global economic powerhouse.

Smaller cities and regions have paid just as much attention to the design of their key museums, also using them as cultural capital for the larger municipal economy. Shenyang's September 18 History Museum (Figure 1), the new Lu Xun Memorial Hall in Shaoxing and Fushun's Lei Feng Memorial Hall are all excellent examples. That Fushun, a depressed city about an hour east of Shenyang and renowned as a coal-producing area with high unemployment rates, would invest so much money in building (and revamping many times) a memorial hall, suggests how important bureaucrats consider these sites to be, to tourism and the local economy, as well as to civic pride and municipal self image.[20] Ever competitive with Shanghai, Beijing has built or is building

17. Typical of the socialist aesthetic is the National Museum of China (formerly the Chinese History Museum and the Museum of the Chinese Revolution), designed by Zhang Kaiji in the late 1950s. There are plans to renovate the museum, including building an addition, before it reopens in 2007, just in time for the Olympic Games. The exterior of the museum will, museum directors have assured the museum community, remain intact.

18. For an excellent collection of essays on this topic, see Michaela Giebelhaus (ed.), *The Architecture of the Museum: Symbolic Structures, Urban Contexts* (Manchester: Manchester University Press, 2003).

19. The architect, Xing Tonghe, was highly conscious of striking a balance between a foreign and a traditional Chinese aesthetic. Although it perhaps cannot compete with the Bund in terms of being a visual icon of Shanghai, images of the museum appear regularly in Shanghai and internationally. The museum appears as the centrepiece of Global Museum's internet banner: http://www.globalmuseum.org/.

20. The Fushun Lei Feng Memorial Hall has competition from Lei Feng's native Wangchang, in Hunan, which also has a memorial hall for their native son. The Fushun hall was built in 1964, and then added on to or renovated in 1969, 1992 and 2002. In its 40-year history, some 47 million people have visited it.

Figure 1: **September 18 History Museum (Shenyang)**

many new museums with interesting and innovative designs, including the remarkable Beijing Capital Museum.[21]

The museum community in China has a new awareness of the importance of unique design in museum buildings and exhibition construction. This is part of a larger wave of interest – one might even called it a fever (*re*) – in design and architecture. Whereas ten years ago you would be hard pressed to find a book on these topics in Chinese bookstores, architecture and design now have special sections with row upon row of books. The Chinese Museum Association (Zhongguo bowuguan xiehui) has a special committee devoted to the "art of exhibition" (*chenlie yishu*) and books are published on the topic of museum architecture and exhibition design.[22] One of these volumes suggests that good design, which is defined primarily as design that is innovative and yet appropriate to the topic, will help save museums from the threat of the market economy.[23] Good design also participates in the market economy by contributing to the cultural life of cities, making them more attractive to tourism, commercial investment and global trade.

21. There is clearly a wealth gap in museum construction. Wealthy cities like Qingdao can afford to build fancy new museums, while smaller towns such as Qingzhou, in the Shandong interior, struggle just to keep their collections intact.
22. Zhao Chungui, "Xu – er" ("Preface, two"), in Jianzhu chuangzuo, *The Architecture and Culture of Chinese Museums*. Zhao's preface to the volume serves as a kind of manifesto for good museum design, which should be "pluralistic," "individualistic," "humanistic," "holistic" and "standardized."
23. Several essays in *ibid.* mention this.

Figure 2: **Nanjing Massacre Memorial Hall (Nanjing)**

The modernist aesthetic in museum design emerged in the early 1980s and is best exemplified by the work of Qi Kang, a Nanjing-based architect who has specialized in museums and memorial sites. Qi's work includes the Yuhuatai Martyrs Memorial Park, the Nanjing Massacre Memorial Hall and the Zhou Enlai Memorial Hall in Huai'an. Qi has a consistent style, but he is also known for thinking hard, sometimes quite philosophically, about designs that are appropriate to the particular mandate of the memorial or museum. Tragedy and horror, in a spirit of humanist sympathy, are beautifully conveyed, for example, in the stark and lifeless, vaguely minimalist, aesthetic of Qi's Nanjing Massacre Memorial (Figure 2).

But most new design is not so intentionally lacking in grandeur. A rather different example of the new aesthetic of modern history museums is the Longhua Martyrs Memorial Park in Shanghai (Figure 3). Like many new museums in China, the aesthetic is a strange brew of modernist grandiosity with the socialist realist heroic. The exhibition hall, which is the centrepiece of a large park filled with artwork and other forms of memorial, is a large glass pyramid in a modernist mode. Its glass and stone style is radically different from the heavy and ponderous style of, say, the classic socialist realist Military Museum in Beijing. Yet, though the style of the building speaks of the modern and the global, the exhibitions inside are devoted to martyrs, the vast majority of whom died fighting for the revolution or leftist revolutionary causes. The principal message is a highly conventional one in Chinese modern history museums: martyrs, those who sacrificed themselves for the collective,

Figure 3: **Longhua Martyrs Memorial Park (Nanjing)**

are the heart and soul of the revolution; commemorating them is to commemorate the revolution itself.

What then is the relationship between the aesthetics of the museum building and the exhibition it houses? Regardless of the content or narrative structure of the exhibition, the modernist aesthetic of the building speaks volumes. First, it marks an explicit rejection of the socialist aesthetic and suggests that the meaning of the exhibition within its walls moves away from standard socialist narratives. The modernist aesthetic also explicitly marks a joining with the world and an implicit rejection of Chinese cultural essentialism. Architectural style can influence museum spectators' experience by changing their framework for appreciating the exhibitions themselves.

More often than not, museums with innovative architectural designs also make use of new exhibitionary techniques. Museums generally are embracing new forms and styles of display, and Chinese museum curators are very much in tune with trends in global museology. There is, to a certain extent, a discernible pattern of "institutional isomorphism," a convergence in behaviour among museum curators and how they shape their exhibitions.[24] Yet Chinese curators must work within a political

24. Sociologists Paul Dimaggio and Walter Powell have argued that increased global interaction in "organizational fields" can lead to a homogenization of behaviour, patterns and tastes, what he calls "institutional isomorphorism." See "The iron cage revisited: institutional isomorphism and collective rationality in organizational fields," in Michael J. Handel (ed.), *The Sociology of Organizations: Classic, Contemporary, and Critical Readings* (Thousand Oaks: Sage Publications, 2003), pp. 243–253. Chinese museums have begun to use Western

system that does not allow them free rein; the design and content of exhibitions in Chinese museums, especially modern history museums, is always a process of negotiation between curators and Party officials. New developments in Chinese exhibitionary practice might converge to a degree with global trends – for example, the style of the Shanghai Municipal History Museum closely resembles that of the Edo-Tokyo Museum in Japan – but local political constraints, cultural traditions and social considerations preclude homogenization.

A typical display in an old-style modern history museum is organized in chronological order, with rooms devoted to moments in a chronological narrative. Though they are not necessarily required to, spectators are generally expected to pass through the rooms in a prescribed order. The rooms are brightly lit, and the visitor can see other visitors as well as the objects on display. Each individual display has small photographs and texts at eye level on the walls, large oil paintings higher up, and artifacts and documents in glass-enclosed cases below. The new aesthetic prefers dimmed rooms with subtle and sophisticated lighting that focuses attention on the objects displayed and makes the viewing experience more personal, akin to the sense of personal connection one gets in viewing a film in a dark theatre (Figure 4).[25] It draws attention to the displays as aesthetic objects and relies less on textual explanations to bring meaning to them. By highlighting the object and enhancing the one-to-one relationship between spectator and object, the new design seems to fetishize artifacts in ways similar to the fetishization of commodities in commercial culture and market economies.

Not surprisingly, the past decade has seen a sharp increase in the use of multimedia and new forms of display technology, especially in new or renovated musuems. Perhaps most obvious is the use of video monitors to show documentary film footage or portions of feature films. Film is often projected on to large screens, as in both the Shanghai and Shaoxing Lu Xun memorial halls which feature footage from Lu Xun's funeral. Some museums have special exhibition rooms for film viewing. The New Culture Movement Museum (Beijing), the Lei Feng Memorial Hall (Fushun) and the Unit 731 Crimes Museum (Pingfang, Heilongjiang) are three examples. The Shanghai Municipal History Museum makes copious use of film and video, including vintage film of scenes from the Shanghai racetrack and a video of the 1981 film version of Mao Dun's *Midnight* (*Ziye*) next to a large model of the Republican-era Shanghai stock exchange.

---

*footnote continued*

design firms in their planning and exhibition design. For example, Gallagher & Associates, a Maryland-based design firm, has been involved in the planning and design of the new Shanghai Science and Technology Museum; Jack Rouse Associates, of Cincinnati, has been involved in designing the new Three Gorges Museum in Chongqing; and BRC Imagination Arts, a multinational design firm, is doing the design of the Great Wall World Cultural Heritage Park.

25. For award winning exhibition designs, see *Zhongguo bowuguan chenlie jingpin tujie* (*Excellent Exhibitions in Chinese Museums: Illustrations and Text*), 3 vols. (Beijing: Wenwu).

Figure 4: **Display from CCP First Congress Meeting Hall**

Dioramas, models and scenes with wax figures are commonly used in Chinese museums today. The Shanghai Municipal History Museum, for example, is almost entirely organized around models. It completely eschews "authentic" artifacts and embraces the patented inauthenticity of recreated scenes. Even museums that treat the most serious of topics now frequently make use of dioramas. For instance, the 731 Unit Crimes Museum has a near life-size scene of Japanese atrocities in a Heilongjiang village, and the Mao Memorial Hall (Shaoshan) has a large bronze diorama of Mao listening attentively to mine workers at Anyuan. Film and video are often incorporated into models and dioramas. For instance, at the Lei Feng Memorial Hall there is a "multimedia scene box" (*duomeiti jingxiang*) entitled "A day in the life of Lei Feng" (*Lei Feng de yi tian*). Before the spectator there is a model of a building with two windows containing monitors with videos showing characters moving from one screen to the other and a voiceover narrating events. At the Shanghai Municipal History Museum, video images projected into a miniature model of a Shanghai slum show the lives of the impoverished slum dwellers. At the Mao Zedong Memorial Hall in Shaoshan an exhibit contains a miniature diorama into which are projected video scenes that recount the story of Mao's efforts to instigate a peasant movement in Shaoshan; the soundtrack includes characters' voices (Mao speaks perfect

Mandarin), a voiceover narrating Mao's efforts and dramatic music. Large dioramas in theatres with accompanying light shows and voiceover narration are also common.

With increased use of film and video, dioramas, scenes, and miniature models, Chinese museums seem to be moving away from the traditional mandate of the museum, which emphasizes the powerful experience of being transported to the past by being in the presence of authentic objects from that past. Authenticity has been replaced by images, models and miniatures – imitations of the real, not the thing itself. One might argue that this marks a move into the postmodern world of the simulacrum and a self-conscious recognition of the essential inauthenticity of all forms of representation, but Chinese museum curators would not see these new forms of exhibition in this way. Rather, they are used to "attract" spectators and lead them to a more "lively," and thus authentic, representation of the past. Yet, in drawing attention away from the authenticity of historical artifacts to the "mediated" nature of representation, these new forms of exhibition contribute to the undermining of established revolutionary history, which is predicated on notions of truth and objectivity.

### Popular Culture, Theme Parks and History

The influence of popular culture is felt strongly in exhibitions throughout China, and not just in terms of the use of multimedia and dioramas; it extends deeper into the very essence of how the material is organized and presented. Some museums – such as the Shanghai Lu Xun Museum – have rejected the still nearly universal practice of structuring their subject chronologically. Whereas the Beijing Lu Xun Memorial Hall and the Shaoxing Lu Xun Memorial Hall make use of the standard chronological approach to Lu Xun's intellectual and literary development, the Shanghai museum takes a more thematic and impressionistic approach. The curators of the exhibit have said they are intentionally using an "expressive" (biaoxian), as opposed to "representational" (zaixian), technique, and indeed much in this museum strikes one as self-consciously different from standard display practices in PRC museums. For example, one of the display spaces in the main exhibition recreates Lu Xun's "iron house" with rusty-looking iron; the observer is made to feel as if living within the tradition that Lu Xun denounced so vociferously in his fiction and essays. Another example is the "True story of Ah Q" display, a white clay diorama of Lu Town, with scenes from Lu Xun's famous novella. There is also a life-size wax figure diorama based on the famous photograph of Lu Xun meeting members of a woodblock artists group. The museum devotes a room to showing a video called Yecao (Wild Grass), which uses imagery from the "Preface" to Lu Xun's collection of prose poems to create a highly abstract visualization meant to capture a feeling of the poem. The film clearly rejects the general tendency in Lu Xun studies to tie the Wild Grass poems explicitly into specific historical moments. Although its style is more serious, the "expressive" mode of exhibition in this museum shows clear traits of popular culture, and these traits help to undermine the standard representation of Lu Xun's life and intellectual development as a from-idealist-to-revolutionary chronology, a narrative that is shaped to a large degree by standard socialist narratives of modern Chinese historical development.

In Shaoxing, there is a very conventional representation of Lu Xun's life in the Lu Xun Memorial Hall, one of the oldest memorial halls devoted to an individual in the PRC. Yet Shaoxing also offers Luzhen, a semi-private, semi-state enterprise 15 miles outside the city at the Keyan Scenic Tourism Area. Luzhen is a life-size re-creation of Lu Xun's fictional town. As you arrive at the main gate, you are presented with five plastic *tongqian* (copper coins). You then pass by a bronze statue of a seated Lu Xun, next to a stone on which are carved the characters *minzu hun* (soul of the people). To the left of the statue is a wall with a citation from "Guxiang" ("Hometown") in which the first-person narrator describes the difference between the hometown he has returned to and the hometown of his memory.[26] To me, this citation sets a nostalgic tone for one's experience in Luzhen. Luzhen is as much about retrieving the past in a rapidly modernizing and commodified society as it is about Lu Xun and his place in modern history.

With your *tongqian* in hand, you then pass through a *pailou* memorial arch into the main commercial thoroughfare of Luzhen. This "commercial street" is lined with shops selling all manner of touristy stuff, only some of which could be said to relate to local Shaoxing culture. You can sip tea in a teahouse or gamble with your *tongqian*. Up and down the street and throughout the town are bronzes statues of scenes from Lu Xun's stories, mostly taken from "The true story of Ah Q." Live characters from his stories also make periodic appearances (Figure 5). As you stroll through the rest of the town, you can visit the Zhao residence, the canal where Xianglin Sao was kidnapped, the Luzhen docks, the Tutelary God temple and the monastery where Ah Q stole turnips.

By far the most interesting part of Luzhen, to my mind at least, is the Madman Memorial Hall (*Kuangren jinianguan*). This is a kind of "house of horrors" that attempts, we are told in the prefatory remarks, to make the spectator feel what it would have been like to live in a "cannibalistic society" (*chiren de shehui*).[27] The preface reads:

How did the feudal ethics eat people? ... Here we use modern technological methods, as well as a variety of artistic expressive methods, to display in a real and lively manner the eaters and the eaten. The exhibit will cause you to feel for yourself – through the sensations of sight, sound, and touch – the true meaning of "Diary of a madman." And in personally partaking in the ten grotesque and bizarre and soul-stirring scenes, you will get an imagistic and entertaining education.

26. It is telling in this regard that the most famous passage from "Hometown," about many men making a path, is not quoted here.
27. James Flath notes that the Liaozhai Hall at the Pu Songling Memorial Garden has a "version of the classic amusement park haunted house with themes drawn from Pu's famous work." See "Managing historical capital in Shandong," p. 56.

Figure 5: **"Ah Q" in Luzhen**

Among the displays in the "memorial hall" are the Worm Cave – where you enter the maw of a great beast until you reach its intestines to "experience for yourself the bloody situation of a man being swallowed and eaten by the old feudal ethics and its dehumanization"; and the Tilted Room – meant to "lead the spectator to experience Lu Xun's upturned, abnormal and distorted psychological world." You can also talk to a model of the madman, who is programmed to respond to set questions. There are grotesque displays of fierce figures eating human hearts, a "special effects garden" that recreates a storm, and a display in which the beams of a room collapse on a madman figure. The final display shows children playing, as a voice recites the famous final line of "Diary of a madman": "save the children."

With Luzhen, especially its Madman Memorial Hall, we see the place of popular culture in new representations of the past. Luzhen is in line with new museums such as the Shanghai Municipal History Museum and to a lesser extent the Shanghai Lu Xun Memorial Hall. Like theme parks around the world, the emphasis is on sensations, feelings of nostalgia and thrills. Luzhen looks authentic on the surface, but it clearly comes across as a theme park – indeed, the term theme park (*zhuti gongyuan*) is frequently used in published discussions about the town. In an interview, Zhou Haiying, Lu Xun's son, recognizes the "disneyification" at work in Luzhen's representation, but he justifies it as an alternative form of representation to that of conventional museums.[28] Indeed, others see Luzhen as a superior form of representation to the "dead" (*siban*) exhibitions found in museums.[29] Although Luzhen has received a lot of attention in the local press – especially when Zhou Haiying was made honorary mayor – the day I was there, there were very few visitors, and the town had an empty and wholly artificial feel. Luzhen evokes a nostalgia for Zhejiang village life that certainly lacks the ambiguity and paradoxical nature of Lu Xun's own relationship with his hometown of Shaoxing, although it should be pointed out that this ambiguity is also lacking in the more conventional and mainstream representations such as that found in the Lu Xun Memorial Hall in Shaoxing proper.

Theme park popular culture competes with museums, and museums have responded by incorporating elements of that culture into their exhibits. But conventional museums, especially well-established ones, are also concerned to uphold their integrity as cultural and educational institutions, and some have chosen to maintain instead a more conventional and academic approach to their topics. This opposition between popular representations and more conventional museums is exemplified perfectly in Humen (Guangdong) and Weihai (Shandong), each with two very different museums devoted to the same topic. In Humen, there are two Opium War museums. The older more established one, in the city centre, presents a rather conventional history of the war, with an emphasis on Lin Zexu's role, and using artifacts, photographs and paintings. The other museum, called the Naval War Museum (*Haizhan bowuguan*), is brand new, next to the Weiyuan Fort and in the shadow of the magnificent Humen Suspension Bridge. Its exhibitionary style leans

28. Zhang Guobin and Zhi Yuanyuan, "Zai Luzhen yu Lu Xun zhi zi mian dui mian: 'Ba Lu Xun huan gei shijie' " ("Lu Xun's son and Luzhen meet face to face: giving Lu Xun back to the world"), *Dujia luyou*, No. 4 (2004), p. 38.

29. Da Hai, "Luzhen: Shi Lu Xun guxiang de zaixian, haishi liti xiaoshuo de changshi" ("Luzhen: is it a representation of Lu Xun's hometown or an experiment in three-dimensional fiction?"), *Dujia luyou*, No. 4 (2004), p. 36.

strongly towards models, dioramas and life-size scenes. In Weihai, two museums present the history of the Sino-Japanese War of 1894–95, with, again, the more established museum offering a more conservative and academic approach, and the newer one showing the pronounced effects of popular culture with massive dioramas of battle scenes and extensive use of multimedia, as well as the relative absence of text.[30] These two examples of parallel museums exemplify the tension between popular and conventional representations of modern history that continues to characterize the Chinese museum world.

### Revolutionary History and the Market Economy

The central message of most revolutionary history museums and memorial sites has been the primacy of the communist revolution to modern Chinese history and the centrality to that revolution of those who sacrificed their lives – martyrs. The Chinese revolution, it should not be forgotten, was motivated by communist ideals of class struggle, collectivism, socialization of the economy and the forging of a new mass culture. Since the post-Mao economic reforms have undermined much of what that revolution originally stood for, the Party and its Ministry of Culture and the Cultural Relics Bureau, which oversees museums, is faced with a dilemma: how to make the history of the revolution appear relevant to people who live in a world that is far removed from the ideals of that revolution without stirring in them revolutionary thoughts that might be turned against the present regime. The essential issue curators faces is, how can revolutionary history, grounded in martyrdom and self-sacrifice, be made to relate to a globalizing market economy that has self-interest as its primary motivating force. In this section, I look at some of the ways (apart from new architectural designs and exhibitionary technologies) museum exhibits attempt to make the leap between the revolutionary past and the decidedly unrevolutionary present.

The Shanghai Municipal History Museum, for example, presents modern history in a way radically different from the temporal narrative that has dominated and continues to dominate Chinese modern history museums. The exhibitions in this museum, which is housed at the base of the Oriental Pearl Tower in Pudong, offers an imitation of the past rather than an "authentic" account of the past through concrete artifacts. It eschews entirely the grand temporal narratives that have generally structured Chinese revolutionary history museums in favour of a spatial mapping of old Shanghai. This emphasis is influenced by the nostalgia for Republican-era Shanghai that raged in popular culture through the 1990s. Its exhibitionary style, dominated by miniatures and models, also demon-

---

30. The two museums are both located on Liugong Island within a few hundred yards of each other. Established in 1985, the Sino-Japanese War of 1894 Museum (*Jiawu zhanzhen bowuguan*) is located in former headquarters of the Qing Beiyang Navy. The newer museum is called the Sino-Japanese Naval Battle Exhibition Hall (*Jiawu haizhan guan*); it was established in 1995 as a joint venture of the Liugong Island Administration and a Guangdong corporation.

strates the influence of forms of popular culture such as the theme park. The miniature, as Susan Stewart argues, is commonly found in capitalist economies and represents a longing to own and possess.[31] The Shanghai Municipal History Museum ends with an exhibition of miniature mansions, famous homes formerly owned by Shanghai's capitalist class. Whereas in earlier forms of exhibition this kind of display would have been presented as a tale of class privilege and oppression, now the miniature homes are like rewards offered to those who work hard in the new economy. In the same way that more conventional history museums have used the past to legitimize the present, the Shanghai Municipal History Museum supports an ideology of entrepreneurship by depicting the Shanghai past as a heyday of commerce and economic development that makes possible a glorious economic future. By glorying nostalgically in the commercial and cultural life of Republican Shanghai, the museum establishes a historical foundation for the ideology of the present market economy.

Now, is this mode of exhibition a trend that will manifest itself nationally or merely the product of a Shanghai local reaction to a nationalist paradigm? Perhaps both. Because it is a local history museum, the Shanghai Municipal History Museum is freer than a national museum to present alternative history.[32] Yet, the Shanghai Municipal History Museum also buys into another paradigm that is consistent with the new state ideology of market reform China: hard work, entrepreneurship and commerce are good and lead to a robust and flourishing society. In looking at the new modes of exhibiting modern history that have emerged in museums in the past decade, we should not assume that their representations are necessarily alternative to official ones.

Yuhuatai Martyrs Park is an example of how a rather conventional exhibition devoted to revolutionary martyrs gets framed in a discourse of economic modernization. The entry hall has an inscription written by Jiang Zemin, which reads: "Keep alive the spirit of the former martyrs, devote yourself to the four modernizations enterprise" (hongyang xianlie jingshen, xianshen sihua shiye), which links the sacrifices of the past to those that need to be done in the present and future. At the end of the exhibit, after numerous displays eulogizing martyrs who died at Yuhuatai (among the most famous being Deng Zhongxia and Yun Daiying), the spectator is presented with a display called "Construction" (jianshe) about present-day Nanjing and its modernization and development projects. The display has nothing explicitly to do with the rest of the

---

31. Susan Stewart, *On Longing: Narratives of the Miniature, the Gigantic, the Souvenir, the Collection* (Baltimore: Johns Hopkins University Press, 1984).

32. James A. Flath has argued that "local" museums in Shandong are moving away from national paradigms. See Flath, "Managing historical capital in Shandong," pp. 41–59. I take issue with Flath's contention that "although the stateist narratives are still promoted in some contexts, that interpretation is now divided by subnarratives that promote a localized and increasingly commercialized interpretation of the past that has a problematic relationship with the nation" (p. 53) or that "increasingly obsolete state narratives based on patriotism, historical materialism, and revolution" (p. 54). What Flath fails to account for, it seems to me, is that the "commercialized interpretation of the past" has national or stateist implications.

exhibit: on the walls are photos of fancy skyscrapers, highway projects and the like; in the middle of the display hall is a miniature model of a developing Nanjing cityscape. With Jiang Zemin's exhortation at the beginning and the modernizing Nanjing display at the end, the Yuhuatai martyrs exhibit is framed by the discourse of modernization and economic development. In this way an exhibit on revolutionary martyrdom of the 1920s and 1930s is made to relate to contemporary society. A spirit of revolutionary self-sacrifice can help build a modern, technologically sophisticated and commercial China. Revolutionary martyrdom is grafted on to the discourse of a market economy.

The Presidential Palace (*zongtong fu*) in Nanjing and its accompanying exhibit on modern history is another case in point. The Presidential Palace is a huge complex of buildings with an interesting history. The site was at various times the palace of a Ming prince, the Liangjiang governor general's residence (taken over by Hong Xiuquan during the Taiping Rebellion), a Republican era presidential palace occupied by Sun Yatsen, later taken over by various warlords and finally the Communists. Opened to the public only in 2003, the compound has several history exhibits: a general modern history exhibit, a Taiping Rebellion exhibit with a focus on Hong Xiuquan, a Liangjiang governor general exhibit, a Presidential Palace exhibit (about the history of the palace), and an Executive Yuan exhibit. Here I focus on the modern history exhibit, which serves as a kind of general introduction for appreciating the entire complex.

The opening display is a general historical overview, offering a standard Chinese Marxist view of the development of modern history from late Qing imperialism and Manchu weakness and ineptitude to the rise and eventual success of the Communist revolution. The exhibition then presents thematic sections, and this is where things get more interesting and less conventional. There are three such exhibits: education, science and technology, and culture; economics; and social classes. These emphasize the great advances made during the Republican period in each area. In a clear shift from earlier representations, the economics exhibit represents the late Qing and Republican periods as a period of incipient capitalism and the burgeoning of national (*guoying*) and private industry (*minying*). There is nothing here about the exploitation of factory workers. We are also presented with a rather positive representation of the rise of the modern banking industry and Nationalist monetary policy. Near the end of the exhibit, there is an inscription by Mao Zedong that reads: "If you work hard, you will not want for food or clothing" (*ziji dongshou, fengyi zushi*). Although it is still common practice in modern Chinese museums to end with a quotation from the Chairman, we can see how Mao's words are being made to fit the free enterprise ethos of contemporary society, where the emphasis is on hard work and self-reliance. At the very end of the exhibit, there is a long citation from Mao's 1945 speech to the Second Plenum of the seventh Central Committee, a text that offers a policy of appeasement to the "national bourgeoisie" and recognizes the necessity of developing capitalism and national industry in

China.[33] Looked at in the context of the exhibit, Mao's rhetoric justifies the rise of private enterprise, which implicitly becomes a historical foundation for the market economy of the present.

In a similar vein, the social classes exhibit is remarkable for the absence of the term *jieji* (class). Instead, the curators opt for *jieceng*, a term that does not recall the Maoist history of class struggle in the same way *jieji* does.[34] Also remarkable is the broadening of what constitutes classes; there are exhibits on "foreigners in China," "rise of the middle class," "intellectuals," and "Qing bureaucrats." There are displays on *xiaceng minzhong* (lower level people), which show the travails of poverty, but the emphasis is on poor people struggling with dignity to work hard under difficult circumstances, something many Chinese today are forced to do.

As a whole, the modern history exhibit at the Presidential Palace gives a far more positive representation of the Republican period than that found in more conventional revolutionary history museums. This may have something to do with what could be called the local effect; Nanjing was, after all, capital of China during a good portion of the Republican period and a more positive portrayal of this period reflects well on Nanjing today. But the positive representation of a capitalist and commercial Republican period is similar in effect (though not in mode of display) to that found in the Shanghai Municipal History Museum. A vibrant commercial past is made to become a foundation for economic development in the present and future.

Sometimes modern history museums stress their relevance to the present in more explicit and specific ways. The Huangpu Military Academy Memorial Hall, for example, presents the military school's history as one marked by a cosy relationship between Nationalists and Communists, and ends its main exhibit with an appeal for Taiwan reunification with the mainland. The Naval Battle Museum in Humen, which recounts the history of the Opium Wars from a naval perspective, also has a large, multipart anti-drug exhibit on the negative effects of drug use in contemporary Chinese society and the state's glorious efforts to eliminate it. Although it does not state so explicitly, the 2004 Red Flag Canal Spirit Exhibit – an exhibition commemorating the 40th anniversary of an earlier

---

33. One passage reads: "China's private capitalist industry, which occupies second place in her modern industry, is a force which must not be ignored. Because they have been oppressed or hemmed in by imperialism, feudalism and bureaucratic-capitalism, the national bourgeoisie of China and its representatives have often taken part in the people's democratic revolutionary struggles or maintained a neutral stand. For this reason and because China's economy is still backward, there will be need for a fairly long period after the victory of the revolution, to make use of the positive qualities of urban and rural private capitalism as far as possible, in the interest of developing the national economy." See *Selected Works of Mao Tse-tung*, 5 vols. (Beijing: Foreign Languages Press, 1975), Vol. 4, p. 367.

34. Dai Jinhua has described how the cultural and intellectual discourse in China of the 1990s veered strongly away from terms such as "class" and "revolution." This was a result, of course, of the historical memory of these terms, but it also marks an ideological position that is consistent with the state's emphasis on entrepreneurship. See "Invisible writing: the politics of Chinese mass culture in the 1990s," *Modern Chinese Literature and Culture*, Vol. 11, No. 1 (Spring 1999), p. 51.

Figure 6: **Xintiandi Development in the Heart of Shanghai**

exhibition about the famed Red Flag Canal and celebrating the economic and social benefits of this canal constructed during the Great Leap Forward period at the place where Henan, Hubei and Shanxi meet – seems a rather patent propaganda ploy to push for the Chang (Yangtze) River water diversion project.[35]

Sometimes the framing of revolutionary history museums with new commercial and market reform messages is not intentional but implicitly suggested by the context in which the museum is situated. I am thinking of the First CCP Party Congress Meeting Hall. Formerly run down and threatened with demolition, the area around the museum was renovated and redeveloped by the Shui On Group (a Hong Kong developer led by Vincent Hong Sui Lo) into a trendy, upscale shopping district called Xintiandi (New Universe) (Figure 6).[36] The museum itself also got a facelift.[37] The area now consists of a whole array of boutiques, restaurants, pubs, galleries and clubs, including the inevitable Starbucks, a nightclub called Ye Shanghai and the Che Guevara tapas restaurant. The district even has its own shop, which sells Xintiandi brands of French wine and other products, and runs a *shikumen* museum, which consists of a renovated *shikumen* residence and displays on the history of *shikumen* and on the redevelopment of Xintiandi. This "tourist destination" clearly

35. I saw the touring exhibit at the Guangzhou Museum in early December 2004.
36. For more information on this firm, see its website, http://www.shuion.com.
37. The museum was reopened after a renovation in May 1999. This included a new building, which was done in a style to match the existing building. For information on the museum, see Ni Xingxiang (ed.), *Zhongguo gongchandang diyici quanguo daibiao dahui huizhi* (*The Site of the First National Congress of the Communist Party of China*) (Shanghai: Shanghai renmin meishu, 2001).

plays on the nostalgia for old Shanghai that has been such an important part of popular culture in this city since the 1990s, but it is also motivated by a sense of global commercial modernity. This duality between nostalgia and global commercial culture seems to have been part of the developer's conceptual design for the area: the northern half preserves the original buildings while the southern half has new buildings in modern architecture and is dominated by a huge shopping plaza. The museum, which sits in the northern half but is right across the street from the southern half, is thus sandwiched between architectural nostalgia for the Republican past and contemporary commercial modernity.

The urban context in which the museum is situated affects the meaning of the museum and its exhibits, which recount the history of the formation of the CCP. The museum and its revolutionary message become part of a larger nostalgia for old Shanghai, filtered through a modern, cosmopolitan consciousness. A visitor who emerges from the exhibition and then strolls around the very attractive surroundings of the Xintiandi district might well think about the CCP's role in making this urban transformation possible. The curators of the museum clearly want the exhibition to be viewed in the context of a historical trajectory. In the hallway before entering the exhibitions proper, one is presented with a series of photographs relating key moments in the history of the CCP/ China, beginning with a photo of the present site and ending with a photo of Tiananmen Square during a recent national day celebration. When I visited the museum in July 2004, there was also a special Deng Xiaoping exhibition. Viewing the museum in the prescribed order, the Deng exhibit was the final thing to see before leaving. The museum as a whole reinforces this idea of a lineage from Shanghai 1921 to the present economic reforms instituted by Deng, the results of which can be witnessed beyond the museum walls in the supremely bourgeois surroundings of Xintiandi.

This raises larger questions. How does the commercialized society in which many urban Chinese live today affect the ways in which they might view and interpret revolutionary history museums? Do Chinese history museums necessarily teach the lessons their curators and/or their Party bosses intend? No doubt individuals' own experience with the modernizing project implemented by Deng Xiaoping and his successors will be the determining factor. A laid-off factory worker or a migrant worker from the impoverished interior might well be cynical and think about how the Party has abandoned its original ideals, whereas a successful entrepreneur might look on the Party's past as necessary stages in its "inevitable" development toward its current economic policies. This is the fine line the Party must navigate in promoting revolutionary history in the market economy. As class divisions remerge, the state whitewashes the very discourse of class struggle that was central to its legitimizing narrative.

# China on the Catwalk: Between Economic Success and Nationalist Anxiety*

## Antonia Finnane

ABSTRACT   In the post-Mao era China competed successfully for a place in the international trade in textiles and apparel, but its economic success has not been matched by recognition of Chinese fashion design on the world stage. One reason for this lies in the obstacles posed by the existing hierarchy of fashion capitals, which has proved notoriously difficult to subvert. Shanghai may mean fashion in China, but unlike Paris, it does not mean that to the world at large. Yet the Chinese fashion industry is also bedevilled by problems of its own. A high degree of national self-consciousness on the world stage is evident in international fashion shows featuring rather predictable pastiches of Chinese culture. It may be the case that state-sponsored nationalism militates against both a more interesting approach to cultural heritage on the part of designers and a more receptive climate for Chinese fashion on international catwalks.

In 2002, Pierre Cardin was questioned about who was likely to lead the international fashion scene in the 21st century. He responded with heartening words for Chinese fashion designers. "I am sure Chinese fashion will become very strong," he said. "I know so much talent in China, maybe it will become one of the leading countries in the world for couture." He concluded, however, on a cautious note: "fashion is not about nationalities, it's just talent."[1]

The latter observation begs questions about the semiotics of international fashion, and particularly about the signifying power of place names. Designs emanating from Paris, New York, London, Milan and Tokyo come with tags announcing their credentials. The cities lend their cultural cachet to both established and emerging designers. This is especially true of Paris, a place so closely identified with fashion as to have become a by-word for it. In contrast, the fashion industry in China barely registers in world consciousness. Western reports on fashion in China routinely sound a note of surprise and discovery, as though Chinese people were still to be seen wearing Mao suits. "Fashion craze sweeps through a new China," announced the *International Herald Tribune* early in 2003, and "Chinese buy into the beauty myth," trumpeted Melbourne's *The Age* a year later.[2] A quarter of a century after the beginning of the reform era, it would appear, China is still "new."

* Research for this article was supported by a grant from the Australia Research Council.
   1. Reuters, in *Renmin ribao* (*People's Daily*), 20 May 2002. http://fpeng.peopledaily.com.cn/200205/20/eng20020520_96074.shtml. Accessed 7 August 2003.
   2. *International Herald Tribune*, 8 March 2003; *The Age*, 14 February 2004.

This newness is nothing very new. "New" Chinas had been appearing on the horizon since the turn of the 20th century, and a fashion industry was apparent in Shanghai at least by the 1920s. It was characterized by mechanized textile production, advertising through billboards and newspapers, the proliferation of pictorial magazines, the emergence of the graphic artist as fashion designer, promotion of retail outlets, competition between local and foreign products, and fashion parades. It is possible to speak of "fashions" in China before this time, but in the 1920s activities surrounding the production and consumption of clothing became systemically linked to the point where a fashion industry can be said to exist.[3]

Given the repeated media reports that people in contemporary China are "discovering" fashion, it is important to recognize this early history. Like the film industry, the fashion industry in early 20th-century China followed closely on developments in the West and was shaped by international and cross-cultural communications, which were maintained to some degree through the early decades of the PRC. While the vestimentary régime in the new "New China" was overtly quite sober, fashions appearing on the margins showed a sensitivity to world as well as to local time.[4] Moreover, China's very large textile industry continued through the Maoist decades to be responsive to a world market, and higher education in the graphic and industrial arts, which supplied personnel to the industry, was (except for the years immediately following the outbreak of the Cultural Revolution) probably stronger than during the Republic.

The fashion industry of the late 20th century did not, then, grow from an acorn, but rather from a neglected sapling. And despite changed world circumstances, in the post-Mao era there was a repetition of features characteristic of the earlier era and of fashion industries every-

---

3. An integrated discussion of these various developments has yet to appear. On local products see Karl Gerth, *China Made: Consumer Culture and the Creation of the Nation* (Cambridge, MA: Harvard University Asia Center, 2003); on advertising, Sherman Cochran, "Transnational origins of advertising in early twentieth-century China," in Sherman Cochran (ed.), *Inventing Nanjing Road: Commercial Culture in Shanghai, 1900–1945* (Ithaca: Cornell East Asia Series 103), pp. 37–58, and also Ellen Johnston Laing, "Visual evidence for the evolution of 'politically correct' dress for women in early twentieth century Shanghai," *Nan nü*, Vol. 5, No. 1 (2003), pp. 68–112. On department stores, see Wellington K. K. Chan, "Selling goods and promoting a new commercial culture: the four premier department stores on Nanjing Road, 1917–1937," in Cochran, *Inventing Nanjing Road*, pp. 1–36.
4. See Tina Mai Chen, "Dressing for the Party: clothing, citizenship and gender-formation in Mao's China," *Fashion Theory*, Vol. 1, No. 3 (2001), pp. 333–360; Antonia Finnane, "Yu Feng and the 1950s dress reform campaign: global hegemony and local agency in the art of fashion," in Yu Chien Ming (ed.), *Wu sheng zhi sheng: jindai Zhongguo funü yu wenhua, 1650–1950* (*Silent Voices: Women and Modern Chinese Culture, 1650–1950*) (Taipei: Academia Sinica, 2003), Vol. II, pp. 235–268. Maris Gillette, "What's in a dress? Brides in the Hui quarter of Xi-an," in Deborah Davis (ed.), *The Consumer Revolution in Urban China*, (Berkeley: University of California Press, 2000), pp. 80–106. Hung-yok Ip "Fashioning appearances: feminine beauty in Chinese communist revolutionary culture," *Modern China*, Vol. 29, No. 3 (July 2003), pp. 329–361.

where. First, designers and models made an appearance – amateur and part-time in the earlier era, professionalized in the later.[5] Secondly, fashion consciousness was and continues to be created by a lively print culture, which to no small degree constituted the world of fashion. Thirdly, fashion was promoted through exhibitions of Chinese textiles aimed at maximizing consumption of Chinese products for the good of the national economy.[6] Fourthly, fashion consciousness was then and is now organized spatially, centred at particular nodes within a national and global network of cities which has changed little since the 1920s. Shanghai in particular was known as the city that "cared only about clothes, not about people," an aspect of its reputation that has not greatly changed. Finally, engagement with world fashion in the Nanjing Decade involved intense national anxieties, which are evident again today.

This said, the fashion industry in contemporary China is distinguished by a world economic context in which the land of floods and famine has become a powerhouse, consuming and producing more each year, not least in the domain of textiles and clothing. This has created a domestic environment favourable to economic success in clothing manufacture. The past quarter of a century has seen a remarkably rapid and surprisingly uncontroversial transformation of popular clothing culture in the world's largest country.

At the heart of China's fashion industry, however, is a sustained tension between satisfaction at economic success in penetrating world markets and nationalist anxiety over failure to win world acclaim for Chinese fashion designs. The short history of Chinese fashion in the post-Mao era reveals a lively local context for diversification of the national wardrobe along lines strongly informed by global trends; but in high fashion there is an acute national self-consciousness. On the international catwalk, Chinese designers recognize that they have to bring something distinctive to clothing if they are to make their mark, and they look to their aesthetic legacy for inspiration. In this, as in some other respects, Japan provides both a model and a benchmark. Japanese designer Issey Miyake had established such a place in the fashion world by 1988 that it could be asked whether he was not "the world's greatest clothes designer."[7] China, despite extraordinary success in penetrating the

5. The earliest identifiable fashion designers in China were graphic artists, often cartoonists, such as Ye Qianyu (b. 1907) and Zhang Guangyu, who provided fashion sketches for magazines and newspapers published during the Nanjing Decade (1928–1937); Ellen Johnston Laing, *Selling Happiness: Calendar Posters and Visual Culture in early Twentieth-Century Shanghai* (Honolulu: University of Hawai'i Press, 2004), p. 189. A second cohort of designers, led by Yu Feng (b. 1916) emerged briefly in the 1950s, during the short-lived dress reform campaign of 1955–56; Finnane, "Yu Feng and the 1950s dress reform campaign."

6. See further below on exhibitions in reform-era China. On the same phenomenon in the Republican era, see Gerth, *China Made*.

7. Georgina Howell, *Sultans of Style: Thirty Years of Fashion and Passion 1960–90* (London: Ebury Press, 1990), pp. 48–52.

world markets in textile and ready-to-wear apparel, is obsessed with its failure yet to have produced an Issey.[8]

*Designing and Modelling Chinese Fashion*

Fashion was one of many areas in which the opening of a dialogue between China and the rest of the world occurred in the late 1970s. Fox Butterfield, China-watching from Hong Kong in late 1978, wrote that "skirts and dresses [were] reappearing recently on Chinese women for the first time in a decade."[9] The cheongsam (*qipao*) was in evidence again, and a Japanese businessman reported having seen women with permed hair, wearing mini-skirts.[10] In the same year, the "Four Modernizations" were proclaimed, establishing the economic context within which the diversification of the Chinese wardrobe was to proceed apace.

The broad contours of the evolving fashion scene in post-Mao China have been described by Xiaoping Li.[11] In brief, after a short period of mainly modification of existing styles and revival of styles of the 1950s (the frock or *bulaji*) or even the 1940s (the *qipao*), closer interaction between China and the West (or Japan) led to the gradual internationalization of Chinese dress, and the "gradual centralization," too, of "Western high fashion."[12] For women, the major change was the legitimation of skirts. By the late 1980s black leather mini-skirts were frequently to be seen, "short till they could be no shorter."[13] Among men, the suit was popularized by Party leaders: when the members of the Politburo appeared at a press conference in 1983, they were all dressed in suits.[14] In 1984, the Beijing Department Store in Wangfujing was selling around 3,330 suits daily.[15] By the end of the decade, millions of men around the country must have been learning how to knot a tie.

The transformation of clothing in the 1980s took place in a society that was repositioning itself in relationship both to the outside world and to its own past, as shown in literature, music, painting and film. Compared to

8. See Lise Skov's excellent discussion of this problem in its Hong Kong manifestation, in Lise Skov, "Fashion-nation: a Japanese globalization experience and a Hong Kong dilemma," in Sandra Niessen, Ann Marie Leshkowich and Carlo Jones (eds.), *Re-Orienting Fashion: The Globalization of Asian Dress* (Oxford: Berg, 2003), pp. 215–242.

9. In 1974 Jiang Qing had promoted a new "national costume" for women: a frock with pleated skirt and wide-lapel bodice, inspired by classical costumes of the Tang-Song era. The frock was worn under duress by girls and women who fell into the domain of cultural activities, including the 1974 Asian Games in Tehran. Antonia Finnane, "In search of the Jiang Qing dress: some preliminary findings," *Fashion Theory*, Vol. 9, No. 1 (2005), pp. 1–20.

10. *New York Times* supplementary material, 16 September 1978, p. 82. *New York Times* was not actually published between August and November 1978 because of a printers' strike. The paper kept all the reports sent in at that time and made them available on microfilm in sequence with the regular issues.

11. Xiaoping Li, "Fashioning the body in post-Mao China," in Anne Brydon and Sandra Niessen (eds.), *Consuming Fashion: Adorning the Transnational Body* (Oxford and New York: Berg, 1998), pp. 71–89.

12. *Ibid.* p. 79.

13. *Zhongguo qingnian* (*Chinese Youth*), No. 1055 (1999/23), special issue, *Bainian shishang* (*Fashions of a Century*), p. 58.

14. *Zhongguo qingnian*, p. 58.

15. *Beijing Review*, No. 43 (22 October 1984), p. 11.

these clearly defined domains of culture, the vestimentary realm was much larger and also rather amorphous. In general, the daily dress of people in China in the 1980s can be said to have shown both a determination to break with the immediate past and, increasingly, a desire to be up-to-date by international standards. Nevertheless, people were constrained by limited spending power and a market flooded with highly standardized garments, so they wore what was available, affordable and conventional, even as conventions were changing with increasing rapidity.

Discrete sectors of the textile and garment industry, however, intruded into the conventionally recognized domains of culture. The flourishing rag trade produced new – in the PRC at least – educational institutions, reading matter and public spectacles, or in other words, fashion institutes, fashion magazines and fashion shows. These provided forums for fashion's engagement with issues of history, identity and culture that were being raised in the arts at large. In the fashion world, the creative artist was the fashion designer, who emerged from the dim offices and factories of the Maoist era to take up one of the more challenging but also more glamorous roles in the reform era economy. The designer's first charge was to produce a new wardrobe for the masses of China, but in a very short time this gave way to the positively Olympian task of establishing China's credentials in the surreal world of international fashion. In this context, Chinese culture in relationship to the past and to the world became an issue as pronounced in fashion as it was in, for example, the films of the Fifth Generation.

Among the 1980s designers, three different generations can be identified, and they brought to their designs different sorts of historical experience. The first, best represented by Li Keyu (b. 1929, Shanghai), was educated in the pre-Liberation period. Members of the third, represented by Liu Yang (b. 1964, Beijing) and Ma Ling (b. 1968, Yunnan), were young enough to have avoided the worst of the Cultural Revolution. The middle generation accounted for the greatest number of designers, all children of Mao's China. The experience of Chen Hongxia, born in Guangzhou in 1957, was not untypical of her generation although slightly unusual among fashion designers. Graduating from middle school in 1973, she spent the next eight years working in the Guangdong Tractor Factory before successfully applying for entry into the Central Academy of Industrial Fine Arts in 1981.[16]

While fashion design was a new area of enterprise to most designers active in the 1980s, the Mao years proved to have provided some foundations for their work. Mass clothing production in the first quarter-century of the People's Republic required few design initiatives, but costume for the stage did demand historical knowledge, imagination and design skills. A number of designers had worked in drama and ballet,

16. Bao Mingxin, Jiang Zhiwei and Cheng Rong (eds.), *Zhongguo mingshi shizhuang jianshang cidian* (*Dictionary of Famous Chinese Fashion Connoisseurs*) (Shanghai: Shanghai jiaotong daxue chubanshe, 1993), passim.

and they turned their skills to good account in the new cultural context of 1980s consumerism. Jiang Jinrui (b. 1950, Beijing), employed in the 1960s in the Beijing New Arts Drama and Dance Clothing Company, was producing award-winning designs in the 1980s.[17] Li Keyu, who in the 1990s was designing clothes unimaginable in her own youth, had originally made her name as a costume designer for revolutionary drama and opera, including the epochal *Red Detachment of Women*.[18]

The training of fashion designers in the early post-Mao years was possible within the established educational complex, which was diversified relatively easily in the face of demands for professionalization of clothing design. A number of the middle generation of designers passed into the fashion industry through the Central Academy of Industrial Fine Arts. In the 1980s, specialization in the field of fashion design in educational institutes became possible. The Central Academy itself established a fashion design department in the early 1980s. In 1988, Chen Hongxia was invited to help in the establishment of a department of design in Guangzhou University.[19] In 1989, Liu Xiaogang became Shanghai's first doctoral student in the area of fashion design.[20] The premium placed on educational qualifications in China was apparent throughout the design industry. A designer such as Jiang Yinmei (b. 1946, Shanghai), who after finishing high school in 1965 was sent off to the Shanghai No. 1 Clothing Factory and never sat another exam, appears to be quite unusual. Jiang made her name while the reform-era fashion industry was in its infancy, winning awards for designs submitted to a Shanghai municipal fashion design competition in 1984.[21]

It is notable that the 1980s designers were mostly women. As the career potential in designing and the importance of fashion in world culture became apparent, male designers increased in number. By 1998 between 6,000 and 7,000 people were registered as professional or amateur designers across China. Men accounted for most of the top names that year although some new female talents – notably the highly-regarded Wu Haiyan from the Chinese Academy of Fine Arts in Hangzhou – had made an appearance.[22] Interviewed in 2004, Guangzhou designer Zhou Guoping noted that girls far outnumbered boys among students at Guangzhou University's fashion school, but that the male students were among the most successful.[23] Questioned on this point, a young woman lecturer in the fashion department of Shanghai's Donghua

17. *Ibid.* p. 221.
18. *Ibid.* p. 118.
19. *Ibid.* p. 164.
20. *Ibid.* p. 86.
21. *Ibid.* pp. 227–28.
22. Kou Zhengling, "Joining top fashion trends: China's clothing industry marches towards the 21st century," *Beijing Review*, No. 3 (19–25 January 1998), p. 18. Prominent male designers mentioned were Zhang Zhaode, Wang Xinyuan, Liu Yang and Du He, all well known already in 1993 (see under individual names in Bao Mingxin *et al.*, *Dictionary of Famous Chinese*). A feature article on Wu Haiyan was published in *China Pictorial*, January 2001.
23. Interview, Guangzhou University School of Textiles and Garments (Guangzhou daxue fangzhi fuzhuang xueyuan), 12 July 2004.

University suggested that men's greater success was because they were more creative. Her own designer of choice, however, was Wu Haiyan.[24] It is probably the case that talented male students receive greater attention than their female classmates, especially in a world where the male fashion designer has such cachet.

As Xiaoping Li points out, there was a "battle over styles" during the 1980s that "was closely related to the issue of national identity."[25] In general, however, Western styles dominated the oeuvre of Chinese fashion designers in the first quarter-century of the reform era. Their role in the market economy was after all to provide smart clothing for the re-emerging bourgeoisie of China and to supply foreign markets with unexceptional, off-the-peg garments. It was in fashion competitions, both at home and abroad, that the Chinese cultural heritage was brought into play. First prize in the Second Chinese Fashion Culture show, held in 1985, went to Liu Ping's ankle-length *qipao*, unconventionally split at the front rather than at the sides and provocatively adorned with a large bow just below the crotch.[26]

Liu Ping's design typified the response of designers to the particular aesthetic demands of formal wear, the most obvious realm in these years for experimentation with "high fashion." From 1979 onwards, the *qipao* provided a repository of elements that Chinese designers have freely raided to produce their various ranges of formal wear. In a glossy publication of a style common in the late 1990s but still unusual at the end of the 1980s, designer Ma Ling provided imaginative designs of evening wear inspired by Tang dynasty costume and – again – the 1930s *qipao*. Glossing her own oeuvre, she wrote: "The glorious history of Chinese clothing culture, the richness of traditional handicraft work – especially embroidery and brocade work – all excite vocal interest in the international fashion world. Chinese fashion must compete in ingenuity and beauty on the world stage."[27]

In time, even the Cultural Revolution was historicized in fashion, but without displacing the *qipao*. Feng Ling, born in 1965, turned from painting to clothes design in the late 1990s. She combined elements of the Mao suit and army uniforms with the *qipao*, using silks and satins to create a sartorial pastiche of references to the Chinese past. Interviewed in 2005, she described her designs in terms commonly used by Chinese couturiers. "My clothes are very 'China,' yet at the same time very modern," she said, "so they can give others a very persuasive hint about today's China … This clothing is very local, special, and Chinese."[28] Like most designers, Feng Ling faces the problem that her compatriots by and large do not want to wear such clothes: 70 per cent of her customers are

24. Interview, Shanghai Library, 16 July 2004.
25. Xiaoping Li, "Fashioning the body in post-Mao China," p. 78.
26. *Shizhuang* (*Fashion*), No. 3 (1985), p. 17.
27. Ma Ling, *Ma Ling shizhuang* (*Ma Ling Fashions*) (Beijing: Ma Ling shizhuang fuzhi youxian gongsi, 1993), p. 77.
28. Priscilla Jiao, "Something old, something new," *That's China* (April 2005), p. 46. http://www.thatschina.net/20054-p46.htm, accessed 20 April 2005.

foreigners. Nevertheless, designers are in tune with Chinese consumers when they return again and again to the *qipao* for inspiration. The quintessential Republican-era garment, it has enjoyed a surge of popularity in recent years and clearly signifies Chineseness more than any other garment from the past.

To advertise their very "China" yet very modern clothes, designers needed Chinese models. Professional modelling was unknown before the 1980s. Assembling for their first class in November 1981, the girl students at China's first school for models were too shy even to remove their jackets because the woollen jumpers they wore underneath would reveal the shape of their bodies. The director had to debrief them. Pierre Cardin, instrumental in the establishment of the school, was present at their first fashion show and stormed his way through the dressing room, which featured a curtain separating male and female models. He pulled the curtain down.[29] This might be regarded as a seminal moment in the transformation of gender relations in China, involving the subordination of conventional ethics of sexual relations to the demands of one of the world's great consumer industries.

Modelling meant both advertising Chinese beauty and attending anew to the question of "what is beautiful in a Chinese woman."[30] In 1984, 18-year-old Deng Ying was an employee in a textile factory, like both her parents. She may have been inspired by the 1983 fashion exhibition in Beijing to apply for admission to the modelling group recently established by the Beijing Textile & Fashion Public Service Centre. Her height – 1.7 metres – must have encouraged her to think that she was an appropriate candidate. She became a favourite model of Beijing designer Li Yanping (b. 1950), who used her to showcase fashionable *qipao* designs.[31]

A decade later, Deng Ying would have been too short to follow such a career. The New Silk Road Modelling Company, established in 1992, featured its 34 top models in a 2001 picture book. The two senior members of the group, each with ten years modelling experience, were both 1.81 metres tall. The shortest models were 1.75 metres and the remainder all 1.77 or above.[32] Correspondingly, the 20 models of the Shanghai Fashion Company, with an average age of 20 years, had an average height of 1.77 metres.[33] Among regional origins of the New Silk Road models, the northern provinces were predominant – Heilongjiang,

29. Xu Wenyuan, *Secai, nülang, wo de meng: shizhuang motuoer zhi lu* (*Colour, Young Women, My Dream: The Fashion Model's Path*) (Zhongguo gongren chubanshe, 1991), pp. 27–28.

30. See Wolfram Eberhard's classic essay, "What is beautiful in a Chinese woman?" in Eberhard, *Moral and Social Values of the Chinese: Selected Essays* (Taipei: Chengwen Publishing Co., 1971), pp. 271–304.

31. *China Reconstructs* (October 1987), p. 15. On Li Yanping, see Bao Mingxin *et al.*, *Dictionary of Famous Chinese*, pp. 126–29.

32. Data from China Pictorial Publications & New Silk Road Models, Co. Ltd (eds.), *Zhongguo xin silu mingmo xiezhen* (*Portraits of China's New Silk Road Models*) (Beijing: Zhongguo huabao chubanshe, 2001).

33. http://www.shanghai-fahion-co.com/biao-yan-dui.htm, accessed 6 October 2003.

Xinjiang, Hebei. Only one model was from south of the Chang (Yangtze) valley.

To height requirements were added certain demands for physiognomy: big eyes, full mouths, prominent facial profiles. Within these guidelines, some variety was required to cover the various sorts of modelling tasks. Among the New Silk Road models, Wang Aiping had a "typically eastern face" and was useful for historical costume displays, while Meng Huan had a "foreign" air. Zhu Tong was celebrated as the only model in the company with single-fold eyelids, a distinctly unfashionable feature that she shared with half the population.[34] However, in general, the models all looked very similar and a group photograph shows that the elements considered essential to Chinese beauty are those set by American pop culture. Chinese were baffled when Lu Yan, with single-fold eyelids and a broad nose, was head-hunted by French modelling agents.[35] The French, of course, were looking for something different, exotic, even primitivist. Chinese designers were quite capable of exploiting difference in their marketing of high fashion, but had yet to reach this stage of self-Orientalism.

Designers and models together inevitably contributed to the conditions within which a certain body type was valorised through the modelling industry. Competing in the international arena, designers produced clothes compatible with international fashion trends – exaggerated and overblown at graphic design stage, thrown into relief on the page by stick-like representations of the human form. Such designs were realizable on the catwalk only on the improbable bodies of exceptionally tall, thin women. This meant revising ideals for a Chinese body that had earlier been established, with marginal differences, during the Republican era.[36] These ideals could now be attained by cosmetic surgery on eyes, noses, navels and finally even legs, stretched millimetre by millimetre to add height to young women dissatisfied with their natural stature. In 2004, an innovative beauty quest in China was held to find the nation's most beautiful surgically modified product.

In the 1980s, Chinese models benefited from the great interest abroad in anything coming out of China. The *Fashion* Magazine Modelling Group was invited to Paris by Pierre Cardin in 1985, and attracted a storm of attention when they rode down the Champs-Élysées in an open-topped car carrying the Chinese flag.[37] Two years later the China fashion scene seemed to have arrived when 19-year-old Peng Li, from the Beijing Modelling Troupe, won an international modelling competition in Naples.[38] But such international successes were rare. After the Tiananmen Incident in 1989 China excited little international interest for some time. It became a very tough environment for both designers and

34. China Pictorial Publications & New Silk Road Models, Co. Ltd (eds.), *China New Silk Road Models*, pp. 23, 47, 55.
35. http://www.china.org.cn/english/NM-e/40994.htm, accessed 20 September 2004.
36. See Eberhard, "What is beautiful in a Chinese woman?" pp. 271–304.
37. *Shizhuang*, No. 23 (1985/4), p. 15
38. *Shizhuang*, No. 35 (1988/4), p. 12.

models, where being Chinese had little cachet and names were more easily made at home than abroad.

*Fashion Magazines*

The uneven struggle between global fashion trends and self-consciously Chinese designs is nowhere better illustrated than in fashion magazines, which from the start gave generous space to designs from abroad and now, after a quarter of a century, are devoted largely to advertising the big international fashion names. The first issue of the first fashion magazine to have been published in many years appeared in 1979, and was soon followed by others. Published first quarterly, then bimonthly, then monthly, costing around 0.5 RMB in 1979 and 1.2 RMB ten years later, these magazines were important conduits of knowledge in an industry struggling to establish itself. They supplied "how to" advice, and introduced readers to current international trends.

For all the actual changes in what people in China wore, a visitor could well have blinked and missed the Chinese fashion scene in the 1980s, especially if the visit was made in the cooler months and to the inland rather than the coastal cities. Looking through magazines, however, would have produced quite a different impression, for they created the imagined fashionable community. Let us "think for a moment of the magazine as a machine that makes Fashion,"[39] although in a simpler way than Barthes famously attempted. Magazines presented a fashionable world much more developed, comprehensible and satisfying than the actual world of fashion. They showed and even explained the seasonal and yearly shifts in style that were fundamental to Fashion, but so hard to detect from the chaotic sartorial spectacle on any Chinese city street. In a very explicit way they structured the nation and the world in terms of fashion, anchoring the new consumer values in a familiar value system that had the nation at its heart.

The fashion magazine of the reform era appeared in bookshops without too much attention. In 1979, *China's Women*, the flagship magazine of the Women's Federation, looked much as it had in the 1960s, before publication was suspended during the Cultural Revolution. The "Four Modernizations" were absorbed seamlessly into a world of workers, peasants and soldiers, each contributing to the new national project through revolutionary will and sheer hard work. The peasant girl gathering the crops wore checked shirt and headscarf; the student turned woodcutter wore Mao jacket and fur cap.[40] In 1981, the first issue of *Modern Dress* (*Xiandai fuzhuang*) informed readers that "girls love dresses," an opinion illustrated with photographs of demure young

---

39. Roland Barthes (trans. Matthew War and Richard Howard), *The Fashion System* (New York: Hill and Wang, 1983), p. 51.
40. "Wei sihua zuo gongxian" ("Making a contribution to the Four Modernizations"), *Zhongguo funü*, No. 250 (1979/6), inside back cover.

women wearing frocks in bright colours with puffed sleeves and frills, or lace trim.

The early fashion magazines were mostly produced by textile and garment manufacturing or trade companies along with higher educational institutions and research groups related to the arts of clothing production. With four to six issues a year, they typically contained a centre spread of colour illustrations of new styles with attention both to local designs and international fashion. The latter appeared outlandish beside the former in the early 1980s but the design gap began to close as the decade wore on and Chinese designers became more adventurous. The Chinese edition of a Japanese fashion magazine was launched in Beijing in 1985, with photographs and patterns entirely from Japanese contributors,[41] and the first issue of a Franco-Chinese co-production, *Elle*, appeared in Shanghai in 1988. These provided a benchmark for international standards in Chinese fashion publishing that Hong Kong fashion magazines had otherwise set (see Table 1).

Apart from the colour spread, 1980s magazines featured a wide range of articles on various aspects of an industry in the process of renovation: textile technology, export standard requirements, Chinese historical

Table 1: **Some Early Reform Era Fashion Magazines, by Year of First Issue**

| Year | Publication | Publisher |
|------|-------------|-----------|
| 1979 | *Shizhuang* (*Fashion*) | China Silk Import and Export Co., Beijing |
| 1981 | *Xiandai fuzhuang* (*Modern Dress*) | Beijing Municipal Clothing Research Society and Light Industry Publishing Co. |
| 1982 | *Liuxing se* (*Fashion Colour*) | China Fashion Colour Society |
| 1984 | *Zhongguo fuzhuang* (*China Garments*) | China Clothing Design Research Centre |
| 1985 | *Denglimei shizhuang* (Chinese edition) | China Fashion Magazine company and Kamakura Bookshop (Japan) |
| 1986 | *Shanghai fushi* (*Shanghai Style*) | Shanghai Muncipal Dress Study Society and Shanghai Science and Technology Publishing Co. |
| 1988 | *Shijie shizhuang zhi yuan* (*Elle*) | Shanghai Translation Publishing Co. and Daniel Filipachi Publishing Co. |
| 1990 | *Shanghai shizhuang bao* (*Shanghai Fashion Times*) | Shanghai Clothing Co. |

*Source:*
Various magazines; Bao Mingxin, Jiang Zhiwei and Cheng Rong (eds.), *Zhongguo mingshi shizhuang jianshang cidian* (*Dictionary of Famous Chinese*) (Shanghai: Shanghai jiaotong daxue chubanshe, 1993).

41. *Shizhuang*, No. 20 (1985/1), p. 2

clothing culture, and nation-wide innovations in the production and marketing of textiles and clothing. An article on the "Red Capital" (Hongdu) clothing store in Beijing early established an unexceptionable model for standards in the retail sector, announcing new styles, quality and customer service as its three points of attention.[42] A photo sequence showed how to iron cloth cut for the manufacture of tailored trousers.[43] An advertisement featured the latest in Japanese sewing machine technology.[44]

Introducing the industry to foreign fashion trends and the structure of the international fashion industry was among the significant services fashion magazines performed. Presented with six different photographs of men in 1985 Parisian fashions, readers of *Fashion* were asked to "spot the difference" between the various combinations of coat, trousers, shirt and tie – a lesson in identifying the detail so important in fashion trends.[45] In the same issue, an article on designing for the clothing export market identified the elements necessary for success, including fashion models, trade exhibitions and fashion shows. This article identified the Soviet Union as an appropriate target for Chinese exports, because the fashion lag between west and east Europe would allow Chinese designers to pick up last year's Western fashions and reduplicate them for the Russian market.[46]

How to design and cut garments that were fitted to the figure was paramount among lessons to be learned by clothing producers, from women making garments for the family to employees of the major clothing manufacturers. The first issue of *Modern Dress* published anatomical sketches of the female human form, showing both skeletal and muscular structure, and provided detailed graphs showing measurements for clothes sizes for both men and women.[47] Patterns with detailed measurements and cutting instructions were a standard feature of all fashion magazines, and were still to be found in the more lavish and expensive publications of the mid-1990s. As the door to international trade opened more widely, Chinese consumers were introduced via fashion magazines to Western paper patterns, especially McCall's.

An innovation in fashion publishing was the launch in 1994 of *China Popular Brand Fashion* magazine (*Zhongguo mingpai shizhuang*). This was a Beijing product, edited by the Chinese Historical Clothing Research Association in conjunction with the newly formed "Chinese Popular Brands Fashion" editorial group. Eight "famous brands" were featured, including the locally successful Aidekang, founded in 1989 with German investment, and Tianma, known for its shirts. The aim of the magazine was to establish brand recognition for Chinese products.[48] This

42. *Shizhuang*, No. 6 (1981/Autumn), p. 6
43. *Ibid*. p. 54
44. *Ibid*. p. 56
45. *Shizhuang*, No. 20 (1985/1), pp. 16–17.
46. *Ibid*. p. 4.
47. *Xiandai fuzhuang* (*Modern Clothing*), No. 1 (September 1981), pp. 8–9.
48. *Zhongguo mingpai shizhuang* (*Chinese Popular Brand Fashion*), No. 1 (September 1994), p. 2.

initiative would appear to be connected with the experience of the head of the Luoman group – also featured in the magazine – when he tried to market modestly priced suits in Paris in 1994. The importance of brand names dawned on him when he failed to attract customers. In 1996, two years after the first issue of the "famous brands" magazine, a similarly named organization was founded, with the same stated aims.[49]

It should be noted that the "famous brands" campaign was conducted in the arena of global fashions. The fashion companies involved were producing suits, shirts, skirts and blouses, and leisure-wear, well-cut from quality fabrics, but overall entirely conventional. The early 1980s magazines had tentatively offered some distinctively Chinese garments. That the "famous brand" companies showed no interest in such experiments was a comment on their realistic understanding of consumer demands, but at the same time showed that they could not bring much to their labels that was new. While price advantage and local know-how would secure them a place in the Chinese market and even permit exports, their brand names were destined to remain in the shadow of the great international fashion labels.

These labels were then proliferating through the top end of the Chinese market, and being promoted in major fashion magazines that were gradually becoming more and more like their foreign counterparts in design and content. By the mid-1990s colour spreads, while continuing to show a regional alertness to Japanese and Korean fashions evident in the 1980s, were dominated by designs from the big European fashion houses such as Versace, Armani, YSL. Street fashion (*jietou shizhuang*) made an appearance in fashion features in 1995–96.[50] The distinction between the colour spread and the more cheaply produced black-and-white pages on coarser paper began to disappear around this time, and full gloss magazines became the norm. The internet started to became a major purveyor of Chinese fashions. Patterns occupied less and less space in popular magazines, finally disappearing from the major titles.

The relationship between what was depicted in the magazines and what people actually wore did not become noticeably closer. In 1996, when the proliferation of glossy fashion magazines and the growing number of specialist clothing shops in big cities might suggest to the casual observer plenty of choice for the consumer, a survey of 200 middle school students by *Zhongguo fuzhuang* found that teenagers were almost universally dissatisfied with the clothing available to them. The magazine summed up their attitude in the words: "We're growing up; we don't want to wear children's clothes and we don't want to wear adults' clothes either. What can we wear apart from school uniform?"[51] The magazine had some useful advice for designers: if the customer was "emperor," as alleged in

49. Claire Roberts, *Evolution and Revolution: Chinese Dress 1700s–1900s* (Sydney: Powerhouse Museum, 1997), p. 99

50. *Shizhuang*, No. 66 (1996/3), pp. 44–47. This issue published the sixth in a series of illustrated articles on street fashion.

51. Gu Qiu, "Shejishi, qing zoujin "shangdi" ("Designers, please draw closer to the 'emperor' "), *Zhongguo fuzhuang* (*China Garments*), No. 1 (1997), p. 32.

the common saying, designers would do well not to maintain their distance. But the magazine itself, of course, could maintain this distance, and probably even depended on it for its readers, who through its pages could move beyond the parochial, mundane world of real made-in-China clothing to engage in a glamorous global culture.

### Sites of Fashion: The Spatial Hierarchy

One of the major achievements of fashion magazines, and of fashion publishing more generally in China, was to produce a spatial understanding of fashion that explained its significance in terms of established urban hierarchies, local and international. In the 1980s, three cities were identified as the recognizable nodes of China's fashion industry. These were Shanghai, Beijing and Guangzhou, all of which combined strong regional roles with national significance as places where China had long conducted negotiations and exchanges with the non-Chinese world. To the extent that they have competed with each other for local and international prominence in fashion, they can be viewed as using fashion to give regional expression to their claims as sites of national culture. But in world fashion, where city names are more important that country names, they have also become the focus of hopes for Chinese fashion fame.

Shanghai's dominance in textile production and established cultural capital has stood it in good stead in the fashion industry. Even in the mid-1970s, it was "a must" for visitors to Shanghai "to buy paper patterns to give to relatives and friends back home."[52] In 1981, "new items, new styles [were] constantly forthcoming" and even the winter wardrobe, in which variety was restricted, featured new styles in new materials.[53] Beijing in that year had nothing to offer by way of comparison, but in the longer term was able to compete because of its capacity to mount exhibitions, develop training institutes, produce literature and supply consumers. It had its own distinctive appeal as the national capital, a city of antiquity and the natural centre of northern culture.

Guangzhou was the strongest performer in the 1980s. It benefited from early reform-era policies that encouraged the development of clothing manufacture in its vicinity, and it had the advantage of being close to Hong Kong, from which it learnt about style as well as about doing business. It became known throughout China as a place where people dressed well, commanding respect even from Shanghainese. Zhang Zhaoda (Mark Cheung), who emerged as one of China's foremost designers in the 1990s, typified the Guangzhou historical experience: he owed his early interest in clothing culture to magazines sent to him by relatives abroad.[54]

52. Yang Yuan (exec. ed.), *Zhongguo fushi bainian shishang* (French title: *Costumes chinois: Modes depuis 100 ans*) (Huerhot: Yuanfang chubanshe, 2003), p. 17

53. Ming Hao, "Shanghai fuzhuang shichang xunli," ("Calling in at the Shanghai clothes market"), *Xiandai fuzhuang*, No. 1 (September 1981), p. 19.

54. *Ibid.* p. 152.

The fashions emanating from these three cities came to be differenti-
ated along regional lines, in time-honoured fashion. The *jingpai* (Beijing)
presented a relatively serious image, the *haipai* (Shanghai) a lively, and
the *suipai* (Guangzhou) a romantic one.[55] Discussions of the fashion
industry have commonly revolved around one or another city, or involved
a comparison of them. In Beijing in the late 1980s fashion-conscious
buyers shopped at "privately run free-market stalls and individual stores"
which purchased garments from all over China. Bright young things in
the suburbs were beginning to produce their own fashion designs, con-
tracting local factories to produce the garments for the market.[56] In
Shanghai, the tailor long continued to be a dominant figure, to the point
where tailored and ready-to-wear garments became a recognized mark of
differentiation between Shanghai and Guangzhou. In Guangzhou, or more
broadly Guangdong, clothing was factory-made, and the locals were
held to have a free and easy approach to what they wore. In Shanghai,
people were "relatively picky and considered," consulted the fashion
magazines, wanted this changed and that altered, and from a long process
of decision-making would emerge in garments "both fashionable and
individual."[57]

Around these nodes a certain idea of fashion was constructed, to be
disseminated throughout urban China via the communication routes that
carried fashion magazines, textiles, T-shirts, jeans and parkas from major
metropoles to small market towns. A Beijing fashion commentator wrote
in 1987 that the gap between clothing trends between cities and rural
areas used to be ten years, and was now five; and between large and
middle-ranking cities had been around five years, but now was only one.[58]
In the 1990s, numerous other Chinese cities became involved in the
fashion industry as local governments across the country promoted
garment manufacture, industry training, trade exhibitions and fashion
shows; but they did little to disturb the existing spatial imagination of
fashion. Summarizing summer trends in 2004, the industry magazine
*View* featured Shenzhen boutiques in its pictorial "window-shopping"
section, but its analysis of major metropolitan fashions focused on
Beijing, Shanghai and Guangzhou.[59]

The spatial understanding of Chinese fashion has been constructed in
parallel with the observed urban hierarchy in international fashion. Ambi-
tions for China's success in world fashion are expressed in terms of the
placement of a Chinese city in the top rank of fashionable cities. It 1996,
it was a matter of great satisfaction in China that Beijing should be

55. Wang Li, 'Woguoren dangjin fushi (duan xiang)" ("Contemporary clothing among
our compatriots: brief reflections"), *Shizhuang*, No. 29 (1987/2), p. 34.

56. Wen Tianshen, "New fashion trends," *China Reconstructs*, Vol. 36, No. 10 (October
1987), p. 67.

57. Yao Zaisheng, "Guangdong de shizhuangchang he Shanghai de caifengpu"
("Guangdong's fashion factories and Shanghai's tailor shops"), *Xiandai fuzhuang*, No. 83,
(1996/6), p. 20.

58. Wang Li, "Contemporary clothing among our compatriots," p. 34.

59. *Liuxing qushi* (*Fashion Trends*), No. 98 (Summer 2004), pp. 219–221. (The English
title given on the cover of the magazine is: *View: International Fashion and Fabrics*.)

included with fashion capitals Paris, New York and Tokyo as one of four cities to host an exhibition of works by young fashion designers from across the world. This was an indication that "China's capital, China's symbol and representative," was on the way to being "a centre of world fashion."[60] In the same year, the second Shanghai International Fashion Expo (or International Fashion Culture Festival) was launched with the mission statement: "We will realize the dream someday, the dream of making Shanghai one of the most important centres of fashion in the world."[61] Eight years later this hope was reiterated in *View*, where Shanghai was described as China's fashion future, on its way to being the world's sixth fashion city after – presumably – Paris, London, New York, Milan and Tokyo.[62]

Of the international fashion cities, Paris and Tokyo loom largest in the Chinese view, Paris because it epitomizes the idea of Fashion, Tokyo because it best represents what China would like to achieve. In 1982, just as something looking like fashion was beginning to appear in China, 12 Japanese designers created a sensation in Paris and placed Japanese fashion in the vanguard of international style.[63] The significance of fashion in the international pecking order dawned on industry participants in the 1980s, not least because Japan – then at peak economic perform-ance – had made its mark in Paris. In 1987 one fashion commentator wrote with wistful optimism: "In the 1980s, Japanese designers greatly influenced world fashion with designs based on traditional Japanese dress. Perhaps in the 1990s or thereabouts, it will be the turn of Chinese designers."[64] In the same year, another commentator reported on the achievements of a designer from the East in the French fashion world. This was Takada Kenzo, the first Japanese designer to make an imprint in Paris.

Japan was an inspiration to China but also a challenge, exciting admiration and resentment in not quite equal portions. In an interview with the International Herald Tribune, Han Feng, born in Hangzhou and now based in New York, criticized Japanese fashions of the 1980s for being "somewhat cold and intellectual," and for being more about the designer than about the people who wore them. Her own aim was "to serve career women, to help them be creative and elegant." This distinc-tion between her project and that of her famous Japanese peers illustrates perfectly Japan's significance in the construction of Chinese identity and the definition of Chinese goals. In the same interview, Han Feng stated firmly: "This is the Chinese century. From now on, the Chinese influence is going to be important in everything."[65] How to convert this

60. *Zhongguo fuzhuang* (*China Garments*), No. 48 (1996/5), p. 12.
61. http://www.shme.com/96sifcf/96sifsf.htm, accessed 3 September 2003.
62. *Liuxing qushi* (*Fashion Trends*), p. 220.
63. See Yuniwa Kawamura, *The Japanese Revolution in Paris Fashion: Dress, Culture, Body* (Oxford: Berg, 2004).
64. Wen Tianshen, "New fashion trends," p. 68.
65. Daisann McLane, "China's new fashion whispers 'Asia'," *International Herald Tribune*, 14 September 2004.

incontrovertible fact into world acknowledgement of Chinese fashion is a question that vexes the industry in China.

*History and Fashion on the Catwalk*

From an early stage of the reborn fashion enterprise, China's fashion future was seen as lying in a successful blend of contemporary international trends with specific Chinese historical and cultural characteristics.[66] The fashion show, with its inherent theatricality, has provided the ideal venue for displaying Chinese culture (almost definitively historical) in various vestimentary forms, sometimes literally through the use of historical costume. To balance the often competing demands of cultural performance and design exhibition has proved difficult. In 1981, the safari suits paraded before Western observers in Beijing were presented by models striking poses from Beijing Opera, specifically in order to place a Chinese stamp on the show but probably with rather comical effect.[67] Although fashion in China has come a long way since 1981, this sort of literal appropriation of culture for the catwalk remains a feature of any Chinese fashion extravaganza.

Fashion shows in China developed in the context of trade exhibitions. From modest beginnings in the 1980s these rapidly increased in number during the 1990s. A 1998 schedule of fairs and exhibitions shows the dates of first exhibition, indicating a growing number of events aimed at the marketing of Chinese textiles and fashion: two in 1993 and 1994, three in 1995, four in 1996 (see Table 2). The exhibitions also grew in scale. The Shanghai International Fashion Expo, launched with great fanfare in 1995, was still a modest affair in 1996. Advertising drew attention to interested regional participants, such as Australia and Japan, and to a few international designers: Oscar de la Renta, Olivier Lapidus, Gerard Pipart. At the 2003 Expo, featuring designs by Givenchy, Vivienne Tam and Vivienne Westwood among others, the exhibition area was nearly double that of 1998, and the number of exhibitors had grown from 370 to 674.[68] By this time, China had become the world's largest manufacturer of clothing and raw textile materials. The steady expansion of exhibitions and trade fairs, serving a rapidly expanding domestic market and accompanied by growing international engagement, was to be expected.

Most of the exhibitions were prosaic in content, directed at maximizing domestic and foreign sales. Fashion shows were a feature of some, but a fashion show might be a very modest affair not at all conducive to making Chinese fashion famous. The Second China Clothing and Textiles Expo held in Sydney in 2002 provides a good illustration. It was

66. Chen Fumei, "Shizhuang biaoyan de qiantu" ("The future of fashion shows"), *Xiandai fuzhuang*, No. 17 (1985/4), p. 9.

67. Tie Ying, "First national fashion show," *China Reconstructs*, Vol. 32, No. 10 (October 1983), pp. 4–5.

68. *Shanghai Star*, 27 March 2003, http:/Nwww.chinadaily.com.cn/star/2003/0327/fa13–1.html, accessed 3 September 2003.

Table 2: **Schedule of Exhibitions and Trade Fairs Related to the Textile and Garment Industries in China, 1998**

| Name of Exhibition | Display | Venue | First held |
|---|---|---|---|
| Dalian International Garment Fair | Clothing, fabrics, wool, leather goods, accessories | Dalian | 1989 |
| Shanghai International Clothing Machinery Exhibition | Sewing, knitting, cutting machines etc. | Shanghai | 1990 |
| China International Clothing & Accessories Fair | Garments, fabrics, accessories | Beijing | 1993 |
| Shenyang National Textile and Clothing Trade Fair | [not stated] | Shenyang | 1993 |
| China International Nonwoven Technology, Textiles and Machinery Exhibition | Nonwovens, technology textiles and machinery, chemical, equipment, etc. | Beijing | 1994 |
| Shanghai International Fabrics and Fashion Accessories Exhibition | Fabrics and fashion accessories | Shanghai | 1994 |
| Shanghai International Fashion Expo | Formal wear, evening wear, bridal gowns, casual wear, children's wear, fabrics, accessories | Shanghai | 1995 |
| China International Trade Fair for Garment Fabrics, Home Textiles and Accessories | Garment fabrics, home textiles, carpets, home textile equipment | Shanghai | 1995 |
| China (Shenzhen) International Clothes Fair | [not stated] | Shenzhen | 1995 |
| Hangzhou Silk Trade Fair | Pure silk underwear, ready-made clothes, garment fabrics | Shenyang | 1996 |
| Dalian International Women's Beauty Commodities Fair | Women's accessories, sanitary and health care articles, bedding, arts and crafts | Dalian | 1996 |
| Dalian International Garment Fair (Autumn/Winter) | Autumn and winter fashions, cashmere and woollen goods, eiderdowns, footwear, hats | Dalian | 1996 |
| China International Lingerie and Beachwear Trade Fair | Lingerie and beachwear | Shanghai | 1996 |
| China International Clothing and Accessories Fair (Autumn/Winter) | Garments, fabrics, accessories | Beijing | 1997 |
| Dalian Silk Fair | Silk apparel and fabrics, silk machinery | Dalian | 1997 |
| China Jewellery, Handicraft and Silk Trade Fair | [not stated] | Tianjin | 1998? |

*Source:*
   www.chinavista.com/business/fairs/textile.

organized by the China Chamber of Commerce for Import and Export of Textiles, an umbrella organization founded in 1998 and boasting "more than 4,600 enterprise members across China by 2002."[69] The expo's glossy brochure showed off Chinese textiles and designs to advantage, with an emphasis on silk garments from export companies in Sichuan, Shanghai and Guangzhou, but the actual exhibition was directed at solidifying the place China had already achieved as a supplier of functional garments and fabrics to the lower end of the global market. The text of the exhibition brochure made this interest obvious. Under the heading "Hot fashion attractions from China," an introduction to the expo noted that "China has ranked first in the world in the export of textiles and clothing continuously for the past seven years. In 2001, the trade turnover in import and export of textiles and clothing in China exceeded US$70.7 billion, with US$54.2 billion in exports and US$16.5 billion in imports."

Eighty-four companies exhibited products ranging from pretty cashmere sweaters made in Inner Mongolia and garish Tweety Bird towels produced in Anhui to sober suits from Hubei. Fashion parades were held on each of the expo's four days. Girl-next-door Australian models walked the catwalk in Chinese-made garments that by and large looked indistinguishable from any designed elsewhere in the world. Watched by an audience largely of Chinese origin, the parade encapsulated the contradictions attendant on Chinese aspirations to place a distinctive mark on global fashion.

In striking contrast to this sort of trade exhibition is the national costume parade, aimed at giving exposure variously to Chinese "traditional" clothing culture, Chinese textiles, and incidentally to the developing modelling industry. The six main fashion shows mounted by the New Silk Road Modelling Company in Berlin in 2001 focused on historical costume. Models mounted striking parades of "dignified" Han, "luxurious" Tang, "delicate" Song, "bold" Yuan, "bright" Ming and "elegantly gorgeous" Qing costume. A Xinhua reporter in Berlin thanked the organizer excitedly with the words: "You condensed our Chinese history and culture into a single fashion show. I felt proud to be Chinese."[70] Similar shows had earlier been organized in Paris and New York in 1998, under the rubric "China Millennium." They have a strategic place in the overall strategy of the Chinese fashion industry, which sees its future as lying in the successful combination of contemporary international fashion trends with uniquely Chinese cultural elements.

The highly self-conscious and uncritical historicism of such extravaganzas can be detected in the work of individual designers. Lu Yue, recognized as one of China's top ten designers in 1997, designs a full

---

69. China Chamber of Commerce for Import and Export of Textiles (Zhongguo fangzhipin jinchukou shanghui), Beijing 2002. Information brochure distributed at the Second China Clothing and Textiles Expo 2002, held at the Sydney Convention and Exhibition Centre, Darling Harbour, 27–30 November 2002.

70. Xin Silu, *Zhongguo fuzhuang zoujin Bolin* (English title: *China Fashion Show in Berlin*), *Zhongguo zhi yi*, No. 85 (2001/12), pp. 70–74.

range of modern clothing, from men's formal suits to women's leisure-wear. Like most of China's top designers, she has had little exposure overseas, but in 1999 and 2000 she showed her "Festival Day" collection in Paris and New York, each time in the context of larger Chinese cultural events. Part of the collection was built around the theme of the "red lantern," made famous in the West by Zhang Yimou's film *Raise the Red Lantern* (1992). Heroine-chic models carrying red paper lanterns, wearing long coats or tunics with loose trousers or very short skirts, all made of red satin, trimmed with fur and embroidered with medallions or chrysan-themums, must have made an impressive sight on the catwalk.[71] This was a predictable assembly of elements that must have left the rapturous audience in its comfort zone. Colours and materials satisfied established expectations of China, and wayward hairstyles did little to disrupt the impression of an updated *Dream of Red Mansions*.

The compulsion to celebrate China's glorious historical culture consti-tutes a problem at the heart of Chinese fashion design. The fact that the industry has not quite succeeded in dovetailing past and present suggests that designers have not yet developed an authoritative, or at least a very interesting, view of their own history. But the politics of international fashion also militate against a ready reception of their specifically Chi-nese designs. Speaking at a fashion conference in 1999, Hong Kong designer William Tang expressed bewilderment that his *qipao*-inspired designs on the Paris catwalk in the early 1990s failed to make an impression. With similar designs a couple of years later, he pointed out, French designers made fashion headlines around the world, inspiring a proliferation of *qipaos* and Chinese jackets in mainstream clothing outlets in the West.[72]

Tang's experience suggests that another obstacle faced by Chinese designers is that they are seen as Chinese, and that reception of their collections is formed by impressions of contemporary Chinese clothing culture in general, if not also of China as an authoritarian state that dictates the limits of individualism and creativity. In October 2003, as part of the "Year of China" in France, the China Association of Fashion Designers mounted a show displaying the work of six of China's top fashion designers. The designs were of flimsy, unremarkable, breast-re-vealing garments such as grace catwalks world-wide in the early 21st century. They could of course be described in terms commonly used to designate such garments: playful, contemporary, understated, whimsical. But the response in France was restrained. Jacques Lévy, director-general of Lanvin, confessed himself an admirer of Chinese creativity in many domains, "but not yet in fashion." The Franco-Swedish designer Marcel Marongiu, head of his own fashion house, commented that Chinese fashion was still at the stage of "basic ready-to-wear." Didier Grumbach,

---

71. Jiang Ye (ed.), *Zhongguo fuzhuang sheji: Lu Yue* (*Chinese Clothing Design: Lu Yue*) (Beijing: Renmin meishu chubanshe, 2004), preface, n.p.n.
72. William Tang, keynote address at the ConsumAsian conference on Fashion in Asia, University of Hong Kong, 23–27 March 1999.

president of the French Fashion Federation, shook his head (one imagines), saying: "It will take a long time before there are any Chinese labels [worth considering]. That takes a long, long time to develop."[73]

Such views are by and large shared by Chinese fashion designers themselves. In May 2002, Suzhou designer Shi Lin wrote an article assessing the present state and future prospects of Chinese fashion in the context of entry into the WTO. Born in 1942, graduating in 1960 from the Central Academy of Industrial Fine Arts, Shi Lin survived the anti-fashion years of the Cultural Revolution to emerge in her 40s as one of China's most promising designers. In 1988 she won a scholarship to study in Japan under the famous designer Kimijima Ichiro.[74] As a front-line participant in the vestimentary revolution of the 1980s, she was manifestly disappointed at the state of China's fashion industry in the early 21st century.

China's dominance in the production of clothing, she wrote, was not in dispute, but was directed mainly at providing run-of-the-mill garments for the daily wear of China's millions. Many clothing companies in China did not have a design section at all. They just bought up hot items from Shenzhen and sold them inland under their own labels, or picked the garments apart to provide the patterns for their own manufacture. Chinese designers had above all to abandon individual dreams of a dizzy ascent to the pinnacle of the fashion world in favour of the hard work of apprenticeship, beginning with "one needle and thread," like Emanuel Ungaro, who spent six years making men's trousers in the House of Balenciaga, acquiring "a fullness of knowledge and experience unattainable from books, to lay the solid foundations for his subsequent success."[75] "Without design, there can be no innovation," she pointed out, "and without innovative undertakings, there is no future." With entry into the WTO, China was facing an ever greater influx of foreign designs: "only by seizing our know-how can we avoid being sunk."[76]

This sense of anxiety and urgency is widely felt through the business world. Nearly a year after China's entry into the WTO, business journalist Chen Shuojian addressed such fears in an article that pointed to the difficulty of assessing exactly what a "national" brand was in the complicated world of multinationals. His purpose was to dispel fears of a "conspiracy" to obliterate Chinese brands and to inspire confidence in an international system that after all had no way of stopping the continual emergence of new Chinese enterprises.[77] In the realm of clothes

73. "La mode chinoise prend son envol" ("Chinese fashion takes off") (5 March 2003), on *France3.fr: un site du groupe France Télevisions Interactive*, http://cultureetloisirs.france3.fr/mode/podiumsdailleurs/103017-fr.php, accessed 3 September 2003

74. Bao Mingxin *et al.*, *Dictionary of Famous Chinese*, p. 50

75. Emanuel Ungaro, b. 1933, founded his own couture house in Paris in 1965.

76. Shi Lin, "Zhongguo shejishi haixu nuli" ("China's designers still have to work hard"), *Zhongguo fangzhi daxue xuebao* (*Journal of China Textile University*), 9 May 2002, http://www.efu.com.cn/info/technique/2002–5–10/8412.htm, accessed 3 September 2003.

77. Chen Shuojian, "Pinpai bu tan guoji" ("With brands – don't talk nationality"), *Da jing mao* (*Foreign Business Monthly*), No. 176 (November 2002), pp. 72–74.

production and fashion design, this analysis seems sound. As the economy grows and the capacity for discretionary spending increases, local designers – including boutique designers – must continue to proliferate.

Chen's realist analysis, however, will not satisfy the collective desire for brand-name recognition, a problem not limited to the fashion world. By the turn of the millennium, after 20 years of almost uninterrupted growth, China had palpably failed to realize its goal of equalling Japan's success in establishing globally powerful companies. In 2003, Japan had 88 companies listed in Fortune Global 500 while China had 11. Analysing the reasons for this failure, Peter Nolan pointed to the intense competition within the world capitalist system in the period that China was opening up. Among the factors favourable to its future success, Nolan identified China's "intense sense of its special place in world history,"[78] presumably on the grounds that patriotism might inspire the sort of efforts in business that in sport won China second place in the Athens Olympics.

In fashion the reverse may well apply. In April 2005, tensions between China and Japan over the content of Japanese history textbooks and the apparently related issue of the future composition of the United Nations' Security Council demonstrated the party state's ability to manipulate popular historical consciousness to its own ends. A more critical or ironic attitude towards their own history and culture than displayed by the Chinese government may be necessary before Chinese designers are able to produce collections capable of impressing the international fashion industry. Naturally, such an attitude cannot be fostered in schools of design alone.

78. Peter Nolan, *China and the Global Economy: National Champions, Industrial Policy and the Big Business Revolution* (Houndmills: Palgrave, 2001), p. 155.

# Popular Music and Youth in Urban China: The *Dakou* Generation

## Jeroen de Kloet

ABSTRACT  The import of illegal, cut CDs from the West (*dakou* CDs) in the mid-1990s marked the revitalization of Chinese rock culture. This article analyses the rise of *dakou* culture in the context of the interrelated processes of globalization and marketization of Chinese culture. Contrary to accounts that proclaim the crisis or death of Chinese rock, this article describes the re-emergence of rock since the mid-1990s. It presents an overview on three different scenes, part of the *dakou* culture among Chinese youth. The fashionable bands are inspired by a cosmopolitan aspiration, the underground bands signify the return of the political and the urban folk singers express a nostalgic longing. All three scenes attest to the current diversity of popular music cultures in China, and are interpreted as sonic tactics employed by Chinese youth to carve out their own space amidst an increasingly commercialized and globalized society.

The scene was rather familiar to me: the punk boys sitting outside the bar "Nameless highland" (*Wuming gaodi*) in Beijing, drinking Nanjing beer from the shop nearby to save money. It was a warm summer evening, 19 June 2004. Today's concert included four bands, all contracted by the local "indie" label Modern Sky.[1] Apart from the Chinese audience, a few foreigners – students, researchers, journalists and, though less so, expats – watched the performance. The scene reminded me of my earlier research trips, when the audience also consisted generally of a mixture of young, hip and predominantly male Beijing youths and curious foreigners.[2] The vocalist of the band Half Man Half Fish (*Renyu*), a band that labels its style as "new industrial metal" (*xin gongye jinshu*), raised his arm, screamed, in English, "I am a Nazi!" and then, to confirm his outcry, pointed at himself. This shock tactic may work in a Western context, but seemed rather out of place in Beijing. Both the statement as well as

---

1. "Indie" is put between parentheses given the involvement of the state in China's record industry: although the most prolific music producers in Beijing – Modern Sky, Scream Records and New Bees – operate relatively independent from the state, *all* music publishers and distributors are state-owned companies. The local labels have recently reduced the earlier prominence of regional and global record companies in the production of Chinese rock, thereby contradicting the trend of the globalization of Chinese economy. See Jeroen de Kloet, "Commercial fantasies: China's music industry," in S.H. Donald, M. Keane and Y. Hong (eds.), *Media Futures in China, Consumption, Content and Crisis* (London & Surrey: Routledge/Curzon Press, 2002), pp. 93–104; and Andreas Steen, "Sound, protest and business – Modern Sky Co. and the new ideology of Chinese rock," *Berliner China Hefte*, Vol. 19 (2000), pp. 40–64.
2. My research on Chinese rock culture started in 1992, when I analysed the reception of Cui Jian among Xiamen youth. Since then I have been following Beijing rock closely. This article is based on research in Beijing, Shanghai and Hong Kong over seven months in 1997, one month in 1999 and two months in 2000 – all part of my dissertation project on Chinese popular music and urban youth culture – and a return visit of three months in 2004.

the presence of foreigners underlines the conspicuous involvement of the West in Chinese rock music, not only at a practical but also, and more so, at a symbolic level.

Over the past decades, disjunctive flows of capital, people, technologies, media and ideologies have been subject to profound changes that have deeply intensified processes of globalization.[3] My return trip puzzled me not so much because so many things were still the same but because so many things had changed since 1995. It is the changes during the 1990s that I want to reflect on in this article. These are mirrored in identity labels that have been used to describe youth cultures in China. Whereas in the early 1990s one could still speak of a *liumang* ("hooligan" or "rascal") generation, around the turn of the century this had changed into the *dakou* generation, named after the cut CDs that were sold illegally on the streets of, among other cities, Beijing. In the first part of the article, I will introduce Chinese rock culture of the early 1990s and its link with *liumang* culture, including brief descriptions of its audiences, releases and performances. The second part discusses the change towards the *dakou* generation at the end of the 1990s.

This change, signalling a rebirth of Chinese rock, contradicts journalistic as well as academic accounts that proclaimed the death of Chinese rock in the mid-1990s. I will argue that *dakou* culture not only illustrates the continuous importance of popular music in Chinese youth culture, but it also signals an increasing involvement with the West, which does not rule out the possibility of voicing out discontent. The *dakou* generation's involvement with the West parallels the increasing marketization of Chinese culture, a process in which the state is deeply implicated.[4] Youth are particularly at the forefront of what Davis calls the consumer revolution of urban China.[5] In the third and final part of my article, I aim to unravel the tactics employed by rock musicians to negotiate globalization and marketization in China – two processes that are closely intertwined. My analysis includes bands of three different scenes that belong to the *dakou* culture: the "fashionable bands" (*shimao yuedui*) Sober (*Qingxing*) and Supermarket (*Chaoji shichang*) express a cosmopolitan aspiration; the underground sound (*dixia yinyue*) of NO and Tongue (*Shetou*) signifies the return of the political; and the urban folk (*chengshi minge*) of Hu Mage and Xiao He are examples of a nostalgic longing.

The three terms that guide the third part of my analysis – cosmopolitanism, politics and nostalgia – are interpreted as *sonic tactics* that are used by musicians and their audiences to navigate through contemporary China in which a state-supported urban consumerism is deeply embedded

3. Arjun Appadurai, *Modernity at Large – Cultural Dimensions of Globalization* (Minneapolis: University of Minnesota Press, 1996).

4. Dorothy J. Solinger, "State and society in urban China in the wake of the 16th Party Congress," *The China Quarterly*, No. 176 (2003), p. 943.

5. Deborah S. Davis (ed.), *The Consumer Revolution in Urban China* (Berkeley: University of California Press, 2000).

in an increasingly globalized capitalist economy.[6] I will show that rock music remains relevant in China, but when compared to the early 1990s, it is dealing with a different society, amidst different forces, in which the marketization and globalization are in full swing. Chinese rock culture serves not only as a prism to grasp these changes, it is also one of its constitutive forces, as it provides a way to be a young Chinese in this globalizing time. The term sonic tactic is invoked to highlight the opportunities offered by popular music for young people to deal with their everyday life.

### Before Dakou

In the wake of Cui Jian – still heralded as the godfather of Chinese rock – a generation of Chinese rock emerged in the early 1990s that attracted a relatively large audience in mainland China. Under the Taiwanese record label Magic Stone, He Yong, Zhang Chu, Dou Wei, Tang Dynasty and Hei Bao became among the most popular rockers and bands of these years.[7] Authenticity is, like in the West, a key element for Chinese rock culture. Two spatial dichotomies propel the quest for authenticity of Beijing rock: the West versus China, and Beijing versus Hong Kong and Taiwan. Being located outside the perceived centre of rock music – the West – rock musicians in Beijing constantly face the danger of being (labelled) a mere copycat of their Western colleagues. Chinese elements are frequently added to both music and image, in particular elements referring to ancient or to Communist China, to authenticate Chinese rock. Bands and singers like Cui Jian and Tang Dynasty have been very keen to make rock with Chinese characteristics. Examples are Cui Jian's references to the Cultural Revolution and his inclusion of "traditional" Chinese instruments and Tang Dynasty's glorification of ancient China. Localization through Sinification is employed to avoid the charge of copying.

The second distinction involves *Gangtai* pop from Hong Kong and Taiwan and rock from Beijing. The pop–rock distinction is anything but typical Chinese; in the West the voice and image of Kurt Cobain is framed differently (that is, more authentic, more true to the inner self) from that of Britney Spears. What is different in the Chinese context, however, is the geographical dimension of this globalized dichotomy: it once again reifies the north – Beijing – as being the cultural centre

6. Wang Hui, *China's New Order* (Cambridge, MA: Harvard University Press, 2003); Jing Wang, "Culture as leisure and culture as capital," *Positions*, Vol. 9, No. 1 (2001), pp. 69–101; John W. Lewis and Xue Litai, "Social change and political reform in China: meeting the challenge of success," *The China Quarterly*, No. 176 (2003), pp. 926–942.

7. For an analysis of the earlier generation of Chinese rock culture, see Andrew F. Jones, *Like a Knife: Ideology and Genre in Contemporary Chinese Popular Music* (Cornell: Cornell University, 1992); Andreas Steen, *Der Lange Marsch Des Rock'n'Roll - Pop Und Rockmusik in Der Volksrepublik China* (Hamburg: LIT Verlag, 1996) and Nimrod Baranovich, *China's New Voices: Popular Music, Ethnicity, Gender and Politics, 1978–1997* (Berkeley: University of California Press, 2003).

of Greater China and the south – Hong Kong and Taiwan – as its commercialized Other.[8] Shanghai is perceived by Beijing rockers as equally desolate in terms of music culture, a judgement that conveniently ignores the importance of Shanghai for the dance and hip hop scenes of China.

Baranovich reads the popularity of Chinese rock in the early 1990s as a continuation of the assumedly more critical and rebellious spirit of the 1980s. According to him, "the rock fad began in the euphoric and carnivalistic spring of 1989, during which it rose to the surface and achieved popularity in the most general public sphere. The intensification of the fad during the early 1990s was a continuation of the process that had started just before and during the movement, but it was also a backlash, a popular expression of anger, defiance, and perhaps a kind of compensation for the failure of the movement."[9] His equation of rock with anger, defiance and frustration reifies a rather univocal, stereotypical reading of it as a rebellious and subcultural sound. Also, by interpreting Chinese rock as a fad, Baranovich not only assumes its temporality, he also exaggerates its popularity in the early 1990s. His reading of the early 1990s as a residue of the spirit of the 1980s is valid, but runs the danger of implicitly privileging the 1980s and its alleged cultural spirit.

The works of Wang Shuo, the hooligan (*liumang*) writer whose books were bestsellers between 1987 and 1992, paralleled the popularity of rock, and "represented the spirit of the alienated, semi-criminal fringe of Beijing youth culture and Chinese urban life in general."[10] The *liumang* was celebrated in the work of Wang Shuo as a person who lives at the margin of urban society, plays around (*wan'r*), has sex, gets drunk and listens to rock music. However, under the forces of commercialization that swept over China after Deng Xiaoping's visit to the southern special economic zones in the summer of 1992 – after which a "socialist market economy ... quickly mushroomed"[11] – both Wang Shuo's and rock music's appeal declined steadily, and with them the *liumang* generation faded away as well. Being marginal was no longer considered a desirable option. "Plunging into the ocean" (*xiahai*), a popular metaphor for engaging in private business, and "linking up with the tracks of the world" (*yu shijie jiegui*) became more popular lifestyle choices.[12]

---

8. For a detailed discussion of these authenticating dynamics, see Jeroen de Kloet, "Authenticating geographies and temporalities: representations of Chinese rock in China," *Visual Anthropology*, Vol. 18, No. 2/3 (2005), pp. 229–256.

9. Baranovich, *China's New Voices*, p. 36.

10. Geremie R. Barmé, *In the Red: On Contemporary Chinese Culture* (New York: Columbia University Press, 1999), p. 79.

11. In Wang Jing and Tani Barlow (eds.), *Cinema and Desire: Feminist Marxism and Cultural Politics in the Work of Dai Jinhua* (London: Verso, 2002), p. 217.

12. Li Zhang, "Spatiality and urban citizenship in late socialist China," *Public Culture*, Vol. 14, No. 2 (2002), p. 312; Zhang Zhen, "Mediating time: the 'rice bowl of youth' in fin de siècle urban China," *Public Culture*, Vol. 12, No. 1 (2000), p. 93.

The mid 1990s were subsequently characterized by a crisis in Chinese rock culture, as critic Zhao Ke puts it:[13]

Even if we are touched by the most pure, the most original rock music, that kind of emotion is still outdated. This era does not belong to those who gather together to scream in one voice. What we need now is individuality, our individual voice. Whether as music, as spirit, or as ideal, rock fulfilled its historical mission in the 1980s.

Rock was considered to be out of touch with the spirit of the 1990s. Its rebellious spirit was perceived to be endangered by the forces of commercialism unleashed at this time, with the Party acting as the invisible puppet-master behind the "gold" screen. As Dai Jinhua phrases it, in the 1990s "the commercial displaces the political."[14] The crisis made people long not so much for the early 1990s, but more for the 1980s, when the culture fever (*wenhua re*) swept over China.[15]

The perceived crisis of Chinese rock in the mid-1990s is shown by the words of DJ Zhang Youdai, who told me:

The new generation does not have their own culture, or their own life; it's consumerism. I think the 1980s were the golden years. People ask me why Chinese rock started in the 1980s. I think you should ask why in the 1990s rock died in China. … In the 1980s young people concentrated more on culture; right now people concentrate on the economy, on making money."

Baranovich interprets the decline of rock along similar lines. To him, it "reflects the fact that young people and others lost much of their past idealism and their will to change things."[16] Instead, according to Baranovich, "commercial" pop from Hong Kong and Taiwan gained popularity in the Mainland, and became the urban sound of the 1990s. He enters the slippery grounds of cultural essentialism by suggesting it may well be the significant cultural, political and social differences between the West and China that prevent rock from becoming a mainstream sound. However, changes over the second half of the 1990s, when Chinese rock witnessed a revival that continues till today, prove that to label rock in China as a fad is inadequate.[17]

---

13. Zhao Ke, "Shijimo yaogun – yaogun xintai yijing guoshile ma?" ("Rock by the end of the century – is the rock mentality outdated?"), *Zhongguo bailaohui* (*Chinese Broadway*), No. 14 (1999), pp. 2–3.

14. In Wang and Barlow, *Cinema and Desire*, p. 216.

15. Geremie R. Barmé and Linda Jaivin (eds.), *New Ghosts, Old Dreams: Chinese Rebel Voices* (New York: Times Books, 1992); Wang and Barlow (eds.), *Cinema and Desire*; Jing Wang, *High Culture Fever: Politics, Aesthetics and Ideology in Deng's China* (Berkeley: University of California Press, 1996).

16. Baranovich, *China's New Voices*, p. 44.

17. Baranovich (*ibid.* p. 48) also notes the danger of sweeping statements when he writes that "the impact of rock, nevertheless, should not be underestimated. It still constitutes a viable subculture in China, especially in Beijing, and although marginal, still exerts, even if only indirectly, some degree of influence on the wider culture."

*Audiences, Releases and Performances*

A brief look at the audiences, the number of releases and the performances already points towards the continuous popularity of rock. In a
representative 1997 survey among 650 Beijing youths, the respondents
were asked to indicate their appreciation of music genres ranging from
Western classical music to Chinese rock on a progressive five-point
scale.[18] Figure 1 shows the popularity of the different genres among male
and female respondents. Pop and rock music are most popular among
Beijing youths; the statistics show that rock – be it from the West or from
China – remains a popular sound for Beijing youth. The popularity of
Chinese rock is as high as Chinese pop, for boys it is even higher. When
compared to the appeal of *Gangtai* pop from Hong Kong and Taiwan,
rock is less popular, but, in particular for boys, the difference is not that
big.[19] Reflecting the composition of rock culture itself, in which female
voices are scarce, the music preference of audiences is clearly gendered:
boys are more into rock, girls are more into pop. The intensity of
involvement with the music is, however, strikingly different, and points
at the importance of rock music. The rock audience is more involved in

Figure 1: **Popularity of Music Genres**

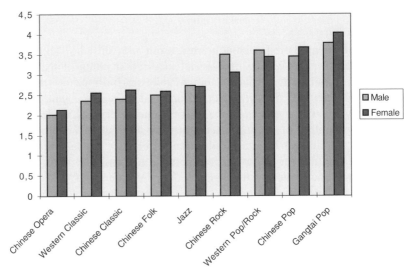

18. The survey was carried out under my initiation and supervision among youths aged
between 15 and 25 years old by a Beijing-based agency, Diamond Consultancy, and was
financed by Philips Sound & Vision. The sample is representative of the variables age,
education and sex. Figures from the real population were obtained from the China Population
Statistics Yearbook 1995 (regarding age) and were calculated by the Beijing Bureau for
Statistics for this survey (regarding education). Figures from the sample differ at most 5%
from official figures. The survey was carried out in five different districts in Beijing; thus
different neighbourhoods are represented.
19. When compared to studies on rock culture, studies on *Gangtai* pop are unfortunately
relatively scarce.

music when compared to the pop audience: they spend 53 minutes a day listening to music, compared to 34 minutes for the pop audience.

The number of releases of Chinese rock grew from just a few in the early 1990s to approximately 40 at the end of that decade, and the increasing number of small record labels means that the figure continues to grow. Sale figures are notoriously unreliable: Tang Dynasty's first album is said to have sold anywhere between 300,000 and 700,000 copies, excluding the pirated versions that are estimated at over one million copies.[20] Chinese sale figures declined from US$127m in 1997 to US$94m in 1999, but grew annually by 21 per cent after 2000 to US$198m in 2003.[21] However, given the increase in rock titles the number of each album sold has decreased. According to estimates from record producers, popular rock albums sell around 100,000 copies whereas more alternative titles reach 30,000 copies. Sale figures of *Gangtai* pop declined over the 1990s but still exceed those of rock: for example, a Jacky Cheung album sold over 2.5 million copies in 1996.[22] Actual sale figures in the cases of both rock and pop are much higher given the prevalence of piracy and more currently illegal downloads. The piracy level in China is more than 50 per cent and includes also the more alternative voices of rock culture.

The promotion of rock in China is severely hampered by the restrictions imposed upon traditional mass media, for which the genre is considered too alternative. Rock performances also suffer from government restrictions. Shows at small venues attract a stable yet relatively small fan audience, but large shows are notoriously difficult (though not impossible) to organize. Nevertheless, since 2000 an annual rock festival has been organized by the MIDI music school in Beijing, This festival, already labelled China's Woodstock, attracts national and international audiences. It was postponed in 2004 for security reasons; according to some sources, its success forced it to move to a larger park,[23] but others suggested political reasons played a role.

Finally, the number of bands and of local independent record companies has also increased since the mid-1990s.[24] Although media coverage is relatively rare, and in particular large-scale performances are scarce, there are no signs of decline. The audience figures are another indication of the continuous popularity of rock.

20. It is also indicative that the International Federation of the Phonographic Industry (IFPI) excludes Chinese sale figures from its regional and world sales overviews since the figures are based on local estimates and considered unreliable, see IFPI, *The Recording Industry World Sales 2003* (London: IFPI, 2004).

21. IFPI, *2004 – The Recording Industry in Numbers* (London: IFPI, 2004).

22. Polygram, *Polygram Annual Report 1996* (Hong Kong: Polygram, 1996).

23. See China Daily, *Festival Goers Sing the Blues,* at http://www.chinadaily.com.cn/english/doc/2004–10/20/content_384075.htm, retrieved 12 January 2005.

24. By now, "China boasts more than 10,000 rock bands. In Beijing, over 2,000 rock bands collectively have at least 10,000 players," according to the, probably positively biased, estimation of Huang Liaoyang, organiser of a rock festival at Helan mountain in Ningxia in August 2004 (in Miao Hong, "Helan mountain – to rock at a music festival," *China Daily,* 6 August 2004, p. 14). An excellent database of Chinese rock culture (in Japanese) can be found at www.yaogun.com.

### The Dakou Generation

To mourn the death of rock and its assumed rebellious *liumang* generation consequently risks missing the birth of new scenes of rock and a more multifaceted *dakou* generation. Although rock may not reach the same level of popularity as it did in the early 1990s, the rise of the *dakou* generation in the second half of the 1990s does mark a new generation of Chinese rock music. China's most prolific rock critic Yan Jun published in 1999 an overview of the bands he considered emblematic of what he called the Beijing New Sound movement.[25] His book is dedicated to the *dakou* generation of China. At more-or-less the same time, Fu Chung, manager of the small Beijing record label New Bees, dedicated his first release of pop-punk band The Flowers to the sellers of *dakou* tapes at Zhongtumen – one of the spots in Beijing to buy them. Among many other meanings, *da* stands for strike, break, smash, attack, and *kou* stands for opening, entrance, cut. Together, *dakou* stands for the cut CDs and tapes that are being sold in urban China, often along with pirated CDs, on a bustling black market (see Figure 2).

Figure 2: **A Dakou CD**

25.  Yan Jun. *Beijing xinsheng* (*New Sound of Beijing*) (Hunan: Wenyi Publishing, 1999).

*Dakou* CDs are dumped by the West, meant to be recycled, but instead are smuggled into China. They are cut to prevent them from being sold. However, since a CD player reads CDs from the centre to the margin, only the last part is lost. *Dakou* CDs enabled musicians and audiences in China to listen to music that was either censored or deemed too marginal by China's music distributors. Examples of titles range from the new wave of Joy Division to the industrial sound of the German band Einstürzende Neubauten and the digital hardcore of Atari Teenage Riot. *Dakou* CDs are, however, not necessarily alternative: Celine Dion and the operas of Wagner have also appeared on the market. But the more alternative titles were picked up by rock musicians and audiences, and consequently became tremendously nutritious for Chinese rock culture, as they opened up a musical space that did not exist officially in China. Inspired by the phenomenon itself, both musicians and audiences picked up the concept of *dakou* and turned it into a signifier for a whole urban generation. As rock critic Dundee explained[26]:

This plastic rubbish dumped by foreign record companies becomes a major source of pleasure for those discontented youths after they switch off their TV. When this plastic rubbish started flowing from the south to Beijing, it actually heralded a new rock era. All the new rock musicians in Beijing have grown up with *dakou* tapes.

It is remarkable that an urban generation chooses to name itself after an illegal product that is dumped by the West. On one internet discussion site, You Dali presents a description of the *dakou* generation that is worth quoting at length. He writes[27]:

Dakou cassette tape, dakou CD, dakou video, dakou MD, dakou vendors, dakou consumers, dakou musicians, dakou music critics, dakou magazines, dakou photo books; this is a dakou world, a new life where you don't even have to leave the country to realize your spiritual adventure. When Americans fiercely give themselves a cut, they also give the world a possibility of communism and unity. The Government doesn't encourage 1.3 billion people to listen to rock and roll. A small bunch of them therefore secretly look for offerings to their ears, to their eyes, to their brains, and to their generation. If you can't do it openly, do it secretly! ... It enables not only part of the population to become rich first, but also another part of the population to become poor first, and it also enables part of the population to become spiritually strong! Dakou products have ushered 1 million Chinese youths into a new wave, a new listening sensibility, a new awareness, a new mind and a new set of values. Whether the dakou generation is a *jinkou* [import] generation or a *chukou* [export] generation confuses quite a few social observers.

This is a parody of propaganda talk, such as the reference to Deng Xiaoping's famous defence of his reform policy, in which he declared that one part of the population should be allowed to become rich first. There is a certain critical irony towards the United States, which "gives itself a cut" and thereby supports a communist world. But at the same

26. Dundee, "Beijing yaogun: smells like teenspirit" ("Beijing rock: smells like teenspirit"), *Yinyue tiantang* (*Music Heaven*), Vol. 31 (1999), p. 28.
27. At www.guangzhou.elong.com/theme/themei48.html, retrieved on 12 July 2000.

time there is a critique of the Chinese state, which, according to this author, restricts the sound of rock. Also, the text evokes feelings of excitement and energy: the idea of being *dakou* seems empowering enough to build one's life on. It is not just a cut in a CD, but an identity that borders on the permissible. It is an identity that is both global and local.

It is also an identity that has moved past the criminal connotations of its predecessor, the *liumang*. Compared to the *liumang* generation, the *dakou* generation is more explicitly geared towards Western musical products: it acknowledges the importance of Western popular music in everyday life. Because of a cut near the edge, a young generation reached the centre of a global music culture. The *dakou* CDs point at the complicated relationship between the West and China, they are a testimony of the importance of the West when it comes to popular music. The cut at the edge, however, can be read as a contradictory sign of localization; contradictory because the cut is made by the West to ensure the CD's destruction, yet appropriated by Chinese youth in a way unforeseen by the manufacturers.

By now, websites such as www.dakou.org and www.dakou.net contain music reviews and message boards both popularizing and commodifying the *dakou* concept, just like the music magazine entitled *Koudai* (a word play of *dakou*) that presents the latest music of the West. The sites are commercial online stores where audiences can buy the latest release of Celine Dion or Kylie Minogue. Rather than following Hebdige's idea that the commodification of a subculture, as illustrated by these sites, results in its disempowerment,[28] it is my contention that the concept of *dakou* culture gathers, ironically through commodification, its subversive power, both against the dominant culture and against its state-supported forces of marketization.

The emergence of the *dakou* generation is very much facilitated by a few local (Beijing) record companies and their managers, most notably Shen Lihui from Modern Sky but also Fu Chung from New Bees, Yan Jun, rock critic and owner of the Subjam label, and Lu Bo from Scream Records. They have been profiting since 1997 from what Shen Lihui calls "a relaxed attitude towards music publishing on the part of political authorities,"[29] a relaxation linked to the dawning of government control after the 15th Party Congress in September 1997. These young entrepreneurs happily "plunged into the ocean" of doing business while simultaneously "linking up with the tracks of the world," thereby facilitating the growth of *dakou* culture.[30]

According to Yan Jun, the *dakou* generation "represents a generation that refuses to be suppressed, that seeks unseeingly, that connects to the underground, that creates marginal culture and lifestyle, that grows

28. Dick Hebdige, *Subculture: The Meaning of Style* (London: Methuen, 1979).
29. Steen, "Sound, protest and business," p. 46.
30. Further study is required to analyse the role of these gatekeepers in including and excluding specific voices in Chinese rock culture, and thereby in defining the field of rock, an analysis in line with Bourdieu's theories on cultural production.

stubbornly, that resists and struggles."[31] His reading presents one side of being *dakou*, it celebrates the rebellious. As my analysis will show, *dakou* culture is more diverse and more ambiguous. In what follows I reveal the variety of *dakou* culture by presenting three different scenes: the fashionable bands, the underground bands and the urban folk singers. These scenes not only account for the current generic diversity of Chinese rock culture, but their sounds, lyrics and images should also be interpreted as tactics through which Beijing youth negotiate "the blessings and the blows of two decades of ever-deepening marketization."[32]

### Cosmopolitan Aspirations: Sober and Supermarket

The record company Modern Sky is clear in positioning its products in relation to the earlier rock bands. Shen Lihui, who is not only the managing director of Modern Sky but also the vocalist of Sober, constantly stresses that he wants more diversity. Steen quotes Shen Lihui from the website of Sober[33]:

One irresponsible shouter is leading a group of headless shouters; this is today's situation of Chinese rock music. At present, the irresponsible shouter has already turned into a chattering old woman. Today, without understanding anything, he is still recovering from the complaints of his childhood. In fact, apart from affirming Freudian science, this doesn't say anything to us. This world has already started to change, and the things he is talking about don't have anything to do with us. ... I think, he or they should go into a museum and get some sleep!

Clearly Shen Lihui is talking about Cui Jian and his generation. Cui Jian responds to this by labelling the new generation "charlatans without culture."[34] The early generation is downplayed as comprising screaming, long-haired individuals. The new (*dakou*) generation on the other hand is said to reflect contemporary urban life: don't take it so seriously, have fun; who cares to rebel if you can revel.

Sober often uses the generic label Britpop to describe its sound. The music of Sober is a postmodern re-appropriation of The Beatles' sound, in ways reminiscent of the music of Britpop bands such as Oasis and Blur. The references to The Beatles are indicative of the cosmopolitan aspirations of Sober. The lyrics of the title song of their 1997 album *Very Good!?* (*Haojile!?*) are:

Your TV set breaks down and your eyes will be cured?
Your watch stops, does this mean that you are happy?

---

31. Yan Jun, "Yongyuan nianqing, yongyuan relei ningkang – 2002 midi yinyuejie jishi" ("Forever young, forever crying – notes on midi 2002 music festival"), in Chen Guanzhong, Liao Waitong and Yan Jun, *Boximiya Zhongguo* (*Bohemian China*) (Hong Kong: Oxford University Press, 2004), p. 176.

32. Solinger, "State and society in urban China," p. 943. Zhang Zhen focuses predominantly on the blows when she writes that "In a society mobilized to plunge into the ocean or to link with the tracks of the world, fear of drowning and the perils of speed have made anxiety a central figure of public discourse." In Zhang, "Mediating time," p. 94.

33. *Ibid*. p. 55.

34. Yan, *New Sound of Beijing*, p. 31.

Does this mean that you are happy?
Very good!? Indeed very good!? Very good!?
To whom do I give Monday and Tuesday?
To whom do I give Wednesday and Thursday? (..)
All right! All right! All right! All right!

The refrain "All right! All right!" is sung in English, giving the song a
cosmopolitan ring. The accompanying video depicts the band in Beatles-
style suits; four young Chinese in a British look with an ironic smile
drawn on their faces. According to Shen Lihui, the song is influenced by
The Beatles, but he considers it postmodern, both in melody and lyrics.

Both Sober and Supermarket are grouped by Yan Jun under the label
fashionable bands (*shimao yuedui*).[35] The ambient sounds of Supermarket
are also referred to as electronic music (*dianzi yinyue*). Supermarket's
1998 debut album *The Look* (*Moyang*) leads the listener to a virtual,
computerized reality. In the linguistically shortest song of the album,
"Explode" (*Baozha*), Supermarket sings:

Right now I'm afraid time may explode
If I'm embarrassed, please don't care.

Clear-cut meanings dissolve in their electronic soundscape. Supermarket
employs a kaleidoscopic sound, linking syntho-pop with dance,
drum'n'bass, and trip hop. This becomes especially clear from their
second album *Weapon 5* (*Wuqi*), on which the electronic aesthetics are
taken even further, as signified by the song titles that run from "S1" to
"S10."

Chinese characteristics are conspicuously absent in both the music and
the image of Supermarket. The group's cosmopolitan position resonates
closely with the aesthetics of Sober. However contradictory it at first sight
may seem, the cosmopolitanism of these *dakou* bands has a clear
nationalistic edge. Shen Lihui has a desire to join the global world of
music by precisely adding a Chinese sound to it: "Until now, the
programming has been dominated by the US, but the next century is
likely to bring a more multicultural mix where American youths will one
day watch Chinese rock bands."[36] And given the current pace of changes
in Beijing, the cosmopolitan aspiration strikes him as closest to reality, as
he explained to me: "I don't think it's necessary to add elements like an
*erhu*, ... Beijing has become very internationalized. ... I feel some foreigners are simply interested in something strange, something exotic.
Music should be true to modern life."

The cosmopolitan aspiration of Sober's Shen Lihui, with its refusal of
Sinification, show that under the current forces of globalization more
authenticating repertoires have become available. Sober's focus on being
modern signifies the longing of the *dakou* generation to become part of
a global youth culture, not on the basis of cultural differences but on the

35. *Ibid.*
36. In Kevin Platt, "China's cutting-edge artists join global village," at
www.csmonitor.com/durable/1998/06/26/fp54s1-csm.htm, 1998, retrieved 14 January 2000.

basis of similarity, of a shared musical culture. At the same time, Shen Lihui's business activities illustrate that this longing goes hand in hand with the practice of "plunging into the ocean" by setting up a private enterprise.

### The Return of the Political: NO and Tongue

The split between the 1980s and the 1990s is often conceived as a shift from the cultural and political towards the commercial and individual. Cui Jian's oeuvre resembles the spirit of the 1980s; in his lyrics and performance the personal and the political are closely intertwined. His lyrics are profoundly metaphorical and often contain a strong political critique.[37] The political voice reappears in the *dakou* generation, but has become more sarcastic and direct, when compared to Cui Jian. To interpret the *dakou* movement as one that lacks a political edge is thus inadequate. The bands NO and Tongue challenge in an underground sound (*dixia yinyue*) and in ironic lyrics the words of Shen Lihui quoted earlier, in which he distances himself from the "irresponsible screams and boring complaints" of the earlier rock musicians. Strangely enough, both bands are contracted by Shen Lihui's label Modern Sky, and can be considered emblematic for the return of the political voice in Chinese rock.

Zu Zhou's NO has been active since 1994, but released its first CD entitled *Missing Master* (*Zoushi de zhuren*) in 1997. By 2004 it had released three CDs. Zu Zhou, born in 1970 in Nanjing, is not only a musician but also a performance artist and writer. His music (for which he uses self-made instruments) and his lyrics are profoundly experimental. His voice oscillates between the very low – resembling, if you like, the voice of Tom Waits – and a high falsetto. As one Chinese critic remarks, "Zu Zhou's uniquely penetrating tenor, like a knife stained with blood and sperm, tears off everything ... His purely despondent bass divulges the loneliness towards the future and the destruction of the will to live."[38] In the song "Representatives" (*Daibiao*) from his third album *Zuoxiao Zu Zhou at Di'anmen* (*Zuoxiao Zu Zhou zai Di'anmen*), he compares Chinese leader Jiang Zemin to both Yeltsin and Clinton[39]:

They asked me when Jiang Zemin would act like Yeltsin
"Ask him. I'll give you comrade Jiang Zemin's contact
I have nothing to do with his business, I have to mind my own"
Just like that, I took them as his enemy
I have mastered the world skilfully
Unlike you

---

37. See Jones, *Like a Knife*.
38. He Li. "Yaogun gu'er" ("Rock'n'roll orphans"), *Jinri xianfeng* (*Today's Avant-Garde*), Vol. 5 (1997), p. 77.
39. See also http://www.zuoxiaozuzhou.com/for an overview of Zu Zhou's lyrics. On the jacket, the lyrics are printed in both Chinese and English. In the Chinese version, the name of Jiang Zemin is left out. The fact, however, that these lyrics do pass censorship is indicative of the relaxation of control over cultural products in China.

The lyrics poke fun at Jiang Zemin. Zu Zhou's lyrics are characterized by a Dadaistic absurdity and, to use his own description, a profound sarcasm that defamiliarizes the familiar. Zu Zhou's music and lyrics can be considered a critical intervention in Chinese popular culture. They signify a dark and falsetto voice of resistance, a voice that, given the publicity Zu Zhou receives in numerous music magazines, is certainly not being silenced.

In one of his songs, Zu Zhou refers directly to Tongue and their Xinjiang background. Tongue's members are from Ürümchi.[40] Their first album *Chicken Coming out of the Egg* (*Xiaoji chuke*) was released by Modern Sky in 1999 and a subsequent live album was published under Yan Jun's label Subjam. Tongue's music is, like Zu Zhou's, full of noise, the tormented voice of leading vocalist Wu Tun strengthening the dark atmosphere the music evokes.[41] Yan Jun writes on the difficulties Tongue's releases face when passing the censorship authorities.[42] He refers in particular to the song "They are coming" (*Tamen laile*), of which the full lyrics run:

The primitive men are coming
The slave masters are coming
The feudal lords are coming
The democrats are coming
Imperialism is coming
Capitalism is coming
Socialism is coming
Communism is coming
They are coming

The upbeat sound turns the song in an underground version of a protest march, almost overruling the gloomy, whiny voice of Wu Tun. At the end of the song – when the last sentence *tamen laile* is repeated all the time – a high pitched screaming voice joins in, after which the song suddenly changes into the tune of the lullaby "Brother John." The switch from a march to a lullaby signifies, in my view, a moment of parody, it pokes fun at all the "isms" that are included in the lyrics of the song, a sonic manifestation of Lyotard's claim that an end of the Grand Narratives such as socialism and communism characterizes contemporary postmodern culture.[43]

---

40. Baranovich (*China's New Voices*, pp. 54–107) elaborates on the link between ethnicity and rock, suggesting that rock serves as an empowering tool for China's ethnic minorities. The presence of non-Beijingers within the Beijing rock culture indeed indicates that rock is a cultural domain that enables musicians to move from the margin towards the centre, but this margin does not necessarily have to be defined in terms of ethnicity, it can also be simply in terms of geography.

41. For a wonderful and subtle analysis of Tongue's work, see Jeroen Groenewegen, "Tongue – making sense of the underground rock community, Beijing 1997–2004," MA thesis, Leiden University, 2005, available at www.keepmakingsense.com.

42. Yan Jun, *Didixia: Xin yinyue chanxingji* (*Underground: A Trip Through New Music*) (Beijing: Wenhua yishu chubanshe, 2002), p. 183.

43. Jean Francois Lyotard, *The Postmodern Condition: A Report on Knowledge* (Minneapolis: University of Minnesota Press, 1984).

Both Tongue and NO are examples of the reappearance of the political in Chinese rock. Their politics are more noisy, more sarcastic and more absurdist when compared to their predecessors, including the poetic, metaphorical lyrics and melodic sound of Cui Jian. They do testify that the displacement of the political by the commercial during the 1990s has not been as absolute as some authors claim. Even more ironically, the two do not necessarily exclude one another; on the contrary, it has been because of the relaxation of government control that small, local record companies could emerge, and eventually contract bands like Tongue and NO. The reappearance of the political in Chinese rock is consequently embedded in a state supported marketization of Chinese culture.

### Nostalgic Longings: Hu Mage and Xiao He

The sounds that carry the labels folk (*minge* or *minyao*), folk-rock (*minge yaogun*) or urban folk (*chengshi minge*) are first and foremost "individual" expressions of urban sentiments. Whereas other genres within Chinese rock are either a direct or a homophonic translation from the English, the term *minge* has a long and complicated history in China. Minorities use it to articulate their local identity, the Han Chinese use it to reify their long tradition, the CCP uses it to propagate communism, and within the rock culture it is used to voice out feelings of urban nostalgia.

Hu Mage is a singer originally from Inner Mongolia, whereas Xiao He moved in 1995 from Hebei to Beijing. The migratory experience is particularly evident in the folk scene with most singers positioning themselves as troubadours from the provinces. Hu Mage's 1998 album *Everyone Has a Little Wooden Stool, Won't Take Mine to the 21st Century* (*Renren dou you ge xiao bandeng, wo de bu dairu ershiyi shiji*) has a white jacket that depicts a childish drawing. The whiteness and the drawing, as well as the hand-written lyrics in the inlay, signify (the longing for) simplicity and purity. In his song "Some potatoes go to the city" (*Bufen tudou jincheng*), Hu Mage starts laughing when he sings:

Next door lives a cultured person, strange, but not really with bad intentions
He says I am hardworking, brave, sincere, simple and without any desire
He shows me an exercise book, full of words
He plays music to me, which I don't like, too noisy

He is like a modern troubadour: the music is plain and simple, only the sound of his guitar accompanies his raw and unpolished voice. He stresses his simplicity by positioning himself in comparison to a "cultured person." His music can be read as a nostalgic longing to retreat from contemporary urban society, towards a place beyond conspicuous consumption, a place that is imagined as one full of serenity and honesty.[44]

---

44. Indicative of the mobility of cultural identities in China is Hu Mage's move towards electronic music in his second album – an album that was generally not well received. He currently operates a popular website that contains, among others, music and film reviews, message boards and chat sites (www.rmage.com).

Xiao He's CD carries an equally long and prosaic title as Hu Mage's: *A High-flying Bird Won't Land on the Back of a Slow-moving Cow* (*Feidegao de niao bu luo zai paobukuai de niu de beishan*). It was released by, again, Modern Sky in 2003. The CD resembles the aesthetics of Hu Mage: this time the jacket is in earth colours, signifying natural-ness, and also includes hand-written lyrics. On the jacket's inlay, Yin Lichuan writes on Xiao He's live performance: "I believe Xiao He can survive in any environment, waiting for every opportunity to have fun and share it with others. Now he is performing in a bar amidst all sorts of people, but he behaves as if he's herding sheep on a little hill slope when he was young, so relaxed, so involved, and so happy."

The last remark again underlines the nostalgic purity of folk, a purity that is often located in the rural, rather than the urban, and in youth, rather than in the adult world. The temporal element in folk's nostalgia remains ambivalent. Drawing on Rey Chow, Helen Hok-sze Leung argues that "nostalgia is not simply a yearning for the past as though it were a definite, knowable object. Rather, nostalgia involves a 'sensitivity to the movements of temporality.' Understood in these terms, a nostalgic sub-ject is someone who sits on the fence of time."[45] The folk singer sits on the fence, his back turned against a time of conspicuous consumption, longing for the innocence of youth and the imagined purity and simplicity of an idyllic life. This longing returns in the lyrics of Xiao He's song "The river of wolves" (*Lang zhi he*), the music of which includes elements of traditional Chinese folk:

The snow that will never melt and remain clean
The river that will never freeze and remain transparent
Wind, please caress her body gently
Make her speak slowly
Through the surface of the river
Through the tree leaves
Through the valleys
As a gift to the forever past
As a gift to the forever future

Both singers evoke – in terms of lyrics, vocals, sound and image – a nostalgic longing for a life beyond the marketization and globalization of urban Chinese society and can consequently be read as a critique on contemporary China. However, ambivalently enough, both singers, in their own life, moved from the geographical margins of China towards its political and cultural centre. This pull to the modern capital comes with a nostalgic longing for a margin that is located in an ambivalent idyllic past.

*Conclusion*

The musical practices that can be grouped under the label "rock culture" encompass a wide array of genres, each with their own sonic

---

45. Helen Hok-sze Leung, "Queerscapes in contemporary Hong Kong cinema," *Positions*, Vol. 9, No. 2 (2001), p. 430.

tactics to negotiate the larger context in which they are situated. The *dakou* culture that emerged in the second half of the 1990s, with Beijing as its epicentre, has refuted the voices that declared the end of Chinese rock. The fashionable bands, in their urge to place China in the world, offer a nationalistic embrace of the cosmopolitan present, as well as a commercial break from an assumedly more rebellious past. The political bands under study present the *dakou* generation with an entirely different set of aesthetics that establish a noisy, ironic and sarcastic critique on contemporary China and the state-supported forces of marketization, which, in turn, have encouraged the establishment of small local record companies and facilitated the return of the political voice in Chinese rock. The nostalgia of urban folk singers delivers less a direct critique than a desire to withdraw oneself from these forces. The modern troubadours move from the provinces towards the cultural centre to articulate their longing for a margin that is perceived to be located in an ambivalent time and place, a more idyllic and ideal China.

All of these rock scenes express a sense of national longing and belonging, though in the case of the fashionable bands this longing paradoxically is articulated through a transnational desire to place Chinese rock on the world map of music. If early rockers and the *liumang* generation have appropriated a Western musical genre to deal with the opening up of a nation towards reform and the world, the later rock scenes and the *dakou* generation are customizing the same genre to negotiate a diversity of longing and belonging in a nation increasingly configured by marketization and globalization. Driven by the same logic, the *dakou* culture itself is threatened to become obsolete, in the words of Yan Jun in 2004: "The *dakou* generation is vanishing. China is changing, the youth is ageing, the market is spreading. Wild thoughts, pledges, poetry and even the suicidal urge have been pushed to the bottom of the box by accumulated wealth. Memory, like first love, is melting in the currents of information."[46] The availability of music through the World Wide Web has rendered *dakou* CDs almost redundant: new songs are just a mouse-click away from Chinese musicians. The West is no longer out there, instead, it increasingly becomes part and parcel of Chinese rock culture and contemporary urban Chinese culture at large, in which China and its Others are being synchronized day after day.[47]

The scenes under study show how popular music is used by Chinese youth to carve out their own space in contemporary China, making use of the possibilities that state-supported, globally embedded processes of marketization offer. The makers and users of such music simultaneously

---

46. Yan Jun, *Ranshao de shengyin (Burning Noise)* (Jiangsu: Jiangsu renmin chubanshe, 2004), p. 174.

47. Synchronization with the West is particular apparent in China's Hip Hop culture. In Yin Tsang, only one out of its four members (MC Webber) is "indigenous" Chinese, whereas MC Sketch Krime works with four 4 MCs from France, Britain, Japan and the US Both Yin Tsang and Sketch Krime released their first album in 2004 under Scream Records.

express and process their daily life experience: a cosmopolitan, national aspiration, a political, ironic critique, and a nostalgic, idyllic longing. Contemporary rock culture in China provides ample evidence that the assumed change from the cultural and political in the 1980s towards the commercial and individual in the 1990s is anything but clear-cut or univocal.

# Reggae on the Silk Road: The Globalization of Uyghur Pop

## Rachel Harris

ABSTRACT    In this article I take examples of popular music recordings released in the Xinjiang Uyghur Autonomous Region during the 1990s and first few years of the 21st century, in order to illustrate the global flows of sounds and meanings which influence Uyghur pop. The disseminatory power of "micro media" (cheap cassettes, VCDs) facilitates the global movement of both musical sounds and political ideas. I argue, using examples of Uyghur reggae and Uyghur belly dancing, that these sounds and meanings are radically adapted and re-signified in the construction of Uyghur identity and cultural politics, in a complex interplay between the global, national and local, and between tradition and modernity. I discuss the gendered expression of Uyghur nationalism in popular song through the iconic figure of the weeping mother, demonstrating the ability of expressive culture (here music) to reveal underlying or underpinning political trends.

In recent years the notion of the Silk Road has enjoyed a new vogue, popularly invoked in a multiplicity of meanings revolving around the region of the former Soviet Central Asian States and China's Xinjiang Uyghur Autonomous Region. These range from the Silk Road Project led by celebrity cellist Yo Yo Ma creating remarkable fusion music from Mongolia to Azerbaijan,[1] package tours transporting American and European citizens to Bukhara and Samarkand, to a 2004 British library exhibition[2] displaying the invaluable discoveries (or outrageous thefts according to your point of view) made by Sir Aurel Stein in the ruins of the ancient Buddhist kingdoms which lie beneath Xinjiang's Taklimakan desert. The most suitable evocation for the purposes of this article, however, is a photo article which appeared in the British *Independent* newspaper in 1998, which deftly illustrated the often surprising pathways of commodities under conditions of globalization on the contemporary Silk Road.[3] The author, James von Leyden, drew readers' attention to the phenomenon of plastic bags advertising The Pet Shop, Pollokshaws Road, Glasgow, which at that time could be found in their millions all over the bazaars of Xinjiang. Contrary to rumour these plastic bags were not part of a container-load hijacked by mujahadin en route to Europe. Their presence in the Xinjiang bazaars was due to a loophole in international trading laws whereby manufacturers could obtain a subsidy if their products were found to be defective. Originally contracted by the Glasgow pet shop to produce 100,000 bags, the supplier in Xinjiang

---

1. http://www.silkroadproject.org/.
2. http://www.bl.uk/.
3. James von Leyden, "Plastic fantastic," *Independent Saturday Magazine,* 21 March 1998.

simply misprinted the telephone number, distributed tens of millions of the bags throughout the region, presumably claimed his subsidy and made a huge killing. As this article will demonstrate, musical sounds, captured in the commodity form of cassettes and CDs, travel by similarly diverse and surprising pathways into Xinjiang.

In his classic study of "cassette culture" in India, the ethnomusicologist Peter Manuel characterized cheap and easily reproducible new forms of technology, like the audio cassettes which spread around the globe in the 1970s, as "micro-media."[4] Micro-media, he argued, stand for "decentralization, democratization and dispersal," providing potential channels for the expression and mediation of local identities, and are theoretically and politically opposed to the old mass-media. Micro-media's oppositional tendencies lie less in the content of the media than in their means of production.[5] Manuel's dualist model of micro- versus mass-media risks over-simplification of the cultural and political complex surrounding recorded music. Nevertheless the concept of micro-media retains its usefulness, and there are numerous parallels between his detailed descriptions of cassette culture in India and the Uyghur scene where cassettes, and latterly VCDs, serve at national level (in the regional capital Ürümchi) as the medium for oppositional politics, and at local level (in smaller oasis towns and villages) to promote diverse and rarely heard subcultural sounds.[6]

The writings of Arjun Appadurai on globalization have informed my understanding of the ways in which global sounds enter and inhabit the sphere of Uyghur pop. Appadurai has suggested that processes of culture production in the changing spatial contexts of globalization have become primarily a question of identity politics, and that electronic media "transform the field of mass mediation because they offer new resources and new disciplines for the construction of the imagined selves and imagined worlds."[7] I have argued in an earlier article that many themes expressed through Uyghur pop are bound up in issues of national or ethnic identity, which in Xinjiang are sharply political.[8] In this article I take examples of popular cassette and VCD recordings released in the region during the last decade in order to illustrate the global flows of sounds and meanings which influence Uyghur pop. I argue that these sounds and meanings are radically adapted and re-signified in the construction of Uyghur identity and cultural politics, in a complex interplay between the global, national (here understood as the Uyghur nation) and the local, and between tradition and modernity.

4. Peter Manuel, *Cassette Culture: Popular Music and Technology in Northern India* (Chicago & London: University of Chicago Press, 1993).
5. *Ibid.* pp. 1–2.
6. Mark Slobin, *Subcultural Sounds: Micromusics of the West* (Hanover & London: Wesleyan University Press, 1993).
7. Arjun Appadurai, *Modernity at Large: Cultural Dimensions of Globalization* (Minneapolis & London: University of Minnesota Press, 1996), p. 3.
8. Rachel Harris, "Cassettes, bazaars and saving the nation: the Uyghur music industry in Xinjiang, China," in T. Craig and R. King (eds.), *Global Goes Local: Popular Culture in Asia* (Vancouver: University of British Columbia Press, 2002), pp. 265–283.

*A Brief Overview of Uyghur Pop Music*

Uyghur music-making traditionally revolves around the *mäshräp* (gathering or party) which draws the local community together for food, music and dancing. Weddings, circumcision parties, the major Islamic festivals and pilgrimages to saints' shrines are also important occasions for music. Singers are accompanied by the long-necked plucked and bowed lutes (*tämbur*, *dutar* and *satar*) and the *dap* frame drum, which are all found across Central Asia, often with the addition of the *skirupka* (violin, from the Russian) or accordion. Kettle drum and shawm bands (*naghra-sunay*) provide raucous, celebratory outdoors music. The singing style is highly ornamented, and the songs often employ the *aqsaq* or "limping" rhythms, which are also found in the rhythms of the Sufi *zikr* chants. Each oasis has its own distinctive musical style and repertoire, ranging from the more purely pentatonic sounds of the eastern town of Qumul (in Chinese Hami), to the modally more complex style of the old Silk Road town of Kashgar in the south-west. Historically, the local kings and elite of the different oases (such as Kashgar, Turpan, Khotan) patronized semi-professional musicians who sang the prestigious Muqam suites. The term is derived from the Arabic *maqām*, but the style is local, indeed each of the major oases boasts its own unique Muqam tradition. Since the 1940s (before the incorporation of Xinjiang into the People's Republic of China) Uyghur traditions have been professionalized and modernized through the Soviet model of state-run performance troupes. Local traditions have formed the basis for new composition from revolutionary folk songs praising Chairman Mao to large-scale ensemble pieces and operas. To this day the troupes perform song-and-dance spectaculars celebrating the region's inclusion in the PRC.[9]

Commercially recorded music in Xinjiang has a rather short history, beginning in the 1980s when recording technologies, especially the cheap medium of cassettes and cassette recorders, became widely available. A visit to Döng Kövrük (in Chinese Erdaoqiao), the main bazaar in Ürümchi, reveals great diversity of music for sale. Most numerous are the locally-produced cassettes of Uyghur pop songs. More traditional-style cassette recordings can also be found: drum and shawm music from Turpan; instrumental dance music for weddings from Kashgar. Cheap VCD technology arrived in Xinjiang in around 1997, and now every music shop in the bazaar advertises its presence with televisions playing videos of the local pop stars, from the ever-popular actor-singer Abdulla Abdurehim to the briefly fashionable Madonna wannabe Aytelan.

Mainstream Uyghur pop marketed within Xinjiang has a wide audience, crossing the generational and the urban–rural divide, although the

---

9. For discussions of professional troupe performance in Xinjiang see Dru C. Gladney, "Representing nationality in China: refiguring majority/minority identities," *Journal of Asian Studies*, Vol. 53, No. 1 (1994), pp. 92–123; Rachel Harris, *Singing the Village: Music Memory, and Ritual amongst the Sibe of Xinjiang* (Oxford & New York: Oxford University Press, 2004); Colin Mackerras, *China's Minority Cultures: Identities and Integration since 1912* (New York: Longman Press, 1995); Sabine Trebinjac, *Le Pouvoir en Chantant: l'art de fabriquer une Musique Chinoise* (Nanterre: Société d'ethnologie, 2000).

more obviously Western-influenced end of the market appeals mainly to urban youngsters. Pop music fills the schedules of Xinjiang's numerous Uyghur-language television channels. Pop singers perform live sets for dancing in high-class restaurants in Ürümchi. Cassettes of pop music fill the bazaars in smaller towns around the region. This broad appeal increases the opportunities for pop performers to disseminate new sounds and ideas. It is impossible to demarcate a clear line between traditional and pop in Uyghur recorded music. Most popular composers strive to maintain some local flavour in their songs. Continuity with tradition lies in the maintenance of traditional rhythms (though the drum machine renders these somewhat inflexible), the use of traditional instruments alongside the synthesizer, the adaptation of specific folk melodies, but especially in singing style and its communication of emotion. Traditional folk songs are frequently set to synthesized beats, regional traditions may be combined with electric guitar and drum set, and new songs are composed with traditional instrumental accompaniment, notably the *dutar* two-stringed lute.

Alongside the locally produced fare on sale in the Uyghur bazaars are numerous imports. Hindi films were the earliest foreign fashion to penetrate Xinjiang after the Cultural Revolution, following the early opening of the Pakistan border, and during the 1980s large crowds could be seen watching them on television in ice-cream stalls in the Kashgar bazaar, or in the pit-stop restaurants for long-distance travellers which line the desert roads. The variety of available sounds steadily increased through the 1990s with the opening of the borders with the Central Asian states, and greater access to Western sounds. By 2001 a hunt along the shelves of a music shop in Döng Kövrük bazaar might reveal the Sex Pistols' *Never Mind the Bollocks* alongside the Gipsy Kings, American country-and-western, Uzbek folk songs and Turkish pop. Inspired by this kind of diversity, the ethnomusicologist Philip Bohlmann has used the image of the Middle Eastern bazaar – with its capacity to collapse the boundaries of time and space, juxtaposing pop tapes and the imam's call to prayer – as a broad metaphor for folk music in the modern world.[10] Although it is not my impression that the Sex Pistols have a big following in Xinjiang, and Uyghur musicians have yet to create their own brand of punk, the arrival of recordings like this into the region is interesting, and illustrative of the contemporary musical "Silk Road" on which it is situated. In spite of government attempts to crack down, the trade in pirate cassettes and VCDs flourishes. The *dakou* CDs, the subject of Jeroen de Kloets's article in this volume, also found their way to Ürümchi in the late 1990s, although here too they are now being superceded by the internet. Uyghurs benefit not only from the very successful Chinese bootlegging industry but also from pirate imports from Pakistan and the Central Asian states. If, as de Kloet argues, the spatial orientation of Beijing's rock scene lies between Hong Kong, Taiwan and the West, then

10. Philip Bohlman, *The Study of Folk Music in the Modern World* (Indiana University Press, 1988), p. 121.

the Uyghur pop scene orients itself by a more diverse range of cultural influences emanating from Beijing, the West, India, Turkey, and the Central Asian states of Kazakhstan, Uzbekistan and Kyrgyzstan.

These diverse sounds are, of course, reproduced and incorporated into their own productions by Uyghur musicians. The earliest releases in the 1980s were dominated by the Russian-influenced waltz-style songs accompanied by the accordion which had first made their mark on the region in the 1950s. Heavy metal began to make inroads into the Uyghur urban youth market in the mid-1990s with the bands Täklimakan and Riwäyat; this kind of sound arrived in Xinjiang via the rock scene of Beijing. Popular flamenco guitar has been greatly in vogue since the mid-1990s. This sound has been incorporated into the Uyghur popular music repertoire by numerous Ürümchi-based singers and instrumentalists, and also by the Beijing-based cross-over star singer Äskär (lead singer of the band *Hui Lang* (Grey Wolf)) who sings both in his native Uyghur and, aiming at the wider market, in Chinese.[11] Äskär has gained fans amongst educated young Uyghurs in Ürümchi who appreciate his experimental musical approach and higher quality production, but his lack of fluency in the Uyghur language and his orientation towards the Beijing rock scene distance him from the wider Uyghur audience.

The Uyghur pop market in Xinjiang also draws on the Uyghur communities in Turkey and across the border in the Central Asian states. One major cross-border success in recent years is the band Dervishes.[12] Formed in July 1999 by four mainly Russian-speaking Uyghur musicians trained in the Almaty Conservatory, the Dervishes music is based in a heavy rock sound mixed with samples from Uyghur folk to Brazilian birembau and London clubland breakbeats. Mirroring Äskär they aim at the cross-over market, singing in a mixture of Russian and Uyghur. Well-known in their native Kazakhstan, they were also in 2003 the most popular band with urban youngsters in Xinjiang even though their music was only available in the region via bootleg recordings. It is telling that the two bands most popular with fashionable youngsters in Ürümchi are both based outside the Uyghur region and neither is at home with the Uyghur tongue. Uyghur musicians working in Beijing and Almaty, especially those educated in the Chinese or Russian language, have greater access to new musical sounds and quality recording equipment, and they best represent for the increasingly outward-oriented urban youngsters the desired combination of modernity and self.

Musical sounds also flow out of the region. In Kazakhstan, where there is a population of some half a million Uyghurs, there is a fairly substantial market in bootleg copies of cassettes released by Xinjiang artists, their covers re-worked to include the Uyghur titles in the Cyrillic lettering employed in the former Soviet states. Uyghur pop music can be

---

11. Äskär, *Tiläg* (*Blessing*) (China: DMVE Co., 2001). Cf. Nimrod Baranovitch, "Between alterity and identity: new voices of minority people in China," *Modern China*, Vol. 27, No. 3 (2001), pp. 359–401.

12. Dervishi, *Dunya* (*World*) (Kazakhstan: Ala Music Enterprises, 2002). Official website: www.show-kz.com/dervishi.

downloaded from several websites maintained by the exiled community in the United States, most of which carry a strong political agenda.[13] Han Chinese pop singers have also drawn on the "exotic" sounds of traditional Uyghur music to infuse their own productions, from the perenially popular songs of the revolutionary era song-writer Wang Luobin[14] to the most recent hit singer, Sichuan-born "Daolang" (whose name is borrowed from the Dolan Uyghurs of the Tarim river), whose songs include rock-style reworkings of revolutionary classics with Uyghur instrumental backing.[15]

### Reggae Re-signified

A closer analysis of two popular songs and their accompanying videos from the mid-1990s serves to illustrate some of the complexities of Uyghur musicians' appropriation of global sounds, and the extraordinary mutability of these sounds and their meanings under conditions of globalization. The ethnomusicologist Veit Erlmann has described the phenomenon of World Music as one of the disjuncture of sounds and meanings. Musical sounds, captured on recording medium and separated from their original sources and contexts, are disembodied. As these disembodied sounds circulate around the globe with increasing ease and rapidity, on cassettes, via broadcast media and over the internet, their meanings are detached and their sounds are re-signified. Erlmann explores how listeners shift the contexts of their knowledge and endow phenomena with significance beyond their immediate realm of personal experience. He suggests, adapting Appadurai's theories of globalization, that World Music invents realities generated by electronic means. Sense manufactured in this way out of discontinuities, he argues, is arbitrary and rampant, and can no longer mediate culture-specific processes of appropriation of the external world; it is neutral ground.[16] These two contrasting, even opposed, examples of musical appropriation illustrate how facets of Uyghur identity are constructed through music from such apparently arbitrary discontinuities.

The first example is a reggae version of a Khotän folk song titled "Qatlima" performed by the singer-guitarist Shiräli. Released in 1995 and a big hit in Ürümchi, this song juxtaposes a reggae bass beat with the lyrics and melody of a popular Uyghur folk song infused with the images and smells of home; *qatlima* is a type of flat bread stuffed with meat and onions commonly baked by Uyghur women in the family home.

---

13. Clearly, the songs of artists working within the PRC appear on such websites without the knowledge or permission of the artists. See for example http://www.uyghuramerican.org/uyghurche/muzika/ or http://www.meshrep.com/.

14. Cf. Rachel Harris, "Wang Luobin: folksong king of the northwest or song thief? Copyright, representation and Chinese folksongs," *Modern China*, Vol. 31, No. 3 (2005), pp. 381–408.

15. http://www.esee.cn/daolang.htm.

16. Veit Erlmann, *Music, Modernity and the Global Imagination: South Africa and the West* (Oxford: Oxford University Press, 1999), pp. 187–88.

"Qatlima" Shiräli; trad.[17]

| | |
|---|---|
| *Qatlimayu qatlima* | Qatlima oh qatlima |
| *Käng eriqtin atlima* | Don't jump over a wide stream |
| *Kelishinggä chay tutay* | When you come I'll give you tea |
| *Yenishinggha qatlima* | When you leave, qatlima |
| *Oti yaman nakhshamning* | My song burns powerfully |
| *Nawasi bu akhshamning* | Joy this evening |
| *Anglap qanmaymän dimä* | Don't say you can't get enough |
| *Mänggu bu küylär sening ...* | These tunes are forever yours ... |

It would be tempting to attribute the appropriation of reggae by Uyghur musicians to a desire to identify with Black Jamaicans as another subaltern minority, but the imagery of the accompanying video suggests that such an identification is far from Shiräli's mind. In the video he appears dressed in cowboy boots and hat, sitting contemplatively guitar in hand on a rock in the middle of the desert. The reggae sounds are subsumed into classic American imaginings of the cowboy and the Wild West. A Uyghur reggae cowboy? Even Shiräli's appropriation of the cowboy imagery owes much to Chinese imaginings of Xinjiang as its own Wild West, as recently reproduced in the martial arts blockbuster *Crouching Tiger, Hidden Dragon*, or as promoted within the Xinjing region through television advertisements for the powerful local brand of alcohol Yili Tequ. But Shiräli is clearly not content to play the Red Indian to the Han Chinese, to be always the Other in Chinese imaginings; he situates himself centrally in his own re-imagining of the American fantasy.

America is not the only object of Uyghur imagining. Another popular Uyghur disco-style release in 1999 featured a remarkable song entitled "Bälli." The term in Uyghur means not "belly" but literally "good, well done!" but its link to belly dancing was clearly underlined by the accompanying video. Belly dancing is not a traditional Uyghur art although it features strongly in Chinese popular culture's imaginings of the region's "exotic" Muslim women, and is promoted for Han and foreign eyes in floor shows in upmarket Uyghur restaurants in Beijing.[18] It is hard to say if the fashion for belly dancing in Ürümchi has come indirectly from such sources or more directly from the Arab world, which has in recent years become a source of inspiration for young Uyghurs. Musical sounds flow into Xinjiang from Saudi Arabia in the form of cassette recordings of Qur'anic recitation which are popular gifts to bring back from the hajj.[19] Also highlighted in official reports is the flow of Wahabbi or fundamentalist propaganda smuggled into the region in video form.[20] Arab states like Saudi Arabia and Syria may be regarded

17. Shiräli, "Qatlima," *Tarim* (China: Xinjiang Nationalities Recording Co., 2000).
18. Nimrod Baranovitch, "From the margins to the centre: the Uyghur challenge in Beijing," *The China Quarterly*, No. 175 (2003), pp. 726–750.
19. Although according to Muslim belief Qur'anic recitation is not properly regarded as music.
20. I have not personally seen any such videos, although I have come across a few videos smuggled into the region from the Central Asian states carrying Christian propaganda.

by the authorities as sources of fundamentalist propaganda and violence, but they are more often regarded by Uyghurs as rich, modern and Muslim, offering alternative models of development for Uyghur society to those promoted by the Chinese state. Orthodox models of Islam emanating from these states have attracted numbers of followers across Xinjiang. Both the full black all-over body covering of the hijab adopted by some Uyghur women returning from the hajj and belly dancing are in vogue in Ürümchi.[21]

### "Mother's White Milk"

Throughout the 1990s, as political tensions increased, the Xinjiang authorities have frequently claimed that malign outside forces are instrumental in spreading separatism in the region, and more recently they have used the global war on terror to reinforce these claims. Following September 11 the authorities have pursued a comprehensive propaganda campaign on the domestic and international front to label all Uyghur opposition, peaceful or violent, as linked to international terrorist networks. The Xinjiang media have carried explicit warnings against the use of micro-media, especially audio and video recordings used to promote religious fanaticism or jihad, and also against popular cultural activities conducted within the region which might be used to encourage opposition.[22] Although productions like "Bälli" have not as yet been considered as oppositional by the authorities, other styles of popular music have been targeted. Several writers working on Uyghur culture and politics have previously drawn attention to the use of veiled metaphors and allusions in the realm of popular song lyrics to reference political undercurrents which cannot be raised in more direct ways.[23] Since the mid-1990s the Xinjiang authorities have become increasingly sensitive to these and increasingly active in suppressing them, but in the post-September 11 period they have been explicitly equated by the authorities with separatism and with Islamic terrorism. This tightening of state control over cultural production in Xinjiang is in direct contrast to the relaxation of controls in inner China since 1997.

The blanket equation of opposition to Chinese rule with global political currents and outside forces is misleading, at least in the field of popular culture, since it is the group of singers whose musical sounds are least

---

21. See Rudelson and Jankowiack's discussion of alternating "soft-hard" government policies towards local Islam and Uyghur contacts with other parts of the Islamic world: Justin John Rudelson and William Jankowiack, "Acculturation and resistance: Xinjiang identities in flux," in Frederick Starr (ed.), *Xinjiang: China's Muslim Borderland* (New York & London: M. E. Sharpe, 2004), p. 301.

22. Nicolas Becquelin, "Criminalizing ethnicity: political repression in Xinjiang," *China Rights Forum*, No. 1 (2004), pp. 39–46.

23. Gardner Bovingdon, "The not-so-silent majority: Uyghur resistance to Han rule in Xinjiang," *Modern China*, Vol. 28, No. 1 (2002), pp. 39–78; Harris, "Cassettes, bazaars and saving the nation," pp. 265–283; Joanne Smith, "Barren chickens, stray dogs, fake immortals and thieves: coloniser and collaborator in popular Uyghur song and the quest for national unity," in Ian Biddle and Vanessa Knights (eds.), *Music, National Identity and the Politics of Location: Between the Global and the Local* (Aldershot: Ashgate, forthcoming).

outward-looking, and whose verbal messages are most bound up with the core concerns of the Uyghur community, who have been most powerful in their expressions of dissatisfaction and most consistently in conflict with the authorities. These singers exemplify the position that some composers and singers occupy in the Uyghur community: one of moral leadership. They perform traditional-style songs set to contemporary lyrics, accompanying themselves on the Uyghur *dutar* two-stringed lute. The best known of these singer-dutarists is Ömärjan Alim from the northern town of Ghulja (in Chinese Yining). A discussion of two of his songs – "Anamni äsläp" ("Remembering mother")[24] released in 1994 and "Kättingiz ana" ("Mother, you have gone")[25] released in 2000 – reveals much about changing attitudes amongst Uyghurs to their political predicament. The songs also reveal, through their musical sounds and their lyrics, the tension between tradition and modernity which informs the constructions of national identity by Uyghur intellectuals, and they show how such tensions are expressed in gendered form.

In terms of discourses of gender revealed through Uyghur song lyrics, male desire is the most common theme, typically expressed in terms of burning fire, suffering and pain. Man is the *ashiq*, the pursuer, inflamed by unfulfilled passion, and woman the *mäshuq*, the object of desire, the pursued, who cruelly withholds herself from the suffering lover. In contrast to this established rhetoric of desire, another image of femininity frequently emerges in Uyghur song: the figure of the idealized mother, invariably depicted as careworn, weeping, nurturing, self-sacrificing. As if in flight from the rhetoric of fire, male singers seem to escape to the comforting figure of mother. In Uyghur songs, in contrast to the flames of romantic love, the mother is essentially wet with flowing tears and white milk, and she is a key signifier in the rhetoric of sentimentality and pathos. This iconic mother figure is often evoked in traditional lyrics, but in contemporary Uyghur pop we find an added layer to the discourse on mother love. Abdumijit Dölätov, a Kazakhstan-based journalist and well-known poet and lyricist for singers on both sides of the border including the Dervishes, is an enthusiastic user of the Mother allegory. In an interview in 2003 he responded to a question on this preference with a political manifesto:

Mother means country, flag, motherland .... Mother is all we have. We are an oppressed people, but the one thing you can't take away from people's hearts is mother, no power can stop mother love.[26]

The "motherland" in question, need it be said, is not the Chinese "zuguo" but East Turkistan, as Uyghurs outside the region commonly term Xinjiang. The notion of Mother as central icon in the nationalist agenda has, of course, precedent in popular cultural representations around the

24. Ömärjan Alim, "Anamni äsläp" ("Remembering mother"), *Pärwayim peläk* (*Destiny Is My Concern*), confiscated: no publishing details, 1994.
25. Ömärjan Alim, "Kättingiz ana" ("Mother, you have gone"), *Tarim* (China: Xinjiang Nationalities Recording Co., 2000).
26. Interview, Almaty, July 2003.

world. In Hindi films, once very popular in Xinjiang, we find central to numerous plots the archetypal and usually embattled figure of Mother who embodies good, tradition and Indian-ness, and whose suffering and eventual triumph provokes strong emotions.[27] Similarly Rey Chow has discussed the use of sentimentalism in 20th-century Chinese literature, writing of a masochistic identification with the fictional Other, where pain and sacrifice are intrinsically maternal and directly equated to political or cultural crisis.[28] The clearest and most emotive expression of this allegory in Uyghur song was voiced by Ömärjan Alim in his mid-1990s song "Anamni äsläp," a lament for mother. Her death clearly symbolizes the death of the nation, and alongside the forceful expression of grief, we can hear a call for vengeance.

"Amamni äsläp" ("Remembering mother") Ömärjan Alim

| | |
|---|---|
| *Köptin beri chushum buzulup* | For a long time I've had bad dreams |
| *Ötär idi ghäshliktä künüm* | I pass my days depressed |
| *Bügün mana shum hävär kilip* | See, today bad news has come |
| *Chüshüp ketti ichimgä ünüm* | Words fail me |
| | |
| *Ana shundaq yärgä kettipsiz* | Mother you went to that place |
| *Ana disäm "hä" dimäydighan* | I call mother, no one answers |
| *Män qaldim bek eghir azapqa* | Heavy suffering has come upon me |
| *Äsläp tolghunup häsrät ...* | Remembering I am sick with grief |
| *äy ... häsrät yäydighan* | ah ... I have eaten grief |
| | |
| *Bu häsrätni kimdin alimän?* | Who will I make pay for this grief? |
| *Bu därdimni kimdin alimän?* | Who will I make pay for this pain? |
| *Täqdir shundaq bulghachqa* | Destiny has turned out like this |
| *Mänmu shundaq dimäy qandaq ...* | And so I will not ask what ... |
| *äy ...qandaq qilimän* | ah ... what should I do |

This song was released in 1994 at the height of Ömärjan's popularity. At that time his cassettes formed a constant soundtrack to the bustle of Döng Kövrük bazaar in Ürümchi, blaring from every cassette stall and restaurant. His songs with their brilliant *dutar* accompaniment and popular style of language, "earthy" as one Uyghur recording engineer put it, also enjoyed unprecedented sales in rural areas.[29] This musical sound, which I described above as "traditional-style," might be better termed a 1990s revival or rather a reinvention of tradition in the sphere of popular culture. In the 1980s, as mentioned above, the dominant style in popular song was the Russian waltz, and traditional Uyghur instruments rarely featured in popular music. The mid-1990s rise of the *dutar*-singers was a response to a perceived need for an authentically Uyghur popular music.

27. Rosie Thomas, "Melodrama and the negotiation of morality in mainstream Hindi film," in C. Breckenbridge (ed.), *Consuming Modernity: Public Culture in a South Asian World* (Minneapolis & Oxford: University of Minnesota Press, 1995), pp. 157–182.
28. Rey Chow, *Woman and Chinese Modernity: The Politics of Reading between West and East* (Minneapolis & Oxford: University of Minnesota Press, 1990).
29. See Harris, "Cassettes, bazaars and saving the nation" for a fuller transcript of this interview.

Based on traditional styles of *dutar* performance, Ömärjan's songs are nevertheless newly composed and deviate from tradition in a number of ways. The bass register of the voice and typically minor feel of the melodies owe more to Western influence than to traditional Uyghur vocal style and modality. Most significantly, this style is not attributable to any one oasis town; it establishes a pan-Uyghur national style which transcends or overlays local traditions, thus increasing the songs' popularity and ability to disseminate political messages.

"Anamni äsläp" was one of Ömärjan's most emotive and radical calls to arms. Its release was probably made possible only because it was produced by a Chinese recording company based in Guangzhou, thus evading the scrutiny of the censor in Xinjiang. In the early 1990s, Uyghur musicians had taken advantage of the burgeoning free market in China to strike recording deals with newly established independent Chinese recording companies from Shanghai to Guangzhou. In the year following the release of "Anamni äsläp" the Xinjiang authorities were already beginning their "crackdown on the cultural market," and it was becoming increasingly difficult to reference Uyghur discontent in the public forum, even through such veiled allegories. After 1995, such out-of-town deals were restricted, and Uyghur language music cassettes and VCDs were only permitted if released by the state-owned Xinjiang Nationalities Recording Company or the Beijing-based Nationalities Recording Company which kept a much tighter rein on the lyrical content of Uyghur cassettes.

Whilst the direct political messages of Ömärjan's most famous songs faded from the forum of popular song into the late 1990s, as a direct result of tighter government control, the number of laments for the death of a loved one in the guise of popular songs has noticeably increased. In the aftermath of 1997 and the brutal suppression of the February demonstrations in Ghulja,[30] it seemed that the Uyghurs had more to grieve about both politically and literally, and these personal laments in the public sphere of pop, without referencing the sphere of public action, were nevertheless expressing a popular grief for which there were few other outlets. In 2001 when I returned to Ürümchi I again met the recording engineer who a few years previously had enthusiastically unpicked for me the political ramifications of Ömärjan's songs. "Things aren't like that any more," he told me, "we were young then. Now we just think practically about how to get our kids to study abroad."[31] This remark was typical of a new mood amongst Ürümchi intellectuals, most of whom had replaced the nationalism of the mid-1990s with an increasingly pragmatic and global outlook.

The muting of nationalist sentiment also had its expression in popular song. In the year 2000 Ömärjan Alim released a new lament for mother. Musically this is a close echo of the earlier "Anamni äsläp," transposing

---

30. Amnesty International, *Gross Violations of Human Rights in the Xinjiang Uighur Autonomous Region* (AI Index: ASA 17/18/99).
31. Interview, Ürümchi, August 2001.

and developing the same melodic material, but in terms of performance style and lyrics a very different mood is expressed. Here again is grief, but it is accompanied not by anger but rather by resignation and nostalgia. The actor in the accompanying video traces a journey from modernity – working at his computer, travelling along the newly built highway – back to the impoverished Uyghur village. Such images typify the experience of Ürümchi-based Uyghur intellectuals. Distanced but emotionally entangled, educated and working in the Chinese-dominated city but brought up in the Uyghur village, the actor makes the long journey from urban modernity returning to rural home, his mother's funeral, and memories of an idealized youth dominated by a caring and inevitably weeping mother. Under conditions of globalization we typically find women positioned as repositories of tradition, a position which inevitably carries an emotional burden, and here "Mother, you have gone" references the singer's complex emotional relationship as urban intellectual with his rural roots, where the mother figure is emblematic not only of nation but also of tradition. What is mourned, it seems, is not only the fading national dream but also the passing of a way of life.

"Kättingiz ana" ("Mother, you have gone")  Ömärjan Alim

...

| | |
|---|---|
| Ketärikän äjäl yätsä dunyadin adäm | People depart this earth when their lifespan is up |
| Qalmaydikän nägadayu hätaki Adäm | Neither the beggar nor Adam can remain |
| Qutulalmasikän bändäng qismätliringdin | None can escape from their fate |
| Bu hayatning shadliqigha yarikän adäm | The joy of this life is shared by all |
| Qaryalmas boldum ämdi didaringizgä | I can no longer see your face |
| Du'a birär pärizäntingiz imaningizgä | Your children pray for your soul |
| Tenich yeting qäbringizdä jan jan ana | Rest peacefully in your grave dear mother |
| Chushlirimdä hämra bolay simayingizgä | In my dreams I will be together with your image |

*Situating the Harem Garden in Guangzhou*

Thus far I have been concerned with Uyghur music and identity politics at national level. Much has been written about the formalization of minority national identities in China, and how they overlay a more complex reality of local, religious and clan allegiances.[32] The reality

32. Dru C. Gladney, "The ethnogenesis of the Uighur," *Central Asian Survey*, Vol. 9, No. 1 (1990), pp. 1–28; Stevan Harrell, "Introduction: civilising projects and the reaction to them," in S. Harrell (ed.), *Cultural Encounters on China's Ethnic Frontiers* (Seattle: University of Washington Press, 1995), pp. 3–36; Justin John Rudelson, *Oasis Identities: Uyghur Nationalism along China's Silk Road* (New York: Columbia University Press, 1997).

underlying the modern concept of "Uyghur music" also displays this kind of diversity. Each oasis town within Xinjiang possesses its own distinctive musical repertoire and style, the Kashgar *uslub* (style) or the Khotan *puraq* (flavour). Local singing style is said to relate to the local dialect, the local environment, even the local character. Certain instruments are found only in one oasis while others are more widespread. Within a single oasis region individual villages may also have their own repertoire of songs or dance suites. Access to rural areas in Xinjiang is not always easy for foreign researchers,[33] but it is of great interest to move beyond the bazaars and the urban spaces inhabited by pop musicians to look at the impact of technology and globalization at local level. What impact are the marketing of global sounds and the production of new popular styles at national level having on contexts of music-making in the oasis villages of Xinjiang? And how are musicians at local level themselves making use of micro-media?

In the small oasis town of Yarkand in southern Xinjiang there is a run of cassette stalls in the dusty back street bazaar. Each one displays several hundred cassettes, mainly Uyghur pop with a few imports from Uzbekistan and India. Here all concessions to copyright have disappeared. The stall owners possess one copy of each cassette, and run off copies to order on the copy machine prominently displayed on the counter. These are sold for about five *yuan*, half the price of the originals available in larger towns. Inevitably quality deteriorates with each copy made; customers take their luck. Also for sale, if you know to ask, held under the counter are boxes full of locally made recordings, not produced or packaged in any way but simply copied on to cassette and marked with fading biro. These cassettes include live recordings of local singers made at *mäshräp* parties and a few recordings of ritual music, local Sufi orders performing the ritual *zikr* at shrine festivals.[34] At this level of the market, where these most local of sounds are transformed into commodities and sold alongside the Ürümchi pop singers, Peter Manuel's theories of technology and hegemony and the role of micro-media in reinforcing and revitalizing local traditions and styles are most applicable.[35]

Yarkand's favourite *mäshräp* singer in 2001 was Änwärjan who, like Ömärjan Alim, plays the *dutar* two-stringed lute; a 20-year-old layabout, according to a local taxi driver who was playing one of Änwärjan's cassettes in his car, who does nothing but play at *mäshräp*, but an undeniable talent. Änwärjan sings in an, to Ürümchi ears, old-fashioned, high-pitched, boyish vocal style which professional singers have cast off in favour of an operatic booming bass. The *dutar* style is typical of this part of southern Xinjiang, the fast $3 + 3 + 2$ beat underlying the four-beat of the sung melody, the instrument tuned in fourths rather than the more

33. Harris, *Singing the Village*, pp. xv–xx.
34. Cf. Rachel Harris and Rahilä Dawut, "Mazar festivals of the Uyghurs: music, Islam and the Chinese state," *British Journal of Ethnomusicology*, Vol. 11, No. 1, pp. 101–118.
35. Manuel, *Cassette Culture*, p. 129.

common fifths, and pitched to suit Änwärjan's voice almost a fifth higher than is common in Ürümchi. The cassettes are recorded live at *mäshräps* and include songs which have been current in this area for several decades, mainly comic and combative love songs using the folk *beyit* poetical form, rich in metaphors and allusions. Yet these cassettes are not recordings of frozen traditions. Like the other pop songs discussed, Änwärjan's songs also reflect and enact contemporary social conditions, but they make an interesting contrast to the songs discussed above. Whereas Shiräli in his reggae-style folk song employed homely lyrics juxtaposed with global sounds, Änwärjan's musical sound is local while his lyrics reach outwards. Also striking at this level is how much less evident the nationalist impulse is. In contrast with the nostalgic home-ward journey undertaken by Ömärjan Alim, Änwärjan's lyrics transport him in progressive stages to destinations outside his local region, repro-ducing the journeys made by Uyghur rural migrants as, impelled by rural poverty and under-employment, they move to the major towns of Xinji-ang in search of jobs or business opportunities, and then "inside the mouth" of the Gansu corridor (*kouli*), eastwards to the cities of central China.[36]

"Shokh dutar" ("Naughty *dutar*") Änwärjan

| | |
|---|---|
| *Yarimning qara sachi* | My darling's black hair |
| *Ashiptu zinga qigä* | Reaches down to her nape |
| *Khäqning yarni yayrim däp* | If I call another's lover darling |
| *Öläymu taya qigä?* | Will I be beaten to death? |
| ... | ... |
| *Oynayli häräm baghda* | Let's play in the palace garden |
| *Bushä Yengishä aldida* | In the town by the new town |
| *Chidimay qalisiz u chaghda* | You won't be able to stand it then |
| ... | ... |
| *Oynayli Mäkitä* | Let's play in Mäkit |
| *Qonashä Yengishä aldida* | In the old town in the new town |
| *Marab qalisiz daldida* | You'll sneak a look behind you |
| | |
| *Bizning balilar yaman balilar* | Our boys are tough boys |
| *Oyanchi yaman balilar* | Good time tough boys |
| *Bizni yaman digänlär* | They say we're bad |
| *Ghajaydu quruq kallar* | They're gnawing an empty skull |
| ... | ... |
| *Oynayli häräm baghda* | Let's play in the palace garden |
| *Ärdawchawda Guwangjuda* | In Erdaoqiao, in Guangzhou |
| *Chidimay qalisiz u chaghda* | You won't be able to stand it then |

---

36. Nicolas Becquelin notes that in southern Xinjiang incomes rest at half of the provincial average, rural under-employment is acute, and up to 45% of the Uyghur population have migrated to towns where they face great difficulties in finding employment; Nicolas Becquelin, "Staged development in Xinjiang," *The China Quarterly*, No. 178 (2004), p. 372.

## The Troublesome Tämbür Technique of Nurmuhämmät Tursun

Also prominent in the display of cassettes in the Yarkand stall are several recordings by one of Xinjiang's most famous *tämbür* lute players, Nurmuhämmät Tursun. Nur was employed by the Xinjiang song-and-dance troupe in Ürümchi until 2001 when he fell foul of the authorities due to his involvement in a New Year concert at which a "separatist incident" occurred.[37] Although he lost his status within the troupe and was banned from travelling abroad, Nur was able to continue his career as one of Xinjiang's most prominent recording instrumentalists until his untimely death in December 2004.[38] He was widely regarded as the finest *tämbür* player in the region, with brilliant technique and a wide repertoire of folk and classical pieces. He was also known for his exploration of new repertoires and his innovative style of playing which encapsulates the ideology of the virtuoso, star performer promoted by the pop music industry. Key aspects of his style include his use of fast riffs and high pitch, and an almost romantic interpretation of the melody, with flexible use of rhythm and prominent vibrato.

Nur's last CD release (an unusual format in Xinjiang) *Kün wä tün* (*Day and Night*)[39] is his most experimental, an extraordinary confection which juxtaposes a medley of popular Spanish tunes[40] with a Pakistani film song dubbed into Uyghur as "Mängülük muhäbbät" ("Never-ending love") which was popular in the region in the 1980s. Alongside these renditions of global melodies performed on the *tämbür* is a radical reinterpretation of a piece at the heart of the classical Uyghur repertoire, "Äjäm."[41] Western purists might find the lush harmonies added by synthesizer the most jarring aspect of this interpretation, but what upsets traditionally minded Uyghur musicians about this is something quite different.

The *tämbür* lute has five metal strings arranged in three courses. The melody is generally played on the highest single string, while the other two paired strings are struck only as drones, punctuating the melody. Nur introduced an original and idiosyncratic strumming of all three courses of stopped strings simultaneously, producing tuned chords. This small innovation produced a disproportionate degree of controversy within Uyghur music circles, in part because he employed it in "classical" pieces like "Äjäm" and the iconic Twelve Muqam suites, and in part simply because of his great influence on young players. Nur had many followers around the region who learned the new style from his cassettes and who have begun to replicate the style on their own cassette recordings. This is the

---

37. See Becquelin, "Criminalizing ethnicity," for further details.
38. Nurmuhämmät Tursun died on 18 December 2004, aged 47 of a heart attack. Obituaries (in Uyghur) and downloads of his music can be found on the Radio Free Asia Uyghur language website: http://www.rfa.org/uyghur/xewerler/tepsili_xewer/2004/12/20/nurmuhemmet-tursun/.
39. Nurmuhämmät Tursun, *Kün wä tün* (*Day and Night*) (China: Nationalities Recording Co., 2003).
40. Most prominently "España cañi" by composer Pascual Marquina.
41. A more orthodox rendition of this piece can be heard on: *Music from the Oasis Towns of Central Asia. Uyghur Musicians of Xinjiang* (London: Globestyle, 2000).

new wave, and it now spreads right across the region. The sometimes bizarre debate which Nur's techniques have provoked illustrates some of the anxieties surrounding Uyghur culture and identity, and it evokes again Veit Erlmann's remarks on the disjuncture of sounds and meanings in global flows of musical sounds and technology.[42]

A Kazakhstan-based Uyghur musicologist with whom I spoke in 2001 was horrified on hearing an example of Nur's new style. "This is how Uyghur music is being infected with Chinese influence these days!" she exclaimed, "he's playing the *tämbür* like the Chinese *pipa*."[43] This remark was revealing of a politically and musically defensive attitude (not to say a lack of familiarity with *pipa* technique) which is commonly found amongst minority groups who perceive their culture and identity to be threatened by assimilation into the larger culture, where any kind of musical innovation is heard as deviation from authenticity and evidence of the encroaching influence of the other culture. The ethnomusicologist Keila Diehl, in her study of Tibetan exile music in Dharamsala, describes an equivalent attitude amongst that highly politicized community which is striking for the vehemence in which it is expressed. Dharamsala musicians situate themselves as preservers of the authentic musical traditions of the Tibetan homeland, which they regard as threatened by Chinese influence. They describe in terms of powerful vitriol the Chinese pollution of their music over 50 years of Chinese rule.[44] As with the Kazakhstan-based Uyghur musicologist, such attitudes are typically expressed by voices from the diaspora who are distanced from the musical changes which occur within the culture. In fact Uyghur musicians within Xinjiang are equally as disapproving of Nur's new style, but less likely to attribute the polluting factor to the Chinese. They, and Nur himself, have acknowledged that the new technique is due less to the pernicious influence of Chinese music than to popular flamenco guitar, in particular the Gipsy Kings cassettes which took Xinjiang by storm in the mid-1990s. It is a feature of the patterns of globalization and Uyghur identity politics that musicians in Ürümchi are more exposed to, and open to, the sounds of popular flamenco than to the Chinese *pipa*.

*Conclusion*

In this article I have attempted to recast the idea of the Silk Road as cultural conduit for musical sounds and meanings under conditions of globalization, describing an electronic "Silk Road" whose routes have less to do with geographical contiguity than with Uyghur musicians' search for self. I have highlighted a few examples of recorded music to illustrate questions of change and continuity in musical practice in Xinjiang in a period of rapidly expanding access and exposure to outside

42. Erlmann, *Music, Modernity and the Global Imagination*, pp. 187–88.
43. Tamara Alibakieva, interview, Washington DC, July 2002.
44. Keila Diehl, *Echoes from Dharamsala: Music in the Life of a Tibetan Refugee Community* (Berkeley, London, Los Angeles: University of California Press, 2002).

influences. These examples show how questions of identity interact with global flows of musical sounds, where certain outside sounds are briefly adopted wholesale but their meanings are subtly altered, and where aspects of global styles are brought into the heart of the traditional repertoire. They demonstrate the ability of micro-media to embody and respond to changing social identities, providing new possibilities for musical and socio-political discourse, although the expressions which emerge through these media are often conflicting and ambiguous. I have tried to highlight the often neglected question of reception and impact on musical life of the broader population outside the urban centres where mainstream recording artists are active, showing how locally produced sounds sit side-by-side with examples of the national style in small town cassette stalls. Equally the role of the individual musician cannot be overlooked in discussions of interactions between the global and the local. Veit Erlmann claims the very idea of locality is a problem, describing "a strange dialectic of the near and far, local and global" where "the making of individual experience may well happen in one place, while its actual coordinates lie in a reality beyond the limited, local space."[45] While young *tämbür* players in Yarkand who pick up the new style from Nur's cassettes may not be aware of their debt to the Gipsy Kings they are certainly aware of the possibilities, and a new verse may easily be added to Änwärjan's song placing the harem garden in New York or perhaps in Saudi Arabia.

45. Veit Erlmann, "How beautiful is small? Music, globalization and the aesthetics of the local," *Yearbook for Traditional Music*, No. 30 (1998), p. 15.

# Not Quite Karaoke: Poetry in Contemporary China

## Maghiel van Crevel

ABSTRACT  Marketization is a prime feature of arts and culture in contemporary China. Strikingly, while avant-garde poetry is hardly involved in this trend, and some of its commentators feel a sense of crisis as a result, it continues to flourish as a small but stable, high-cultural niche area that boasts increasing textual richness and a well-positioned constituency. An explanation of this phenomenon must take into account multiple re-inventions of traditional Chinese notions of poetry and poethood, amid rapidly changing circumstances throughout the contemporary era. Less culturally specific but no less essential, another factor is the very nature of the genre of avant-garde poetry in its social context and of artistic experiment *per se*, creating a problem for cultural analysis that makes numbers the measure of all things.

### Two Red Flags

*We*
*The youngest citizens of the Republic*
*Know how in the long river of history*
*The venerable older generations*
*Weathered battle after battle of blood and fire*
*The slowly rising five-star red flag*
*Once again makes us shed hot tears*
*Ah, salute!*
*The five-star red flag*
*As before the eyes of each of us*
*Images from the long night*
*Flash up in multitudes ....*

*behind the provincial government building*
*behind the trees and the lawn*
*in a small open space*
*sits a red flag limo long discarded as useless*
*that's weathered untold years of wind and rain*
*rusty to the point of being unrecognizable*
*you get all cynical again*
*but it's really not worth it*
*let's make our way in*
*let's sit in it*
*let's enjoy it together*
*and then ponder it*
*and finally dissolve in*
*this scrap-metal*
*modern sculpture*

On the left, above, is an excerpt from Gui Xinghua's (1948) "Manifesto of youth," a book-length poem composed in 2002 at the request of the Chinese Communist Youth League.[1] It is straightforward political lyricism (*zhengzhi shuqing shi*), commissioned and sanctioned by the "official" (*guanfang*) politico-literary establishment. It is a socio-moral policy document in verse.

---

1. Gui Xinghua, *Qingchun xuanyan* (*Manifesto of Youth*) (Shanghai: Shanghai renmin, 2002), p. 19. All translations are mine.

On the right is "Red Flag limo in wind and rain," written in 2000 by controversial poet and polemicist Yi Sha (1966).[2] It is roughly 600 times shorter than "Manifesto," and as different from political lyricism as it could be in all other respects, too. Although included in an officially registered publication, it qualifies as "unofficial" (*fei guanfang*) by virtue of its thematics: irreverence, with some condescending nostalgia, for a socialist past symbolized by the decrepit Red Flag limo.

In their radically different framing of the Chinese flag, these two poems indicate the range of claims currently laid to modern poetry in China, from vintage orthodoxy to roguish avant-garde. I focus on the "avant-garde" end of the scale, meaning a broad category grounded in local literary history after literature's emancipation from political control, rather than in (international) discourse on aesthetics: a mixed bag of texts also called "unofficial," in the sense indicated above, as well as "experimental" and "post-Mao." Initially, they were held together in a negative definition by their *in*-compatibility with orthodox cultural policy since Mao's 1942 Yan'an Talks, and their formation of a circuit of *un*-official publications, with the journal *Today* (*Jintian*) (1978–80) as its fountainhead. But the impact of orthodox poetry in contemporary China is now too limited to make it the (negative) measure of all things. Since the mid-1980s, the avant-garde has outshone orthodoxy, to audiences in China and elsewhere. Developments over the last quarter of a century justify the study of various trends in poetry with the simple qualification that orthodoxy is not among them, rather than stressing that every single one of them is different from orthodoxy.

Marketization is a prime feature of arts and culture in contemporary China. This article shows that, while avant-garde poetry is hardly involved in this trend, and some of its commentators feel a sense of crisis as a result, it continues to flourish as a small but stable, high-cultural niche area that boasts increasing textual richness and a well-positioned constituency. An explanation of this phenomenon must take into account multiple re-inventions of traditional Chinese notions of poetry and poethood amid rapidly changing circumstances throughout the contemporary era. Less culturally specific but no less essential, another factor is the very nature of the genre of avant-garde poetry in its social context and of artistic experiment *per se*, creating a problem for cultural analysis that makes numbers the measure of all things.

After a quick rehearsal of some well-known socio-political context, the article moves on to textual trends and examples of individual oeuvres, metatextual (self-)images of poetry and poethood, and a closing statement.

---

2. Yi Sha, *Yi Sha shi xuan/Yisha's Poems* (*Poems by Yi Sha*) (Xining: Qinghai renmin, 2003), p. 155.

*Context: Times of Mind, Mayhem and Money*

In the title of this section, mind refers to the 1980s, mayhem to the bloody suppression of the 1989 protest movement remembered as June Fourth, and money to the 1990s and beyond. The 1980s saw a gradual end to the subordination of literature to politics, and exhilaration in the life of the mind that expressed itself in a (high) culture craze or (high) culture fever (*wenhuare*).[3] In poetry, this was visible in frenzied activity. June Fourth and re-intensified repression in the next few years meant a shocking end to the decade, and traumatizing disillusionment for large parts of the intelligentsia. Its reflection in poetry is complicated by the fact that the portrayal of government action as violent and repressive remains taboo in any type of writing. As regards the atmosphere on the poetry scene, June Fourth was a catalyst in the transition from extraverted exaltation in the 1980s to more private and sober if not sceptical and cynical moods in the 1990s. In society at large, the 1990s and the first years of the 21st century saw the rise of consumerism, entertainment, (new) media and popular culture, as marketization and commodification swept through all spheres of life, including elite practices in literature and art.

Contextual factors across the contemporary period may be summed up as follows. While continuing to rely on mechanisms of literary (self-)censorship, political interest in poetry has declined, in a trend from totalitarian *pre*-scription of obligatory forms and content to authoritarian *pro*-scription of dissent on politically sensitive topics. After high social visibility in the 1980s, poetry has been subject to overwhelming competition by other distractions. The constituencies of the official and unofficial circuits are no longer mutually exclusive, and interact in various forms of mutual recognition. Nevertheless their distinction, though blurred, has certainly has not disappeared, and the unofficial circuit retains its importance to this day. It does so not just "against the gloomy backdrop manufactured by the state," as Geremie Barmé suggests, but by providing publication opportunities and a lively poetry climate that are crucial to individual poets' development.[4] Poetry's relation to foreign literatures, most of all an ineradicable generalization called "the West," has shifted from the uncritical celebration of cultural imports in the early 1980s to the problematization of source and target cultures, and to re-assessment of Chinese cultural identity in an age of globalization.

*Text: From Elevated to Earthly and from What to How*

This section identifies two overall trends in contemporary poetry, and samples its diversity in four individual oeuvres.

---

3. Jing Wang, *High Culture Fever: Politics, Aesthetics and Ideology in Deng's China* (Berkeley: University of California Press, 1996).
4. Geremie R Barmé, *In the Red: On Contemporary Chinese Culture* (New York: Columbia University Press, 1999), p. 206.

Poetry's development since the late 1970s has been explosive. Amid a jumble of styles, two trends may be discerned: from elevated to earthly and from what to how.

Since the early 1980s, poetry can be viewed as a spectrum between the outer limits of two divergent orientations. This is manifest in poets' and critics' frequent use of dichotomies such as these:

| | | |
|---|---|---|
| heroic | versus | quotidian |
| literary | versus | colloquial |
| cultural | versus | anti-cultural or pre-cultural |
| lyrical | versus | anti-lyrical |
| mythical | versus | anti-mythical |
| sacred | versus | worldly |
| utopian | versus | realist |
| absolute | versus | relative |
| elitist | versus | ordinary |
| academic | versus | authentic |
| westernized | versus | indigenous |
| central | versus | local |
| northern | versus | southern |
| mind | versus | body |
| intellectual | versus | popular |

These dichotomies apply to subject matter and style, and often run parallel to one another. Together, the items on the left and those on the right represent the two orientations which I call the elevated and the earthly[5]: not pigeonholes, but co-ordinates in a multi-dimensional body of texts. In principle, they can be applied to literature and art from any time or place and there is nothing inherently Chinese or poetic about them, but poetry in contemporary China brings them to mind with particular force. Without essentializing, it is safe to say that the overall trend has been away from the elevated and towards the earthly. Again, this may be contextualized in a deconstruction of "serious" literature and art in various genres and media that has been going on for decades in global as well as local (Chinese) settings, but the dialectic of the elevated and the earthly is notably relevant for Chinese poetry today.

By a trend from what to how I mean a development away from straightforwardly paraphraseable, often historically-referential subject matter and towards the elaboration of individual style, including things like (experimental) idiolect, thematics, figures of speech, and aural and visual poetic form in the broadest sense. In the 1970s and the early 1980s, the message dominated the medium, but the balance has shifted, especially since the 1990s. Hence, while basic knowledge of recent Chinese history is indispensable for reading the earliest contemporary poems –

---

5. There is an obvious connection with research on other literary genres presented in Ban Wang, *The Sublime Figure of History: Aesthetics and Politics in Twentieth-Century China* (Stanford: Stanford University Press, 1997) and Xiaobing Tang, *Chinese Modern: The Heroic and the Quotidian* (Durham, NC: Duke University Press, 2000).

especially the best-known specimens of Obscure poetry (*menglong shi*) – it is no longer so for many works from later years. Often, China is simply not there. When it *is* there, for instance in Lower Body (*xiabanshen*) poetry, its manifestations tend to be explicit, eliminating the need for the reader to supply plausible interpretations: say, the Cultural Revolution for the "black night" in Gu Cheng's "A generation" and the "ice age" in Bei Dao's "Answer."[6] Neither trend is constant, absolute or irreversible, but this is what a bird's eye perspective on the past quarter of a century shows.

Four samples of poetry, below, illustrate Pierre Bourdieu's position that by themselves, neither determinist reflectionism nor the romantic myth of the creative genius – that is, views of literature as social documentation and as the expression of all-powerful, individual orig-inality – will usually suffice to explain literary texts.[7] Apart from the fact that they were originally written in Chinese, all four texts can be sensibly linked to China, meaning that their authors are mainland Chinese. Yet, China is not enough, and individual creativity must feature in any discussion of these texts *qua* poetry.

A glimpse at a few salient texts cannot represent anything like the full body of poetry in contemporary China, or even all its major dimensions. The selection of the samples below, all from the late 1990s and later, is informed by the following considerations. Xi Chuan (1963) and Yu Jian (1954) have been the most influential poets writing in China since the early 1990s, and are important representatives of the elevated and the earthly trends, respectively. Yin Lichuan (1973) is a prominent voice within the Lower Body troupe that scandalized and delighted the poetry scene in 2000–2001. Yan Jun (1973) has made a name for himself by innovative, audio-visually supported poetry performance, which he is now taking to foreign audiences.

*Xi Chuan.* This is one of the 99 stanzas of Xi Chuan's "What the eagle says," dated 1998[8]:

*Shall we not read the map? At sorrow lies the first crossroads, with a road to song and a road to bewilderment; at bewilderment the second crossroads, with a road to pleasure and a road to nothingness; at nothingness the third crossroads, with a road to death and a road to insight; at insight the fourth crossroads, with a road to madness and a road to silence.*

One of Xi Chuan's enigmatic prose poems that invite and yet resist interpretation, "What the eagle says" strikes something of an expository

6. Yan Yuejun, Gao Yan, Liang Yun and Gu Fang (eds.), *Menglong shi xuan* (*Obscure Poetry*) (Shenyang: Chunfeng wenyi, 1985), pp. 1 and 122.

7. See Pierre Bourdieu, *The Field of Cultural Production: Essays on Art and Literature*, ed. and intro. Randal Johnson, various trans. (Cambridge: Polity Press, 1993), p. 34 *et passim* in parts I-II.

8. Xi Chuan, "Ying de huayu" ("What the eagle says"), in *Di san jie Aiwen wenxue jiang banjiang hui* (*On the Occasion of the Awarding of the Third Aiwen Literary Prize*) (Beijing: Aiwen wenxue yuan, 1999), stanzas 25, 56, 58. For a complete translation, see *Seneca Review* Vol. 33, No. 2 (2003), pp. 28–41.

pose. In an aestheticized repetition of syntactic patterns, it has much to say about identity, language and the human condition. On closer inspection, it flouts the rules of expository logic and celebrates ambiguity, paradox and contradiction, making it pseudo-philosophy (*wei zhexue*)[9]: playful, down to earth, generated by its own musicality as much as anything else. The speaker is a mental-linguistic agency without a home of its own, roaming between man, beast and thing:

*Thereupon I shun my flesh, and turn into a drop of perfume, actually drowning an ant. Thereupon I turn into an ant, drilling my way into an elephant's brain, upsetting it so that it stamps all four of its legs. Thereupon I turn into an elephant, my entire body exuding a great stench. Thereupon I turn into a great stench, and those who cover their noses when they smell me are men. Thereupon I turn into a man, and a plaything of fate.*

…

*Thereupon I turn into my posterity and let the rain test if I am waterproof. Thereupon I turn into rain, and splash upon the bald head of an intellectual. Thereupon I turn into that intellectual, detesting the world and its ways, pick up a stone from the ground and hurl it at the oppressor. Thereupon I turn into stone and oppressor at the same time: when I am hit by me, that sets both of my brains roaring.*

In the body of the poem, the eagle alternates between a clichéd, dignified abstraction of eaglehood and an individual, imperfect animal. The latter dies, and its feathers end up "in the living room of a white-collared beauty." In the context of present-day China, that brings to mind the new rich, unimpressed by eaglehood but happy to pay for an eagle hide as a piece of interior design. The opposition of the intellectual and the oppressor suggests another possible association with the poem's place of origin. Then again, neither the new rich nor intellectuals and oppressors live only in China.

*Yu Jian.* Thus begins Yu Jian's 71-line poem "Outside the poet's scope: observation of the life of a raindrop," dated 1998[10]:

right   it's going to rain
the poet on a bar stool in the coffeeshop
shoots a glance at the sky   quietly mumbles
and his tongue withdraws into the dark
but back in those dark clouds   its life   its
drop-by-drop tiny story   is only just beginning
how to say this   this sort of small thing   happens every moment
i'm concerned with bigger things   says the poet to his female reader
obedient to that invisible straight line   coming down
maintaining consistency   with surroundings   equally perpendicular to the earth
just like the poet's daughter   always maintains consistency with kindergarten

---

9. Xi Chuan, *Da yi ru ci* (*This Is the Idea*) (Changsha: Hunan wenyi, 1997), p. 5.

10. Yu Jian, *Yi mei chuanguo tiankong de dingzi/A Nail through the Sky: Shiji 1975–2000* (*A Nail through the Sky: A Collection of Poetry from 1975 to 2000*) (Kunming: Yunnan renmin, 2004), pp. 327–29. For a complete translation, see the Appendix to this article.

*and then    in skies twisted by pedagogy*
*becoming twisted    it cannot but become twisted*

In his patiently insistent tone of voice, characterized by the absence of punctuation and the use of multiple spaces instead, Yu Jian makes room for the conventionally trivial and the quotidian. The parallel stories of poet and raindrop come together when, at the end of its short but eventful life, the raindrop leaves a wet mark on the poet's trouser leg. The text exemplifies the phenomenon of objectification in Yu's poetry: the presentation of everyday human realities as "objectified" away from habitual perception and interpretation, as well as imaginative attention to (inanimate) objects. In this poem there are several shifts from the poet as the grammatical subject to the raindrop that remain unmarked by personal pronouns, one of them in line 9, cited above (*obedient ...*). This is the reflection in syntax of objectification, levelling out hierarchies of the lofty and the lowly. As in his earlier work, a milestone being "File 0,"[11] Yu Jian shows that language is not a transparent, neutral and reliable tool for describing "reality," its distortion of experience being particularly effective in institutionalized discourses such as political ideology and formal education. In this sense, awareness of the importance of politically correct usage (*tifa*) in such discourses in China may help to shape our reading. Yu's own manipulation of language is apparent in the mixing of registers, such as when he says that the raindrop "divorces itself from the [revolutionary] ranks" (*tuoli le duiwu*). "Outside the poet's scope" contains verse-internal statements about poethood, saying that the poet

*at the same time as writing poetry*
*also serves in an association    he has a membership card*

and that

*... our poet    rebels    howls*
*and then becomes legitimate    moves up in the world*

Yu Jian's dismantling of clichéd, heroic visions of poethood recalls Xi Chuan's caricaturing portrayal of the intellectual and the oppressor, but the resonance of Chinese contexts does not make their poetry quintessentially Chinese. One feature of poetry in contemporary China as compared with earlier days is that it contains plenty of irony. In that respect and others, poets such as Yu Jian and Xi Chuan have opened new perspectives, starting in the 1980s and coming into full swing in the 1990s.

*Yin Lichuan.* In the work of younger authors, who build on that of their predecessors and grew up at a time when solemn, socio-political ideology was quickly losing ground, irony goes without saying and cynicism is never far away. This is evident in Lower Body poet Yin Lichuan's use of orthodox phraseology, in poems that fly in the face of orthodoxy by using "unhealthy" and "debauched" subject matter and cruel humour, such as

11. *Dajia (Grand Master)*, No. 1 (1994), pp. 48–58. For an English translation, see *Renditions*, No. 56 (2001), pp. 19–57.

"Why not make it feel even better" (dated 2000).[12] This poem features lazy instructions to a clumsy man by a woman maximizing her sexual pleasure, in the process ridiculing a polemic of "popular" (*minjian*) and "intellectual" (*zhishifenzi*) poetics that dominated the poetry scene from 1998 to 2000. But there is more to Lower Body poetry than irony, cynicism and sex: it reflects dark sides of life in China's big cities, seen from within the ideological vacuum surrounding the urban young. Shen Haobo, the driving force behind the Lower Body, combines theatrical, rude machismo with angry rants on social injustice, and Yin Lichuan alternates her caustic descriptions of sex, love and bourgeois lifestyles with sensitive portrayals of low life in the urban jungle: junkies, prostitutes and a small-time city thief.[13] She stands out in the Lower Body troupe by her regard for poetic form, in ditty-like repetition, rhythm and rhyme. In "Still wet with paint," dedicated to "NN, NN and NN," lines 3–9 are syntactically and rhythmically identical, and end in the same character (*du*)[14]:

*reach out your hands*
*tear off your face*
*measure its depth*
*increase its strength*
*rule out its filth*
*master its truth*
*shorten its length*
*repair its width*
*reject its worth*
*then put it back on*
*(handle with care)*
*fix its expression*
*aim it at nothingness (that is, all mortal beings)*
*and be so kind as to reach with your tongue*
*to feel if your face is still there*
*and whether or not it is there*
*right where it is right then*
*please put your palms together*
*and you will certainly feel*
*your own devout and valiant expression*
*like a signboard still wet with paint*
*on which everyone wants*
*to leave a pawprint*

After the opening phrase, the perfect cliché for a sentimental vision of love or compassion, *tear off your face* is of shocking brutality. One's presentation to the world as a mask leads into issues of identity. Is the face-mask still there? Can one see oneself? Has the mask taken over? Can

12. *Xiabanshen* (*The Lower Body*), No. 1 (2000), pp. 58–59. For a translation of "Why not make it feel even better," see the Appendix.
13. Yin Lichuan, *Zai shufu yi xie* (*Feel Even Better*) (Beijing: Zhongguo qingnian, 2001), pp. 183–84. For a translation, see the Appendix.
14. *Lan* (*Blue*), No. 6 (2002), pp. 112–13.

one *be* oneself? The final scene bespeaks disgust at being touched by others wanting to leave their mark, however literal or figurative.

*Yan Jun.* Xi Chuan, Yu Jian and Yin Lichuan are accomplished reciters of their own work, Xi Chuan the most musical and Yu Jian the most theatrical. If Yin Lichuan likes to preface her readings by saying she isn't much good at them, that is part of her performance, in which she studiously keeps her eyes on the page and away from the audience: the detached, monotonous use of her voice combines with bleak subject matter to produce an effect that is at once humorous and painful. One poet whose readings are positively sensational is Yan Jun, who is also an active critic, publisher and artist on the unofficial music scene, and uses audio-visual media to support his recitals. His poetry brings to mind intertexts from China and elsewhere, ranging from Li Bai to Xi Chuan, William Burroughs and Allen Ginsberg. It breathes a jumpy, unruly type of social engagement that reflects current developments in urban China, not unlike that found in Lower Body poetry. Here is a stanza from "Against all organized deception"[15]:

*against advertisements, against forgetfulness. against tearing up anyone's ID and ugly face. against coming through meteoric showers clad in a golden cape but forgetting your daughter's name. against carnivores dancing. against computers dying. against living like a sickle. against night fragrance dying at night. against faddish magazines and dotcoms. against day-dreaming, see-through garments, the heart exploding like goose feathers .... drink killing a man from ten steps away .... dumb shits ruling the world .... porn magazines for exam papers .... against fear.*

Yan Jun's multi-media performance tallies well with contemporary cultural trends. Yet, it remains high art just as much as Xi Chuan's, Yu Jian's, Yin Lichuan's and most other contemporary poetry.

### Metatext: Images of Poetry and Poethood

Metatext, or discourse on contemporary poetry, can include everything from one person's inability to name a single author to someone else's full scholarly genealogy of the poetry scene ever since its 1960s underground beginnings, and from theories of writing to *ad hominem* polemics on poethood.

*What others think.* The textual trends from elevated to earthly and from what to how decrease readership in the light of a traditional Chinese poetics, which continues to have considerable influence: poetry as the epitome of serious, high art and inherently incapable of aspiring to any other status, literature to convey the Way (*wen yi zai dao*), and insight

---

15. Yan Jun, *Cishengbo (Infrasonic Sound)* (Beijing: unofficial, 2001), pp. 149–152. For a complete translation and the sound recording of an April 2003 performance, see the MCLC Resource Center (online): "Publications."

into the poet's exemplary morality and worldview as well as his (*sic*) personal position within a stable conception of social order.

This helps explain why the general public's perception of contemporary poetry is characterized by prejudice and disregard, if not sheer ignorance. To most Chinese, *poetry* means "classical poetry." Few people know that there is such a thing as modern poetry beyond the products of the 1920s–30s New Culture movement and communist cultural policy since the 1940s, and perhaps the work of Bei Dao, Shu Ting, Gu Cheng and Haizi in the 1970s and 1980s. With the exception of Shu Ting, whose work bridges the gap between orthodoxy and archetypal Obscure poetry, these poets are remembered primarily for their extra-textual impact: Bei Dao's "dissidence" and legendary success abroad, and Haizi's and Gu Cheng's dramatic suicides, the latter coupled with Gu's murder of Xie Ye, his wife. If people do know about contemporary poetry, even if they have not read it, they usually assume that whatever is being written now cannot possibly compare to the New Culture Poets, much less to scores of premodern greats. The poets' own relation to their premodern predecessors is ambiguous. No contemporary poet will question the beauty of classical poetry, other than in theatrical contexts such as the Lower Body manifesto.[16] Simultaneously, they experience the classical tradition as near-insurmountable and hence a potential source of frustration. This is reinforced by the aforesaid prejudice, disregard and ignorance.

So why was there a full house when in 2003, with minimal preparation and publicity, a new Beijing mega-bookstore specializing in anything but high literature organized a reading called "Open your eyes – Chinese poetry after SARS," in which most if not all participants were avant-garde poets?[17] Cynically put, any standing that the Poet retains beyond the poetry scene may be a *misunder*-standing based on traditional expectations, and part of the audience would have been disappointed to find that the reading included idiosyncratic texts failing to touch on topics of general concern like the SARS crisis and the infrastructural face-lift of the capital.

More to the point, even if the avant-garde cannot dream of the number of readers that classical poetry continues to satisfy, it is in fact a small but tenacious industry in its own right, a high-cultural niche area populated and held together by highly educated and well-connected practitioners and supporters. The latter include editors, individual and institutional financial sponsors, and specialist and amateur readers, meaning professional critics and scholars as well as dedicated fans: many university students and generations of graduates, and generally those whose lifestyle means being *au courant* with high-cultural development. The China cliché is true yet again: while the poetry crowd might barely constitute even a single-digit percentage of the population of a few big cities, not to mention less poetically inclined parts of the country, that still means a

---

16. *Xiabanshen*, No. 1 (2000), pp. 3–5.
17. Haidian Book-Buying Center (Haidian goushu zhongxin), 6 June 2003.

sizeable reference group in absolute numbers. What is more, they are influential in terms of symbolic capital.

Yet, since the 1990s, even specialist readers have despaired at what they perceive as a "crisis" in poetry.[18] Writing in 2003 on a Nanjing-based group of novelists, Henry Zhao dismisses poetry as self-indulgent and inconsequential[19]: "They were all formerly poets who made their name in the late 1980s … In the 1990s they turned to fiction, knowing that writing poetry is now very much a narcissistic 'kara-oke' art."

Although Bourdieu may not have had karaoke in mind, it certainly comes under "production for producers,"[20] exemplified by the avant-garde. In that sense, Zhao's metaphor makes sense. Inasmuch as karaoke means performing *other* people's words and music, it does not. As for the notion of production for producers, it is useful but hyperbolic, and only accurate if we take into account the likelihood that proportionally, in poetry there are more readers/consumers who are also writers/producers than in other genres and media of literature and art – virtually all of them amateurs, unknown outside a small number of more or less private readers, if any. But that qualification is not enough. Measured by individual and multiple-author collections, unofficial and official journals and websites, the contemporary Chinese poetry scene has, quite simply, displayed vitality and resilience all along, albeit with notable changes from the 1980s to the 1990s and beyond.

As for poetry's high visibility in the 1980s – outside the "in-crowd audience" for karaoke, so to speak – apart from hard-core enthusiasts who came mostly from artistic and academic circles, it is doubtful that many readers forayed far beyond the best-known specimens of Obscure poetry: Bei Dao's "Answer," Shu Ting's "Motherland, my beloved motherland," Gu Cheng's "A generation," Liang Xiaobin's "China, I've lost my key," Mang Ke's "The vineyard," Jiang He's "Monument," Yang Lian's "We, from our own footsteps … ." and a few other quickly canonized texts, most inviting socio-historical, allegorical readings to do with the Cultural Revolution.[21] More fundamentally, the widespread attention to poetry in the 1980s, however shallow or profound, was really an anomaly, well captured by the metaphor of culture craze or fever. It resulted from a happy meeting of the public's hunger for cultural liberalization and poets' sheer activism before other distractions had begun to compete. From the rise of Obscure poetry to the failed 1983–84 government campaign to "eliminate spiritual pollution," this was in part a reaction to extreme repression and monomaniacal prescriptions for literature and art during the Cultural Revolution, the memory of which made the experiment extra thrilling. The second half of the 1980s became a time of exhilaration and unprecedented freedoms: an exuberant

18. One of many examples is this editorial contribution to *Shikan* (*Poetry*), No. 9 (1998), pp. 4–8: "Zhongguo shige xianzhuang diaocha" ("Investigation into the current state of Chinese poetry").

19. Henry Zhao, "The river fans out: Chinese fiction since the late 1970s," in the *European Review*, Vol. 11, No. 2 (2003), p. 203.

20. Bourdieu, *The Field*, p. 39 *et passim* in parts I-II.

21. Yan Yuejun *et al.*, *Obscure Poetry*, pp. 1, 42–43, 122, 148, 190–92, 247–48.

life of the mind unfolding in borrowed time, before mayhem and money made themselves felt. By contrast, production for producers – as qualified above – may in fact well be the normal situation for a poetry that claims no social significance and is not controlled by a politico-literary establishment.

Zhao's metaphor is defensible in that poetry will not draw large crowds, and neither will karaoke. The term "in-crowd audience," above, covers settings from a handful of people in a private room to the entire clientele inside a bar with public karaoke facilities, whose joint spectatorship is to some extent coincidental. But whereas successful karaoke operations make money, avant-garde poetry is unmarketable in terms of economic capital, making it the foremost example of what Bourdieu calls the reversion of the economic world.[22] As such, inside China, poetry is different from fiction and film and, to a lesser extent, from most drama, art and rock-n-roll. At any rate, Zhao's contention is inspirational in that it offers avenues into discourse on poetry, but poetry is not quite karaoke.

As for internationalization and foreign audiences, poetry's economic unmarketability stands out when compared to the successes of Chinese film and visual arts, whether in public places such as cinemas, galleries and museums, or in private ones like the homes of wealthy individuals. Yet, through translations, international festivals and writerships-in-residence, Chinese poetry has made itself heard and seen inside a long list of foreign poetry scenes – which tend to be equally unmarketable in economic terms. Foreign audiences of Chinese literature at large offer another piece of interesting evidence on marketability. Crudely speaking, what they know is classical poetry and contemporary fiction.

In sum, the general public is largely ignorant of contemporary poetry, and some of its (specialist) readers are angry, disappointed or at a loss. These things reflect only part of what others think – here, I will not dwell on poetry's many optimistic readers – but they are acutely relevant to what poets think. In that quarter, too, I will only highlight a small number of currently conspicuous issues.

*What poets think.* The first two authors featured in the previous section, Xi Chuan and Yu Jian, have extensive explicit poetics to their name. In Xi Chuan's poetry, a lofty image of eaglehood can be dismantled by the vulgar reality of an eagle hide. Similarly, his poetics contains relativizing, ironic passages, this one from 1995[23]:

There are indeed those who announce that although they do not write poetry, they are poets.

22. Bourdieu, *The Field*, ch. 1.
23. The following three quotations come from Xi Chuan, "Guanyu shixue zhong de jiu ge wenti" ("On nine issues in poetics"), in *Shanhua* (*Mountain Flower*), No. 12 (1995), pp. 61–66; "Yishu zishi" ("The author's explanation of his art") (dated 1986), in Xu Jingya *et al.* (eds.), *Zhongguo xiandai zhuyi shiqun daguan 1986–1988* (*Survey of Chinese Modernist*

to balance solemn, sometimes grandiloquent claims. In 1986, he writes:

The poet is both god and devil.

And in 1999:

When the strong poet touches iron, it turns to gold.

By contrast, Yu Jian, writing in 1997, holds that the poet is no more than a processor of language, a craftsman anchored in everyday reality who uses language to "retreat from metaphor," indeed as "a method to eliminate the imagination": nothing like a tragic genius who writes in autumn or by moonlight – and nothing like an alchemist. But Yu Jian's poetics is no more unequivocal than Xi Chuan's. Yu's exercises in demystification are invalidated by pompous statements that bespeak the romanticism they claim to oppose. In 1999, he calls poetry[24]

a movement of language that cuts through forgetting and returns to the home of being ... an original truth of the world, the light emitted by wisdom and the soul.

These remarks may serve to outline Xi Chuan's and Yu Jian's orientations, and show the usefulness of the elevated and the earthly as co-ordinates in not just text but also metatext. Poetics of the elevated are powerfully present in what Michelle Yeh has called the cult of poetry in contemporary China, with its origins in the 1980s, granting the poet superhuman status and as such a cult of poet-*hood*. Its impact in the 1990s and beyond is manifest in the continuing worship and mythification of poets like Haizi, whose apotheosis was occasioned by his suicide at the age of 25 in March 1989, and Hei Dachun, on account of his bohemian lifestyle.[25] Recent years have shown aggressive, concerted efforts at the earthly end of the spectrum, with Yu Jian as the most prolific contributor. Natural tension between the earthly and the elevated grew into all-out conflict in 1998–2000, in the polemic of "popular" and "intellectual" mentioned earlier in connection with Yin Lichuan's poetry, as a particularly intense metatext.

The polemic showed that for all their self-proclaimed ordinariness, members of the earthly camp still view poethood as a superior quality of extraordinary importance and social relevance. As for authors of elevated persuasion, the special status of the poet has always been among the tenets of their poetics. Perhaps the need to reclaim something of the dwindling visibility of poetry and poet-*hood* is extra pressing for the earthly polemicists in the light of their much-vaunted ability to stay in

---

*footnote continued*

*Poetry Groups, 1986–1988*) (Shanghai: Tongji daxue, 1988), p. 361 and "Shige lianjinshu" ("The alchemy of poetry") (revised ed., dated 1999), in Xi Chuan, *Shuizi* (*Water Stains*) (Tianjin: Baihua wenyi), pp. 223–28.

24. Yu Jian, "Cong yinyu houtui" ("Step back from metaphor"), in *Zuojia* (*Writer*), No. 3 (1997), p. 72 and "Chuanyue Hanyu de shige zhi guang" ("The light of poetry, cutting through the Chinese language"), in Yang Ke (ed.), *1998 Zhongguo xinshi nianjian* (*1998 Yearbook of China's New Poetry*) (Guangzhou: Huacheng, 1999), pp. 11, 13.

25. Michelle Yeh, "The 'cult of poetry' in contemporary China," in *Journal of Asian Studies*, Vol. 55, No. 1, pp. 51–80.

touch with the realities of everyday life (in China) and the "ordinary people" – whose ignorance of their art would be all the more painful. The textual trend from what to how, then, has a metatextual pendant in one from what to who.

Since roughly 2000, the promotion of poethood has also found expression in the visual presentation of poets and their publications. Young authors such as those in the Lower Body troupe and generally the generation "born after 1970" (*qiling hou*) were the first to include all manner of photographs and spectacular formatting in journals like *Poetry Text*.[26] Older poets and publishers have adopted similar styles for book publications, such as poetry collections by Yi Sha and Yu Jian, and anthologies of the Coquetry School (*sajiao pai*) edited by Momo.[27] There is also the newly popular genre of illustrated memoirs and informal histories, regaling stories of the avant-garde from its underground origins to the present day, for instance by Zhong Ming, Liao Yiwu, Mang Ke and Yang Li.[28] This visualization is in part explained – especially for the younger authors, to whom it would come naturally – by overall cultural trends, with other media encroaching upon the hegemony of the written word. It is, however, also a strategic exercise in image-(re)building in order to sustain readership, or indeed spectatorship.

Photographs and other illustrations come in three types. The first is hip, stylized, sometimes theatrical and provocative portraits, individual or collective, typical of *Poetry Text* and kindred publications: a loud, visual

**Figure 1: "…. hip, stylized, sometimes theatrical and provocative portraits …."**

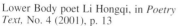

Lower Body poet Li Hongqi, in *Poetry Text*, No. 4 (2001), p. 13

"Li Hongqi killing himself," in *Poetry Text*, No. 4 (2001), p. 12

26. *Shi wenben* (*Poetry Text*), e.g. No. 4 (2001).
27. Yi Sha, *Poems*; Yu Jian, *Shi ji yu tu xiang/Anthology and Image* (*A Poetry Collection with Images*) (Xining: Qinghai renmin, 2003); Momo (ed.), *Sajiao* (*Coquetry*) (Hong Kong: Shishang zhoukan, 2004), two issues to date.
28. Zhong Ming, *Pangguan zhe* (*Onlooker*) (Haikou: Hainan, 1998); Liao Yiwu, *Chenlun de sheng dian: Zhongguo 20 shiji 70 niandai dixia shige yizhao* (*Sunken Sacred Palace: A Portrait of Erstwhile Underground Poetry in the 70s of the 20th Century*) (Urumqi: Xinjiang qingshaonian, 1999); Mang Ke, *Qiao! Zhe xie ren* (*Look at Them All!*) (Changchun: Shidai wenyi, 2003); Yang Li, *Canlan: di san dai ren de xiezuo he shenghuo* (*Splendour: The Writing and the Lives of the Third Generation*) (Xining: Qinghai renmin, 2004).

extension of poetry-as-performance, vaguely showcasing rock-n-roll life-styles (Figure 1). The second is a mix of pictures taken at public events – poetry readings, conferences and so on – on the one hand, and banal snapshots on the other, mostly recent but sometimes including family-album-type childhood pictures, facsimiles of the poet's hand-writing and so on, as in Yi Sha's and Momo's recent books (Figure 2).

Figure 2: "…. **family-album-type childhood pictures** …."

Controversial poet and polemicist Yi Sha at age eight, when he first went to school, and age nineteen (inset), when he entered university. In Yi Sha, *Poems*, p. 30 + 1.

Figure 3: "…. public occasions that definitely belong to literary history …."

Mang Ke (28) and Bei Dao (29) at the time of founding *Today* [ca 1978], in Mang Ke, *Look*, p. 21.

The Coquetry School in 1986, in Momo, *Coquetry*, inside cover.

The third type, in the upsurge of poetry memoirs, is that of (group) portraits to mark public occasions that definitely belong to literary history, as opposed to the here-and-now (Figure 3). It will be hard to distinguish from the second once both may reasonably be called "old."

The transition between what is experienced as past and present is gradual, and a poet like Yi Sha has been around for a good ten years. Still, pictures of Yi Sha are not the same as pictures of underground poets in the 1970s, such as Bei Dao and Mang Ke, whose work would soon change overground literature forever. The latter point to moments in poetry that are definitely past and have left their mark, and can claim stable historical significance. Something similar holds for the facsimile, in Yang Li's book, of an April 1989 letter to Wan Xia by Luo Yihe, describing Haizi's suicide in some detail shortly after the event (Figure 4) – as opposed to, say, that of a handwritten "representative work" (*daibiao zuo*) from 1990 by Yi Sha that, for all we know, may have been copied out anew in 2003 for his latest book (Figure 5). On that note, many pictures in Mang Ke's memoirs are fairly recent, but have been reproduced in sepia colours and less-than-perfect focus, conjuring up the image of a past that is barely retrievable and therefore all the more special (Figure 6).

To recall Zhao's karaoke metaphor once more, one reading of banal snapshots in the New Look Books portrays poets as addressing an audience of friends and colleagues, even if their performance is musically/photographically and historically insignificant. Another reading, that fits squarely with strategic image-(re)building vis-à-vis an audience beyond the in-crowd, draws on the continuing currency of poethood as a thing of extraordinary importance, especially in earthly circles: if the picture is of a poet, that should automatically make it interesting, even if

Figure 4: **"…. Luo Yihe … describing Haizi's suicide in some detail …."**

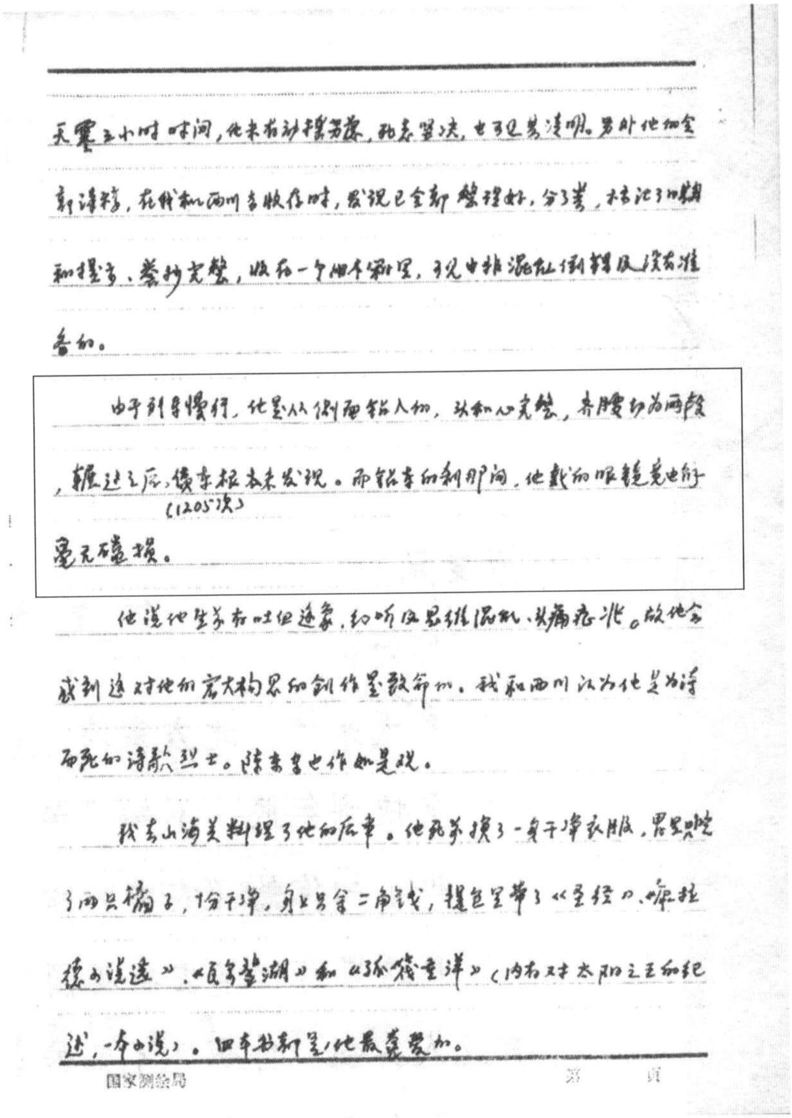
[illegible]五小时时间，他[illegible]，斗志坚决，也可见其清明。另外他的全部诗稿，在我和西川去收存时，发现已全部整理好，分了类，标记了日期和提要，誊抄完整，收存一个个本子里，[illegible]。

由于列车慢行，他是从侧面卧入的，头和心完整，身腰切为两段，辗过之后，货车（1205次）根本未发现。而卧车的刹那间，他戴的眼镜竟也都毫无碰损。

他说他生前有吐血迹象，幻听及思维混乱、头痛症状。故他会感到这对他的宏大构思和创作是致命的。我和西川认为他是为诗而死的诗歌烈士。陈东东也作如是说。

我去山海关料理了他的后事。他死前换了一身干净衣服，[illegible]了两只橘子，十分干净，身上只有二角钱，挂包里带了《圣经》、《康拉德小说选》、《瓦尔登湖》和《孤筏重洋》（内有对太阳之王的纪述，一本小说）。四本书都是他最喜爱的。

国家测绘局 第 页

Luo Yihe's letter to Wan Xia. The highlighted paragraph reads: "The train was going slow, and [Haizi] had thrown himself [under the wheels] from the side. His head and heart were intact, but he had been cut in two at the abdomen. The freight train crew (it was the 1205 service) never realized he had been run over. And in the instant that he had thrown himself [under the wheels], the glasses he was wearing had not even been cracked or damaged." In Yang Li, *Splendour*, p. 16.

all the poet does is eat a bowl of noodles (Figure 7). Notably, while the professional quality of author portraits on book covers has improved across the board, exponents of elevated poetics appear much less frequently in this process of visualization.

Figure 5: "…. a handwritten 'representative work' from 1990 by Yi Sha …."

Hand-written version of Yi Sha's most famous poem, "Starve the poets" (1990). In Yi Sha, *Poems*, p. 30 + 3.

(Self-)images of contemporary poethood, then, have seen multiple re-inventions. In early Obscure poetry, there is the humanist spokesman for the emancipation of art, akin to political activists of the 1978–79 Democracy Wall and the Beijing Spring, and to some extent still operating on the terms of the Maoist discourse he seeks to question. From the

Figure 6: ".... conjuring up the image of a past that is barely retrievable ...."

From the left: Xi Chuan, Tang Xiaodu (at the back), Mang Ke (on the swing) and Zhang Renping gathered in Baiyangdian, on one of several 1990s nostalgic trips made by members of the Beijing poetry scene to this Hebei fishing village, where Mang Ke and other budding poets had been "rusticated" during the Cultural Revolution – this one took place in 1998. In Mang Ke, *Look*, p. 112.

mid-1980s on, when overt political messages have all but disappeared, opposing constructions of the poet emerge: elitist high priest of a cult of poetry, and avowedly "popular" demystifier-cum-desecrator invoking the realities of everyday life. The 1990s bring the disintegration of groups and "isms," and a shift toward individual efforts incapable of claiming social significance and not necessarily aspiring to do so anyway. The turn of the century shows efforts at image-(re)building, partly in reaction to the poet's increasing removal from centre stage in society at large, and partly reflecting overall cultural trends: visualization, but also things like the increasing popularity of personal columns in lifestyle magazines.

My generalization of masculine pronouns for the poet is a reflection of near-exclusive male dominance of the metatextual arena, all the more remarkable in the light of women poets' textual contributions to the avant-garde.[29] Female poets appear less inclined – or less driven by

29. Cf. Yeh, "The 'cult'," p. 75. For women's poetry, see Jeanne Hong Zhang, *The Invention of a Discourse: Women's Poetry from Contemporary China* (Leiden: CNWS, 2004).

Figure 7: "…. even if all the poet does is eat a bowl of noodles …."

"[Poet Han Dong] eating," in Yang Li, *Splendour*, p. 295.

compulsive ambition, and aspirations to priesthood or desecratorship – to leave their mark on the debate, in spite of occasional attempts by male metatextual activists to enlist their female colleagues for the cause. Zhai Yongming's refusal to take sides in the "intellectual"–"popular" polemic is a case in point.

Poets' recent image-(re)building facilitates a modest, politically disinterested celebrity discourse and commodification of contemporary poethood, a category that has travelled all the way from the proud and righteous to the hip and shameless. Any understanding of its versatility, not to say its frantic leaps and bounds amid diverse and conflicting stimuli, must draw on Michelle Yeh's identification of modern Chinese poets' identity crisis, beginning early in the 20th century and evolving up to the present day, triggered and perpetuated by unceasing social, political and cultural upheaval,[30] and exacerbated by the recent impact of capitalist market ideology. Poets sustain the importance of poethood – whether as representing (traditional) cultural essence, (modern) national salvation or (contemporary) individual identity – by cherishing it as an abstraction, made concrete and interpreted in different ways that succeed one another or co-exist.

30. Michelle Yeh, *Modern Chinese Poetry: Theory and Practice since 1917* (New Haven & London: Yale University Press, 1991), ch. 1.

*Whose Margins?*

In metatextual matters, then, poetry remains part of a society whose values and styles are changing fast. While any attempt at marketization – in the sense of generating real money, not just fame and free meals – would be doomed, the genre has had some success in the celebrity discourse noted above, and in new media. Online poetry scenes are beyond the scope of this article.[31] Suffice it here to note that they are extremely active in uploading poetry texts and metatexts, both those first published on paper, often before the internet era, and those that first – or only – appear online.

These things work differently for different generations and inclinations, as evidenced by the poets discussed above. Yu Jian can be seen to *adapt*, actively working towards a hip presentation in his general pursuit of publicity, through sheer noise and notoriety if need be. Yin Lichuan and Yan Jun, whose age more naturally puts them in touch with rapidly expanding youth culture, *help constitute* socio-cultural change; Yin's poethood especially is inseparably linked to the internet. As for Xi Chuan, he is typical of reticence at the elevated end of the spectrum in matters such as the visual presentation of publications and events.

For the other three poets and many more, there is a potential discrepancy between text and metatext: high art and low readership on the one hand, and celebrity discourse and commodification of poethood on the other. Even if the numerous visitors of poetry websites are added to those who read poetry on paper, the fact remains that beyond the field of restricted production, texts by the avant-garde are incompatible with overall socio-cultural trends whose dominance is defined by numbers. While this holds for poets from all quarters, it is exemplified by the self-proclaimed "popular" poets. Yu Jian's claim that classical poetry was part of the everyday life of ordinary people in the Tang and Song dynasties and that the right kind of contemporary poetry operates "among the [ordinary] people" is unconvincing. When Yin Lichuan says that for all its professed anti-elitism, Lower Body poetry, including that of "popular" firebrand Shen Haobo, hardly reaches beyond an elite audience, that is easier to believe. That Lower Body poetry's relative accessibility allows it to count more of Bourdieu's "non-producers" among its readers than Xi Chuan or a typical poet's poet like Che Qianzi does not change this.[32]

Questions of the type "whither poetry?" occur frequently in mainland-Chinese critical discourse, and trigger discussions in which the value of poetry's development to date and the desirability of this or that one among its possible futures are linked to socio-cultural trends. This

31. See Michel Hockx's contribution to this volume, and Michael Day's poetry chapter at www.sino.uni-heidelberg.de/dachs/leiden.
32. Yu Jian, "The light," p. 12; Yin Lichuan, question-and-answer session, Gent, De Centrale, May 2004 and That's Beijing (no author's name), "Beijing writers face a dilemma," in *China Daily*, 2 April 2004.

happens through lament – or jubilation – over poetry's *in*-compatibility with these trends, but also through the confident assertion of its ability to ride the tide and avoid falling behind the times. Rather than appraising the suitability of various poetics to their physical surroundings, and deploring or celebrating the fact that there are more people who watch television than poetry readers, we may simply observe that starting in the 1980s, and especially in the 1990s and beyond, a large number of authors have written a wide variety of avant-garde poetry that continues to appear with reputable publishing houses, and sustains a dedicated, well-positioned audience. Equations of the 1980s with the rise of contemporary poetry, and of the 1990s and beyond with its decline, say something about context, not text or metatext.

Let us return to the two red flags. The publication of Gui Xinghua's poetry is the product of government policy; that of Yi Sha's, the product of a publisher's decision. The latter is informed by considerations of prestige, at a time when automatic government subsidies have long been a thing of the past, and any expectation to make money from poetry is as unrealistic as ever under normal circumstances, as opposed to the anomaly of the 1980s or people's fascination for self-killing poets. Some rank and file avant-garde publications would not appear without external sponsors, but publishers will pay prominent poets for the rights to their work, without such sponsorship. Be all that as it may, to make numbers – money, print runs, readership – the measure of all things, in this case of the "relevance" of a poetry whose objectives do not include traditional and orthodox ideals of broad recognition and dissemination as an instrument of social morality, is socio-economic reductionism, of limited analytical and interpretative power. Bourdieu is keenly aware of this: witness his definition of the literary field as[33] "a separate social universe having its own laws of functioning independent of those of politics and the economy." Yet, subsequently he writes that to understand literature is to understand "how it is defined in relation to the field of power and, in particular, in relation to the fundamental law of this universe, which is that of economy and power."

Throughout the 20th century, Chinese-poetic modernity proved difficult to combine with traditional poetics summed up in the notion of literature to convey the Way. Seen in that light, and that of Bourdieu's "fundamental law," poetry's oft-noted marginalization in the 20th century is a valid, indeed an ineluctable notion. But with an eye to its inclinations since the 1980s, and to radical changes in relations between social, political, economic and cultural forces at work in contemporary China, one might well ask: Whose margins? What makes socio-economic discourse and power relations the centre? Lest we dispense with the notion of artistic creativity by reducing it to a flaw in the fabric of an all-encompassing economic "rationalism," we should be wary of an argument that

---

33. Bourdieu, *The Field*, pp. 162–64.

may appear plausible enough, but is in fact deeply problematic. For anything like a comprehensive understanding of contemporary Chinese poetry, it makes no sense to apply criteria informed by forces that are largely alien to its development: orthodoxy and marketization. "Is this poetry suitable for conveying the Way?" and "does this poetry sell?" are the wrong questions.

*Who cares?* Answering the wrong questions would be turning a blind eye to a demonstrably thriving if rather self-contained cultural scene, and do little more than reaffirm disparaging comments on the "relevance" of (modern) poetry that are something of a genre in themselves, across diverse cultural traditions – as are, conversely, apologies for poetry. If there is a need for either, there is nothing Chinese about that.

Alternatively, while recognizing changes in the cultural landscape that surrounds and obviously affects poetry in contemporary China, we may wish to leave sufficient room for approaching it on its own terms, as gleaned from the niche where it finds itself. Not as some gratuitous assertion of the absolute autonomy of high art, but as an attempt to grasp what this poetry means, and how it works, and for whom.

*Appendix: Poems by Yu Jian and Yin Lichuan*

"Outside the Poet's Scope: Observation of the Life of a Raindrop"
by Yu Jian

*right   it's going to rain*
*the poet on a bar stool in the coffeeshop*
*shoots a glance at the sky   quietly mumbles*
*and his tongue withdraws into the dark*
*but back in those dark clouds   its life   its*
*drop-by-drop tiny story   is only just beginning*
*how to say this   this sort of small thing   happens every moment*
*i'm concerned with bigger things   says the poet to his female reader*
*obedient to that invisible straight line   coming down*
*maintaining consistency   with surroundings   equally perpendicular to the earth*
*just like the poet's daughter   always maintains consistency with kindergarten*
*and then   in skies twisted by pedagogy*
*becoming twisted   it cannot but become twisted*
*not in order to graduate   but in order to retain its wetness*
*it has not yet the ability to choose its locus*

*it does not know as of yet    that whatever its choice*
*to fall down is all that is within its rights    or maybe it knows*
*but then again    how to stop    here*
*everything is going down*
*happy little princelet    in self-styled coronation*
*on the verge of an overcast sky    lithely flashes by*
*divorces itself from the ranks    turns into a tiny tail*
*stuck upward    flattened out    twisting up again*
*lashing out    experiencing the freedom*
*and the unreliability of open space*
*now    it seems that it can do as it pleases*
*in a small space in the world    neither up nor down*
*junior high school student out of class    on the road between home and the classroom*
*the poet maintains his composure    sizing up his reader's chest like an honest man*
*but it dares not indulge in enjoyment of this wee bit of freedom*
*in the end having to become an appendage of something else*
*in the end having to team up    with one colossus or another*
*petty lowly luminophor*
*firefly fearful of individualism*
*longing for surveillance by the lights of summer nights*
*just like the poet    at the same time as writing poetry*
*also serves in a certain association    he has a membership card*
*descending faster now    losing all freedom*
*at the moment of gliding into the ground    the nature of an object*
*in the end is only grasped    on the verge of death*
*the little raindrop    has finally caught hold of an iron-wire clothes-line*
*to change its previous course    now moving across*
*beginning to absorb smaller compatriots*
*gradually swelling    hoarding them into a*
*small transparent bundle    tied on the back*
*seeking support    gliding on    collecting more*
*fatter than before    and heavier too*
*it seems that it's turning into another kind*
*pearl    grape    transparent little calabash*
*or something else    it seems that it can choose anew*
*this right moves it to flaunt its talents    and possess its own form*
*while doomed to fail for want of the final touch    the weight of this form*
*has long ago determined that it's all downward    a heaven-granted pitfall*
*just like our poet    rebels    howls*
*and then becomes legitimate    moves up in the world*
*with his aestheticist pen    giving his reader an autograph*
*desperately grasping at everything within reach*
*but the connection with the iron-wire grows ever thinner*
*heedlessness    in order to grow bigger and fuller*
*and once grown to the full    drop off    now that is death*
*the body quivers    turns into a thin thread again*
*travels along that still invisible*
*straight line    falls on the earth*
*like a snake that exists for just one second*
*the body moving    only to disappear*
*but that does not entail its failure*
*it has remained wet throughout*

*in this life   its victory is never to have been dry*
*its time   means water retention   up until it*
*turns into other water   splashed on the bottom of a trouser leg*
*of the poet who has just left the coffeeshop   to leave a wet mark*

\*

## "Why Not Make It Feel Even Better"

by Yin Lichuan

*ah   a little higher a little lower a little to the left a little to the right*
*this is not making love   this is hammering nails*
*oh   a little faster a little slower a little looser a little tighter*
*this is not making love   this is anti-porn campaigning or tying your shoes*
*ooh   a little more a little less a little lighter a little heavier*
*this is not making love   this is massage writing a poem washing your hair or your feet*

*why not make it feel even better   huh   make it feel even better*
*a little gentler a little ruder a little more intellectual a little more popular*

*why not make it feel even better*

\*

## "Small-Time City Thief"

by Yin Lichuan

*out of a fistful of last year's snow*
*you squeeze a lump of black mud*
*absolute emptiness. you can't find a stone to kick*
*so your hands and feet stay in line straight through*
*the streets are swept too clean to offer you shelter anymore*
*the buses are no longer crowded*
*you just can't get used to the girl selling shoes saying*
*how are you, or to the shop*
*selling not steamed rolls but hamburgers*
*fuck! all these things have changed*
*and nobody's talking to you*
*big brother's gone to vietnam for big money*
*brother two has his own gang now, brother three's been taken in*
*brother four's been run over by a car, brother five's back in the fields*
*and you've no place to go. in 1968, you were born here*
*you're a city citizen, you've built your own life since you were little*

*you're no cheat no burglar no adulterer you're chaster than a monk*
*you walk past the police, careful now*
*but they don't even look at you*
*your steps are slowing down, people swirling*
*past you all the time. you sit down*
*in the city park, the fence hurting your ass*
*for the first time you wonder about your beloved trade*
*nobody needs you now. you were born at the wrong time*

*

# Virtual Chinese Literature: A Comparative Case Study of Online Poetry Communities*

## Michel Hockx

ABSTRACT  This article looks at the practices of communities that employ internet technologies in order to produce, distribute, consume and value Chinese poetry. The article is in three parts. The first part provides a brief general overview of the current state of research about the Chinese internet. I take issue with the dominant tendency of English-language research to focus almost exclusively on questions of censorship. The second part looks at the development of "web literature" (*wangluo wenxue*) in China, briefly outlining the meaning of the term and the content of a protracted debate about web literature that took place in 2001. The debate illustrates the limited extent to which web literature is able to distinguish itself from conventionally published literature. Paradoxically, this has led to "web literature" becoming a recognized genre within print culture. In the final part, I compare a PRC online poetry community with a similar community based in the USA. I conclude by arguing that previous scholarship's biased focus on the transformative aspects of cyber culture has made it difficult to gain a clear insight into the many positive and culture-specific features of Chinese web literature.

Discussing the distinction between web literature and literature is as boring as discussing the distinction between web love and traditional love.   ----"wwwmm"[1]

According to statistics from the China Internet Network Information Center (CNNIC) there were by the end of 2004 approximately 668,900 websites on the Chinese world-wide web.[2] It is reasonable to assume that a good proportion of these contain content that can be described as literary. The intention of my research, and of this article, is to study the practices of communities that employ internet technologies in order to produce, distribute, consume and value literary products. In this article, my emphasis is on poetry communities. As is shown in Maghiel van Crevel's article in this volume, the genre of poetry, often seen as culturally marginal, continues to occupy a significant niche in PRC elite culture, with some of the most avant-garde groups making good use of

---

* I am grateful to Charles Laughlin for his perceptive comments as the discussant for the first draft of this paper during the IIAS workshop in October 2004.

1. Quoted from an article entitled "Wangluo wenxue" ("Web literature"), originally published (possibly under a different title) in *Zhonghua dushu bao* (*China Reading Journal*), 10 October 2001, reproduced online, URL: http://www.china.org.cn/chinese/RS/65142.htm. The reproduction does not mention the name of the article's author. "wwwmm" is the screen name of one of the participants in the 2001 debate about web literature, discussed below.

2. Information provided on the CNNIC website, URL: http://www.cnnic.net.cn/download/2005/2005012701.pdf. Most general sources on the Chinese internet referred to in this article were traced using the resources available to members of the Chinese Internet Research Group. For more information about this group, see URL: http://groups.yahoo.com/group/chineseinternetresearch/.

websites to disseminate and discuss their work and ideas. However, poetry (both modern and classical) also continues to have a more popular appeal among young educated urbanites who gather in virtual communities as part of their lifestyle, without displaying any obvious interest in being avant-garde. It is the latter type of community that I intend to discuss in this article.

The article begins by providing a brief general overview of the current state of research about the Chinese internet. I take issue with the dominant tendency of English-language research to focus almost exclusively on questions of censorship. By foregrounding censorship and by highlighting what does not appear on the Chinese internet, attention is taken away from what does appear. For research on contemporary Chinese web literature this exclusive focus on censorship issues is unnecessary as censorship is a fact of life for Chinese writers and it does not make their work less valuable or interesting.

The article then looks at the development of "web literature" (*wangluo wenxue*) in China, briefly outlining the meaning of the term and the content of a protracted debate about it that took place in 2001. The debate illustrates the limited extent to which web literature is able to distinguish itself from conventionally published literature. Paradoxically, this has led to "web literature" becoming a recognized genre within print culture.

In the remainder of the article, I compare a PRC online poetry community with a similar community based in the United States. The comparison further emphasizes the limited distinctions between online and printed literature. It also confirms that, as many have begun to suspect, the supposed "globalness" of internet technology does not remove clear cultural differences.

## Research on the PRC Internet

The CNNIC statistics mentioned above estimated the number of Chinese internet users at 94,000,000. As is well-known (and as is the practice in some other countries) these users do not have access to the world-wide web in its entirety, as the content of non-PRC sites is continuously monitored, filtered and, if deemed necessary, blocked.[3] Perhaps because of the world-wide web's reputation of being an exceptionally permissive and uncontrollable space, most researchers of the Chinese internet so far seem to be predominantly interested in methods and technologies of control and censorship, that is, in what does *not* appear on the Chinese web, rather than what does. If initially China watchers were optimistic that the advent of the internet in China would promote freedom of speech and create niches for free thinkers

---

3. For an ongoing analysis of web content filtering in China and other countries see Jonathan Zittrain and Benjamin Edelman, "Empirical analysis of internet filtering in China," URL: http://cyber.law.harvard.edu/filtering/china/.

to express their opinions, recent research seems to deny these expectations, demonstrating instead the effectiveness of state control of the internet in China.[4] Among the 138 items on Randy Kluver's "Bibliography on the internet in China,"[5] which lists English-language studies of the Chinese internet, the vast majority deal with issues of state control versus civil liberties, with e-commerce and economic aspects the second most popular topic. References to research on cultural production on the Chinese internet are almost absent, nor can they easily be found elsewhere. A notable (and very recent) exception is Michael Day's annotated archive of avant-garde poetry websites that is part of the "Digital archive for Chinese studies (Leiden Division)."[6] That project, however, also appears to be largely motivated by the fear that government repression will cause websites to disappear without warning: it is mainly an archive of dissident voices. That such disappearances can be immediate and extensive became clear to me on 20 September 2004 when I tried to access some of the tens of thousands of personal web pages (including 2,372 pages classed as "literature" and 25,699 pages classed as "personal manifestos" (*geren xuanyan*) hosted by the Chinese commercial ISP 533.net. They had become inaccessible. An announcement by the ISP explained that it had ceased its free web hosting service with immediate effect because of "problems with the contents of a small minority of the pages" and that it would henceforth only provide web space for paying customers providing full proof of identity.[7]

Following this, similar announcements began to appear on the websites of many Chinese ISPs, discussion forums and chatrooms. The government policy of making service providers, forum moderators and chatroom operators legally responsible for any "inappropriate content" appearing on their sites has obviously led to extensive self-regulation. The demand for users to provide full proof of identity acts as a deterrent to those possibly planning to post or host (politically) subversive content. Service providers, moderators and operators appear willing to co-operate with the authorities in this way in order to keep their sites up and running. In the context of this volume, this is one example of how the state in contemporary China continues to exercise control over culture, especially popular culture, by appealing to cultural

4. For examples of this approach, see for instance Jeroen de Kloet, "Digitisation and its Asian discontents: the internet, politics and hacking in China and Indonesia," *First Monday*, Vol. 7, No. 9 (2002), URL: http://firstmonday.org/issues/issue7_9/kloet/index.html and Lokman Tsui, "Big Mama is watching you: internet control and the Chinese government" (Leiden: Unpublished MA thesis, 2001; downloadable from URL: http://www.lokman.nu/thesis/).

5. This list is available to members of the Chinese Internet Research Group mentioned above. My comments here are based on a visit to the (continuously expanding) list in September 2004.

6. URL: http://www.sino.uni-heidelberg.de/dachs/leiden/poetry/index.html.

7. The URL of the announcement, being the page that would appear regardless which personal web page one was trying to access, was (and perhaps still is) http://ads.533.net/gonggao/.

brokers' interest in maintaining a stable marketplace for their enterprises.[8]

## Web Literature: Production-Oriented Analysis

Although the preference for censorship-oriented research is under-
standable, there are good reasons to argue for the viability of a more
production-oriented approach, that is, an approach that looks at what
*does* appear in Chinese web space. Foremost among those reasons is the
fact that all Chinese literature of all dynasties and periods has been
produced under conditions of state censorship and this has never prevented scholars and critics from taking it serious as literary work, nor has
it prevented Chinese writers from writing and readers from reading.
Censorship of the internet does not necessarily confront Chinese writers
and readers with an unfamiliar situation. Censorship is the norm, rather
than the exception.

A second (related) reason is that censors and their practices can and
should be studied as part of literary practice as a whole, whether in print
culture or in cyber culture. There is no reason to ignore censorship but
there is similarly no reason to overemphasize it or isolate it from the
practices of other agents within the literary field.

Thirdly, the particular type of censorship practised in China is, for
better or for worse, one of the things that make contemporary Chinese
web literature different from that of other countries (cultures, language
communities). This would support the suggestion that there is such a
thing as "PRC web culture" despite the fact that the world-wide web is
supposed to work against such nation-based distinctions.[9]

Finally, content analysis of literary websites is important because it
aids our understanding of how internet technologies, as distinct from print
culture technologies, are challenging familiar concepts of literature, not
just in China but everywhere in the world. It is this final point that
reverberated most strongly during a lively debate about web literature on
the Chinese internet in 2001.

## The PRC Web Literature Debate

In as far as I can claim to have an overview of the large amount of web
space devoted to the debate about web literature, it began on one of the
discussion forums (*luntan*), sometimes referred to as "bulletin boards"

---

8. It might be mentioned in passing that the techniques used by the Chinese government
here are not new. Similar policies, based on mutual interest of government and ISPs, were
arrived at in Western countries in order to suppress illegal content such as child pornography
or terrorist manuals. The difference is of course that the Chinese government's definition of
what constitutes "inappropriate content" is much wider.

9. Here the formulation of my argument is indebted to Jeroen de Kloet's research cited
above.

or BBS[10]) of the popular Shanghai-based website "Rongshu xia" ("Under the banyan tree") (URL: http://www.rongshu.com or http://www.rongshuxia.com).[11] The debate was sparked by a short post (*tiezi*) to the forum by the author Chen Cun, known to some as the "father of Chinese web literature," presumably because he was the first well-known contemporary author to switch to the new medium.[12] I have been unable to retrace the original post, but its content has been copied in many places. It reads as follows:

> I go online and visit Under the Banyan Tree because I want to see what web literature is really like. I have high hopes for it. But web literature these days is starting to make me reconsider. If the highest achievement of web literature is to publish traditional books offline, if that is what qualifies you as a writer and allows you to brag, then is there still a web literature? Its freedom, its randomness and its non-utilitarian nature have already been polluted. Although I understand these changes, it is still not what I hope to see. Web literature is already past its prime. What Laozi called the period of utter innocence [*chizi zhi xin*] has vanished too quickly.[13]

Chen Cun, who later withdrew from the management of "Under the banyan tree," a site which he had founded and funded, provided with this post an (in my view) accurate assessment of the position of web literature within the Chinese book market. In 2001, and probably still nowadays, it was the case that the main measure of success for a web literature author was to have his or her works appear in print. "Under the banyan tree" itself played a major part in developing these practices, as it published regular book collections of its best online works and secured generous funding from the German Bertelsmann Book Club who used the site to enter the Chinese (printed) book market. It is understandable that someone like Chen Cun, who probably saw himself as a representative of a literary avant-garde, was attracted by the possibilities that HTML writing offers for literary experimentation, ideally leading to novel ways of writing making full use of the characteristics of hypertext and hypermedia. Such writing did indeed not or hardly develop on the Chinese internet. The bulk of web literature, including much online writing that presents itself as new or shocking, is plain (or "linear") text rather than ("non-linear") hypertext.[14]

10. In Western cyber-circles, the term "BBS" (bulletin board system) is considered somewhat outdated, referring as it does to the text-only interactive systems of the 1980s and 1990s. In East Asia, however, the acronym is still popular and used to refer to both text-only and multimedia online forums. Cf. the article "Bulletin board systems" on *Wikipedia*, URL: http://en.wikipedia.org/wiki/Bulletin_board_system.

11. For a partial content analysis of this website, see Michel Hockx, "Links with the past: mainland China's online literary communities and their antecedents," *Journal of Contemporary China*, Vol. 13, No. 38 (2004), pp. 105–127.

12. Chen Cun's status as an important contemporary author is confirmed by the inclusion of one of his stories in Howard Goldblatt (ed.), *Chairman Mao Would Not Be Amused* (New York: Grove Press, 1995).

13. Quoted from the article entitled "Web literature," see n. 1.

14. This is true, for instance, of the "happening" avant-garde website called "Shi jianghu" ("Poetry vagabonds"), which consists entirely of poems that adhere to the print culture format, despite their often highly unconventional content. (Indeed, the group also publishes

The crossing-over of web literature authors into print culture led, however, to an unusual phenomenon which continues until the present day. Within print culture, "web literature" has become a genre of its own. When I visited Beijing in 2002, I was struck by the fact that the literature sections of all major bookshops had shelves devoted to "web literature" just as they had shelves devoted to, say, "Chinese poetry" or "foreign fiction." The category also appears as a genre category on some online Chinese bookshops. In short, for a web author (*xieshou*) to become successful in print culture there is an additional hurdle to overcome: even if one does manage to publish one's work in print it might still carry a generic label that distinguishes it from "real" literature. On the other hand, for web authors to have this kind of entry point into print culture at all is convenient and valuable. As Howard Becker points out in an article about English-language hypertext fiction, the challenges faced by American web authors are much greater.[15] I return to this comparison below.

Many of the thousands who responded to Chen Cun's post after it was first published disagreed with his pessimism. However the most frequently seen response, documented in online articles and in newspapers into which the debate spilled over by October 2001, was that the internet was after all only a medium (*zaiti*) for literature. Those who held this view argued that literature was literature no matter how it was distributed and that web literature, rather than being on the way out, was to have a glorious future. Although the enthusiasm for web literature does seem to have diminished since 2001, the sheer number of literary works produced for the various online forums on a daily basis is still staggering.[16]

Below, I take a closer look at the practices of a typical Chinese literary website, making a straightforward comparison with a similar American website. Despite the continued adherence to the print culture format, the actual practices of the Chinese website occasionally diverge from the print culture paradigm, especially in the realm of criticism and valuation.

## Online Poetry Communities

The following sections briefly describe the practices of two online literary communities, one hosted on a server located in the United States

---

*footnote continued*

a normal printed journal.) In September 2004, the site was no longer accessible at the old URL (http://www.wenxue2000.com – this instead linked, ironically, to the text of a poem by Li Bai). Alternative URLs were available, leading to a collection of old work (http://sh.netsh.com/bbs/3307/) and to a new discussion forum (http://my.clubhi.com/bbs/661502/). In December 2004 the old site was accessible again. At the time of writing (March 2005), it has once more disappeared, but the other two URLs mentioned above remain valid. The translation "poetry vagabonds" for *shi jianghu* was suggested to me by Maghiel van Crevel.

15. Howard S. Becker, "A new art form: hypertext fiction," URL: http://www.soc.ucsb.edu/faculty/hbecker/lisbon.html.

16. For an overview of related articles see "2001: Qingsuan wangluo wenxue" ("2001: liquidating web literature"), URL: http://www.booker.com.cn/gb/paper253/1/.

and using the English language (http://www.everypoet.com) and the other hosted on a server in the People's Republic of China and using the Chinese language (http://www.chinapoet.net). Both communities boast a large membership,[17] have well-designed websites and apparently a solid financial basis, gained from advertising, donations or the sale of web hosting services. They are independent domains and therefore different from the smaller communities that one finds on portals such as Yahoo. Both sites are dedicated to the genre of poetry, usually a marginal and elitist literary genre, which however seems to enjoy a remarkable popularity online.

The description below is in the form of a straightforward comparison between the US site and the PRC site. It points out where practices are identical or similar, and where they diverge as a result of cultural factors. I look at practices surrounding the production and distribution of poems as well as practices of valuation ("symbolic production"[18]). Following the example set in Howard Becker's book on "art worlds,"[19] I try to take into account all the skills and tools that are needed to bring an online poem into being. I also refer to a more recent essay by Becker about "hypertext fiction," already mentioned above. In that article, Becker argues that hypertext fiction, being non-linear writing requiring special software to create, special distributors to sell and special reading strategies to enjoy, is a truly new art form in the sociological sense. The world of printed literature has no way of accommodating it within the existing forms of organization and co-operation between its agents. As mentioned above, such innovative forms of online literature have not yet emerged in the PRC. Similarly, the practices described below are only partially innovative in comparison to those of offline publishing.

### Hardware and Software

The basic material condition for the authors of online poetry is to have a computer with access to the internet. For most people in the United States and for increasing numbers of people in the urban areas of China,

17. When I visited the sites in May 2004, over 15,000 members were claimed to subscribe to the forums on the Chinese site; over 18,000 members were claimed to subscribe to the main forum (the "Poetry free for all") of the US site. When I visited both sites again on 20 September 2004 both were claiming a membership of over 19,000. At the time of writing (March 2005) the American site has "over 21,000 members." The Chinese site boasts 23,267 subscribers. It has, however, temporarily stopped accepting new subscriptions. Although no reason for this is given, the appearance of a two-line slogan under the announcement ("Let us jointly establish a healthy, civilized, law-abiding poetry community. Actively suppress and eliminate bad information and lend your strength to the cleaning up of the web environment") suggests that in this case, too, state intervention has brought about stricter self-regulation.

18. I borrow my usage of this term from C.J. van Rees's model for the description of literary communities. See for instance C.J. van Rees and Jeroen Vermunt, "Event history analysis of authors' reputation: effects of critics' attention on debutantes' careers," *Poetics*, Vol. 23, No. 5 (1996), pp. 317–333.

19. Howard S. Becker, *Art Worlds* (Berkeley, Los Angeles, London: University of California Press, 1982).

computers are affordable and internet access is cheap and convenient. Membership of the two poetry websites discussed here is free, as is publication of one's work on the site. This means that most of the cost of making this kind of literature available is incurred by those who run the website. Their position combines that of publisher and book seller in the print culture system. In the PRC case, this means that the website is also subject to censorship regulations. The front page displays, at the bottom, a state registration number and a link to the government website listing the domain registration details of the site.

The basic material conditions for hosting a website like this are server space and software. Large interactive sites that generate much server traffic, like the two sites under discussion, are generally not hosted free by internet service providers. The software needed to operate the interactive forums is also not freely available. However, compared to any kind of print culture venture, the direct costs of running sites like this is small. The American site (Figure 1) seems to derive at least part of its income from advertising in banners and pop-up windows. It also offers members the opportunity to make donations. Initially, the PRC site had very few advertisement banners. In Figure 2, a screenshot of the front page of the PRC site taken in April 2004, the only advertisement present is the one on the right-hand side in the middle, advertising a printed anthology of best works from the site itself. During later visits to the site in September and December 2004 and March 2005 I noticed an increasing number of

Figure 1: **Front Page of** *everypoet.com*

Figure 2: **Front Page of** *www.chinapoet.net*

advertisements on the front page, presumably an indication of increased popularity. The PRC site also functions as a company offering paid web hosting services. It is unclear in the case of both sites to what extent the enterprises are profit-making or rather based on generous investment of time and personal funds by enthusiastic individuals.

Both sites provide copious information about famous poems and poets, this being an indication of their relative closeness to the print culture tradition. The main attractions of the sites, however, are the "poetry forums" (*shige luntan*). These are interactive message boards dedicated to different poetic genres, styles and themes. In China at the moment such message boards are hugely popular and literary forums such as the ones discussed here can be found on almost every portal.[20] The software used by both sites appears to be identical, with the first point of entry being a page listing the various available boards and inviting the user to choose which one to read or contribute to (Figures 3 and 4). These listings also provide some statistical information about the forums, such as the number of posts and threads they contain. In both cases, the lists also provide the screen names of the moderators of each of the forums.

20. To mention just one fairly unexpected example, the website of the All China Lawyers Association (ACLA) runs a lively literary forum where lawyers can publish and discuss their own literary writing. URL: http://www.acla.org.cn/forum/postlist.php?Cat = &Board = 2.

Figure 3: **(Partial) List of Discussion Boards on** *everypoet.com*

| Forum | Posts | Threads | Last Post | Moderator |
|---|---|---|---|---|
| **Amorphous All-Purpose Anarchy** | | | | |
| **General Poetry** — Poets and poetasters of the Internet, unite! Post here if you're not looking for extensive critical commentary. You may prefer our more relaxed Pink Palace of Positude. | 11905 | 2280 | 05-25-2004 07:50 AM by Artemisia | , Donner, KAIYL, Harry R, HowardM2, Julie, Kim, Scavella |
| **General C&C** — The first stop for less experienced poets desiring constructive critical commentary. Please and read and respect these Groovy Guidelines for Gen C&C. | 26826 | 4435 | 05-25-2004 04:10 AM by Citybreak | , Donner, KAIYL, Harry R, HowardM2, Julie, Kim, Scavella |
| **Another General C&C** — Egad, the traffic. This new General C&C forum has exactly the same aims and guidelines as the other one. Take your pick! | 12875 | 1847 | 05-25-2004 07:44 AM by Mister Micawber | , Donner, KAIYL, Harry R, HowardM2, Julie, Kim, Scavella |
| **Scansion Mansion** — Are your rhymes wrenched? Your ends stopped? Does your rhythm have no spring? Hightail it to this stress-filled forum for metrical poetry. Please respect the House Rules. | 4136 | 466 | 05-24-2004 04:34 PM by Steph#2 | , Donner, KAIYL, Harry R, HowardM2, Julie, Kim, Scavella |
| **Charon's Leaky Schooner** — Let's get pithy! A teaching forum. 40 post minimum. READ THIS FIRST! | 1932 | 229 | 05-23-2004 08:11 PM by Lola Two | , Donner, KAIYL, Harry R, HowardM2, Julie, Kim, Scavella |
| **High Critique** — A place for critical commentary, mainly for the more than merely moderately experienced. Park your ego outside, embrace critical commentary, and read these. | 10841 | 1592 | 05-25-2004 08:30 AM by kekala | , Donner, KAIYL, Harry R, HowardM2, Julie, Kim, Scavella |
| **Merciless & Possibly Painful Critique** — For the more experienced, thicker-skinned, and stronger-willed. Do not post here unless you have a burning desire to improve your poetry. Please read. | 8798 | 1160 | 05-24-2004 05:42 PM by Lola Two | , Donner, KAIYL, Harry R, HowardM2, Julie, Kim, Scavella |

Figure 4: **(Partial) List of Discussion Boards on** *www.chinapoet.net*

| | | | | |
|---|---|---|---|---|
| □ 我爱论坛 | | | | |
| 【 论坛办公室 】 ▷ 社区事务的公告处，社区用户的求助处…… | 李可可 风中百合 管理者 | 今日： 25 主题： 1942 回复： 14940 | 主题：注册ID为 … 最后发表：蓝蓓 2004年05月25日 09:49pm | |
| 【 站点会议室 】 ▷ 管理员讨论区 | 李可可 管理者 | 今日： 7 主题： 538 回复： 4532 | 主题：最后发表：一剑 2004年05月25日 10:28pm | |
| 【 论坛诗歌精华区 】 ▷ 论坛的优秀诗歌，年度选刊和网刊的备选。 | 管理者 | 今日： 0 主题： 1118 回复： 7525 | 主题：公告：短诗比赛 … 最后发表：一剑 2004年05月25日 08:31am | |
| □ 诗歌论坛 | | | | |
| 【 中国诗人青梅煮酒 】 ▷ 主要用来发表诗歌批评和鉴赏。【 陈仲义评论专栏 】【 毛翰评论专栏 】 | 刘水 吴铭越 | 今日： 12 主题： 1392 回复： 7189 | 主题：[原创]请诸位续贴 最后发表：将进酒 2004年05月25日 09:28pm | |
| 【 古风悠扬红楼结社 】 ▷ 古风尤存，古韵永久。古典诗歌发表园地。【 红楼藏书阁 】 | 田牧 歌乐人生 月白风清 | 今日： 142 主题： 13964 回复： 59877 | 主题：独钓 最后发表：一还 2004年05月25日 10:11pm | |
| 【 中国诗人一百单八将 】 ▷ 各路豪杰，不分门派，啸聚于此，替诗行道。More… | 吴铭越 任轩 李三林 More… | 今日： 108 主题： 16903 回复： 65011 | 主题：卑微者之歌（系 … 最后发表：老灰 2004年05月25日 10:29pm | |
| 【 先锋一派大闹天宫 】 ▷ 新形式、新体验诗歌的尝试。 | 评论者 佟声 sunnight | 今日： 82 主题： 7229 回复： 35093 | 主题：◇相遇和离别是… 最后发表：傲天 2004年05月25日 10:26pm | |
| 【 我手写我心 】 ▷ 都市，情感，校园，生活，青春的情感。【 左後街書房 】 | 天堂马匹 光头子青 月牙儿 More… | 今日： 230 主题： 19919 回复： 101202 | 主题：[原创]想哭，你 … 最后发表：山野清风 2004年05月25日 10:25pm | |

*Agents*

The moderators are the key agents involved in the running of this kind of online poetry forum. Combining the roles of editors and censors in print culture, they decide which posts are and which are not included but they do so (at least in the forums discussed here) *after* the original post has been submitted.[21] In other words the moderators' main task is to screen submissions and to ensure that their content is suitable and appropriate for the forum to which they have been sent. The content of this task might vary from removing obscene or abusive messages to moving a poem to another forum where it more appropriately belongs. In the case of the Chinese site, the moderators are also responsible for ensuring that submissions do not violate government censorship regulations.[22] As is the case in most internet communities, the moderators are themselves regular contributors or visitors to the site. It is unlikely that they receive more than token remuneration for their efforts. This is consistent with Becker's model of art worlds: if one wants to do things within an art world that are unconventional (such as publish online rather than in print) one must be prepared to do a lot of the work oneself, since other agents within the community might not be willing (or be trained) to provide the assistance you need.

The key agents in keeping these sites alive are of course the members contributing to the forums, either by submitting their own work or by commenting on other work posted. As mentioned before, contributions to the forums are represented as threads – as a series of individual posts on one topic – normally a poem submitted by one of the members, who, by doing so, starts a new thread. A typical forum on the US site (Figure 5) shows the title of the post/poem, the screen name of the author, the number of replies to the original post, the number of times the thread has been visited, the screen name of the last person contributing to the thread and the date and time when that last contribution was made. Various symbols on the left-hand side indicate various aspects of the status of the thread. For instance, the yellow folder symbol turns into a symbol of a flaming folder if the thread is "hot," meaning it has been responded to or visited more than a certain number of times.

---

21. For a more detailed discussion of the various control mechanisms of online discussion forums in China, see Wenzhao Tao, "Censorship and protest: the regulation of BBS in China people daily," *First Monday*, Vol. 6, No. 1 (2001), URL: http://www.firstmonday.dk/issues/issue6_1/tao/index.html.

22. It is likely that especially the Chinese site also screens submissions with automatic filters to remove posts containing certain words or terms that are deemed unacceptable. It has recently been suggested that all Chinese messenger services, chatrooms and message boards are forced to operate filters based on a single list of "forbidden" words put together by the authorities. This list was retrieved by Chinese hackers and reproduced in full on various websites. (See Xiao Qiang, "The words you never see in Chinese cyberspace," *China Digital News*, 30 August 2004, URL: http://journalism.berkeley.edu/projects/chinadn/en/archives/002885.html. ) However, I have certainly seen some of the "forbidden" words on message boards; following the publication of the list, others have reported successfully using them in Chinese cyberspace. It is more likely that the list (with entries ranging from "democracy" to "masturbation") only applies to the messaging software (QQ) in which it was found, or that the report was a hoax.

Figure 5: **List of Threads on a Discussion Board on** *everypoet.com*

Poems at the Poetry Free-for-all > Amorphous All-Purpose Anarchy > High Critique

(Moderated by: Donner, garvg, Harry R, HowardM2, Julie, Kim, Scavella)

POST NEW TOPIC
Subscribe to this Forum
Mark this Forum Read

| | Thread | Thread Starter | Replies | Views | Rating | Last Post |
|---|---|---|---|---|---|---|
| | Sticky: On posting to the higher critical forums | Scavella1 | 0 | 3532 | | 01-09-2003 08:18 AM by Scavella1 |
| | Sympathy in Paradise | kekala | 3 | 112 | | 05-25-2004 08:30 AM by kekala |
| | When a Boy Becomes a Man | RainKing1 | 2 | 87 | | 05-25-2004 12:17 AM by StevenDSchroeder |
| | World without Glasses | StevenDSchroeder | 4 | 238 | | 05-24-2004 10:18 PM by StevenDSchroeder |
| | Of Half-castes and Rabbits | Melanie | 5 | 327 | | 05-23-2004 12:37 AM by Melanie |
| | Dining alone | Searcher | 12 | 406 | | 05-21-2004 09:45 PM by Searcher |
| | In Alexandria: A Dialogue (Revised) | Jee Leong | 3 | 199 | | 05-19-2004 09:38 PM by Jee Leong |
| | The Old Man and the Sea | Saluda | 8 | 419 | | 05-15-2004 04:27 PM by Saluda |
| | Haggis Supper | romac | 9 | 522 | | 05-14-2004 04:50 PM by romac |
| | Mordechai Vanunu is Free | Marc Adler | 6 | 343 | | 05-12-2004 07:21 PM by bloodthirstybitch |
| | Talking to Lord Newborough | David Anthony | 14 | 477 | | 05-10-2004 06:51 PM by David Anthony |
| | (Revised from C&C) The Dualist | vox | 6 | 231 | | 05-09-2004 08:41 PM by Kaltica |
| | Of This Lyric | Jee Leong | 7 | 530 | | 05-08-2004 07:05 PM by Jee Leong |

Figure 6: **List of Threads on a Discussion Board on** *www.chinapoet.net*

★中国诗人论坛★ ▶ 【 中国诗人一百单八将 】 → 浏览论坛主题          标记论坛所有内容为已读

当前没有公告                                              回原窗口    查看所有的主题

目前论坛总在线 141 人，本分论坛共有 7 人在线。其中注册用户 1 人，访客 6 人。今日新贴 108 篇 ［显示详细列表］ 刷新

发表文章     发起投票                              本版精华 ▼   本版管理员列表 ▼   服务日志

| 状态 | 主 题（点心箭符为新闻方式阅读） | 作 者 | 回复 | 点击 | 最后更新 | 最后回复人 |
|---|---|---|---|---|---|---|
| | [公告] 说发帖—SOS这里不是巴格达—— ... | 黑山老妖 | 6 | 87 | 2004/05/25 21:45 | 蓝雪 |
| | ❷审鱼——给沈鱼的生日 NEW! | 吴铭越 | 3 | 17 | 2004/05/25 19:51 | 白白的黑色 |
| | 仙—— 写给她 NEW! | 野城 | 3 | 30 | 2004/05/25 12:31 | 静月 |
| | 镜像时代（选五） | 李三林 | 5 | 39 | 2004/05/25 20:31 | 马科 |
| | [原创]整理一下：诗100首 | 芦花 | 5 | 47 | 2004/05/25 11:04 | 李三林 |
| | 守备第三师 | 铁哥 | 2 | 23 | 2004/05/24 11:09 | 李三林 |
| | 卑微者之歌（系列长诗《盛宴》之三） NEW! | 老皮 | 2 | 13 | 2004/05/25 22:29 | 老皮 |
| | 夹缝（外两首） NEW! | 马科 | 3 | 23 | 2004/05/25 22:11 | 沉香木 |
| | [原创]哎，日子 NEW! | 心太软 | 2 | 6 | 2004/05/25 21:35 | 心太软 |
| | [原创]傻孩子，我也没有见过上帝 NEW! | 海之子 | 2 | 10 | 2004/05/25 21:10 | 马科 |
| | 飞飞，菲菲（组诗之三，四，五） NEW! | 东子 | 2 | 6 | 2004/05/25 21:08 | 马科 |
| | [原创]站在岸上看水 NEW! | 向复春 | 2 | 8 | 2004/05/25 21:06 | 马科 |

A typical forum on the PRC site (Figure 6) looks much the same. Apart from some additional symbols (which I am still looking to understand completely), the same information is provided about the various threads. As the word "thread" itself indicates, the poems submitted and the responses by other users are organized in a linear fashion, in chronological order. In other words, the threads themselves are not hypertexts. Nevertheless, the possibility of direct interaction between poet and reader/critic is unusual when compared to print culture. This is discussed in more detail below.

*Symbolic Production*

The main attraction for poets of publishing their poems on a website like this, rather than in a smaller writers' discussion group or on their own personal website, is the opportunity to expose their work to, obtain feedback from and get in touch with a community of poetically minded individuals. Since "being published" is the easiest thing in the world on the internet, at least part of the attraction of these websites has to be the idea of belonging to a community and obtaining some sort of recognition. Interestingly, though, a poll asking members to indicate their main motivation for writing poetry, carried out by the US site (Figure 7), shows that "emotional catharsis" was considered by a majority to be their main drive. It should be noted, though, that the answers "to get published" or

Figure 7: **"Why do you write poetry?"** (from *everypoet.com*)

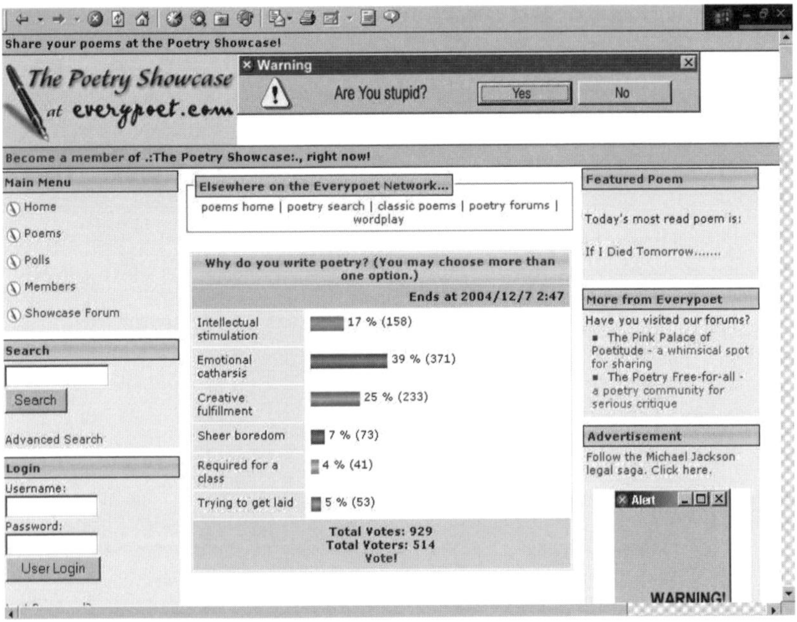

"to belong to a community" were not given as possible options to respondents.

Unlike most print culture communities, symbolic production in these online communities is not carried out by specialized critics but by other authors (that is, members who themselves are contributing poetry to the site), presumably because it is difficult to find specialist critics willing (or able) to take on the task. Moreover, it is normal for authors to respond directly to comments on their work, which is a new function not available in print culture. The moderators of both sites (themselves also authors and contributors) play a crucial role in attributing recognition to members' works as they decide which posts or threads are selected for inclusion in regularly published anthologies (the US site[23]) or on a special board for the best of Chinapoet. This special board in turn provides material for the editors of the two web journals (*wangkan*) which Chinapoet strives to publish each month, one for modern poetry and one for classical poetry.[24]

The web journals are edited by a small group of moderators. The contents of the journals represent only a very small part of what is contributed to the site every month. The works (poems and essays about poetry) are presented on nicely designed web pages that do not have any interactive functions, that is, they can only be read and not commented on. The web journals are not unlike printed literary magazines of the kind that appeared in China in the 1920s when new printing technologies (and New Literature) were spreading. Those magazines, too, were low-cost ventures produced by small editorial collectives participating in a literary economy that valued swift and frequent production. Furthermore, the fact that editors select a tiny proportion of work submitted to them for inclusion into a journal is also not dissimilar from the editing process of a print culture journal. The main difference, however, is that in this case all contributions get published on the site first. To have one's work included in the site's web journal is probably the highest possible form of symbolic recognition that a contributor to Chinapoet can obtain within the site itself. Other literary websites in China have web journals as well and some of them are important mouthpieces for groups that have little access to, or interest in, official print culture. On the other hand, the format of the web journals is so devoid of interactive characteristics that they can also be seen as possible stepping stones into print culture. They could simply be (and presumably sometimes are) printed off and enter the offline literary world. Unlike the world of hypertext fiction discussed by Howard Becker, the world of online Chinese poetry on the whole displays

23. Information based on my April 2004 visit to the US site. During a visit in December 2004, I failed to detect references to such anthologies. During that visit the US site did have special boards in which some of its best contributions were preserved. Members were not allowed to add work to those boards, but were allowed to submit comments as usual.

24. Recent issues of the site's web journals (starting from the August 2004 issue) are accessible through links on the page listing the discussion forums: http://www.chinapoet.net/cgi-bin/leobbs.cgi. I have been unable to find an index page of all issues published so far. It is possible that publication did not start until August 2004.

no intention to break away from print culture paradigms, making the boundaries between the two much more fluid.

The web journal phenomenon is worthy of further separate investigation. A useful question to ask would be whether or not the editors' selection of works for inclusion in the web journals is influenced by the valuation of those same works by contributors to the discussion forums. It is likely that a certain amount of recognition derives from the statistics indicating how often a poem has been read and commented on. I noticed that, as I was browsing the forums, I was generally inclined to click on threads with high statistics, assuming that they would be more interesting or controversial than others. Naturally these numbers can be manipulated by the author, if he or she simply keeps going back to the thread to add new posts. The US site has a rule against such behaviour and moderators are authorized to delete any posts from authors other than those directly responding to critical suggestions from other posters. Moreover, it also asks of each member not to post more than one poem per forum per day, and to post three responses to other people's work for each original poem posted. Clearly, the US site values the "mutual aid" aspect of the site and is wary of becoming merely a showcase of aspiring poets' work or (the other extreme) a glorified chat room. No such rules can be found on the PRC site,[25] which does, however, as mentioned above, have strict rules for the content of posts, based on government censorship regulations.

*Censorship*

Figure 8 shows the rules for submission to Chinapoet (as downloaded in April 2004). There are two main parts. One part lists all the content that is not allowed on the site, including "writings violating the PRC constitution, the policy of reform and opening up and the four cardinal principles," "writings attacking the PRC government, the Chinese Communist Party and its leaders," "writings propagating violence, superstition and licentiousness," "writings exposing state secrets" and (lastly) "all other content forbidden by law." The second main part lists all types of screen names that members are not allowed to use, including "names, stage names and pseudonyms of Party and government leaders or other celebrities" and "names of state institutions and other institutions." Most importantly, however, and mentioned three times in bright red font, the site is closed to any and all content alluding to the outlawed *falun gong* movement. The last line states unequivocally: "This site does not welcome *falun gong*. If we see one we delete one" (*jian yi shan yi*).

This is not just paying lip service to government campaigns. When doing research on another paper on web literature three years ago, I found that *falun gong* members and sympathizers were indeed using freely accessible bulletin boards to spread information about their movement

---

25. During my last visit to the PRC site, in March 2005, a notice had appeared informing users that no more than three posts per member per day would be allowed. There was however no encouragement for users to post more responses to other poems.

Figure 8: **Rules for Contributors (from** *www.chinapoet.net*)

and to denounce government oppression. Failure to remove such contributions in time might lead to a website being closed down. The alternative to outspoken warnings like the one cited above would be to renounce the open character of the forums and screen every contribution before publication, a step which Chinapoet obviously is not willing or able to take, since it would place a much heavier burden on forum moderators. As shown above, there is now a tendency among Chinese ISPs and forum hosts to add membership registration to its strategies of keeping out unwanted content and avoiding legal responsibility.[26]

## Cultural Differences

A comparison of the content of some of the threads on the two sites reveals some more cultural differences. At the moment I can only characterize these as differences between the cultures of the actual sites, although the Chinese site confirms ideas I have about the cultural specificity of modern Chinese literature and criticism as a whole. Empirical support for those ideas awaits, however, a much more comprehensive reading of these and other websites.

26. As I was making revisions for the final version of this article (in March 2005), there was an uproar among China's "netizens" about the restrictions imposed on popular discussion forums at Qinghua, Fudan and Nanjing Universities. In this case, the restrictions (suspending off-campus access and making full registration of members compulsory) appeared to have been imposed directly by the authorities, rather than being the result of self-regulation.

Figure 9: **Comments on a Poem (from *everypoet.com*)**

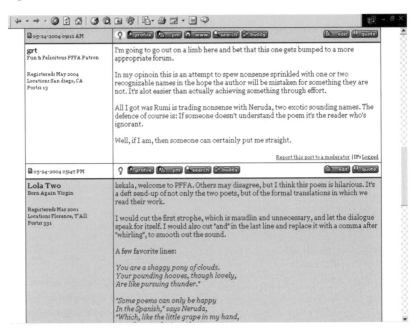

Substantial differences are noticeable in the area of symbolic production. Figure 9 shows a part of a typical thread on the US site. The
discussion focuses on whether or not the poem is "good enough" to be
included in this particular forum, which is meant for "more than merely
moderately experienced poets" (Figure 10). Responses to poems are very
specific as to which words in which lines might be changed or omitted.
In general, the US site strongly propounds the notion of poetry as a craft
or skill which requires considerable training and investment of time and
which needs to be subjected to harsh criticism in order to be able to
improve. In fact, the US forums are partly subdivided on the basis of the
harshness of criticism allowed to be submitted to threads, with the most
fiercely critical forum presented as the one to which only the best
poets/critics should contribute.

On the PRC site, the issue of skill and discussions about the right word
in the right place are much less prominent, although they do appear in the
forum dedicated to those writing in the classical style, which of course
has very strict prosodic rules. The feedback on poems in the modern
poetry forums is much less normative, and often consists of one-liners of
the type "I like this poem" or "I don't like this poem," without going into
much detail. Questions of content and personality are also often debated.
A typical example is shown in Figure 11, which shows two responses to
a simple poem (not shown) expressing love for a woman. The first
response basically dismisses the poem as romantic rubbish. The second
response points out that this would be the case if the poet had been a man,

## Figure 10: **Posting Guidelines, "High Critique" Forum,** *everypoet.com*

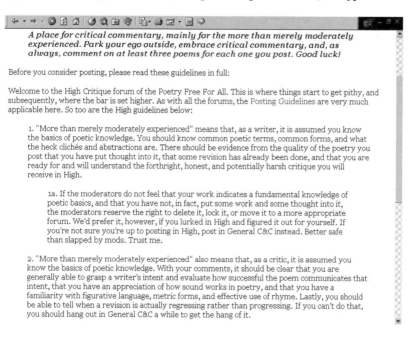

*A place for critical commentary, mainly for the more than merely moderately experienced. Park your ego outside, embrace critical commentary, and, as always, comment on at least three poems for each one you post. Good luck!*

Before you consider posting, please read these guidelines in full:

Welcome to the High Critique forum of the Poetry Free For All. This is where things start to get pithy, and subsequently, where the bar is set higher. As with all the forums, the Posting Guidelines are very much applicable here. So too are the High guidelines below:

1. "More than merely moderately experienced" means that, as a writer, it is assumed you know the basics of poetic knowledge. You should know common poetic terms, common forms, and what the heck clichés and abstractions are. There should be evidence from the quality of the poetry you post that you have put thought into it, that some revision has already been done, and that you are ready for and will understand the forthright, honest, and potentially harsh critique you will receive in High.

1a. If the moderators do not feel that your work indicates a fundamental knowledge of poetic basics, and that you have not, in fact, put some work and some thought into it, the moderators reserve the right to delete it, lock it, or move it to a more appropriate forum. We'd prefer it, however, if you lurked in High and figured it out for yourself. If you're not sure you're up to posting in High, post in General C&C instead. Better safe than slapped by mods. Trust me.

2. "More than merely moderately experienced" also means that, as a critic, it is assumed you know the basics of poetic knowledge. With your comments, it should be clear that you are generally able to grasp a writer's intent and evaluate how successful the poem communicates that intent, that you have an appreciation of how sound works in poetry, and that you have a familiarity with figurative language, metric forms, and effective use of rhyme. Lastly, you should be able to tell when a revision is actually regressing rather than progressing. If you can't do that, you should hang out in General C&C a while to get the hang of it.

## Figure 11: **Comments on a Poem (from** *www.chinapoet.net*)

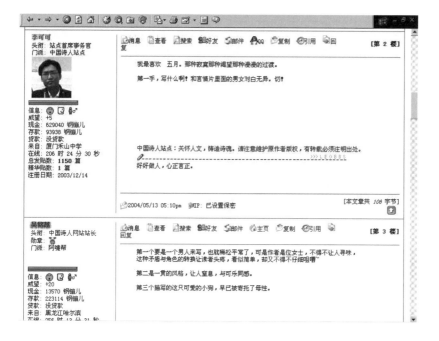

Figure 12: **List of Threads, Poetry Translation Forum,** ***www.chinapoet.net***

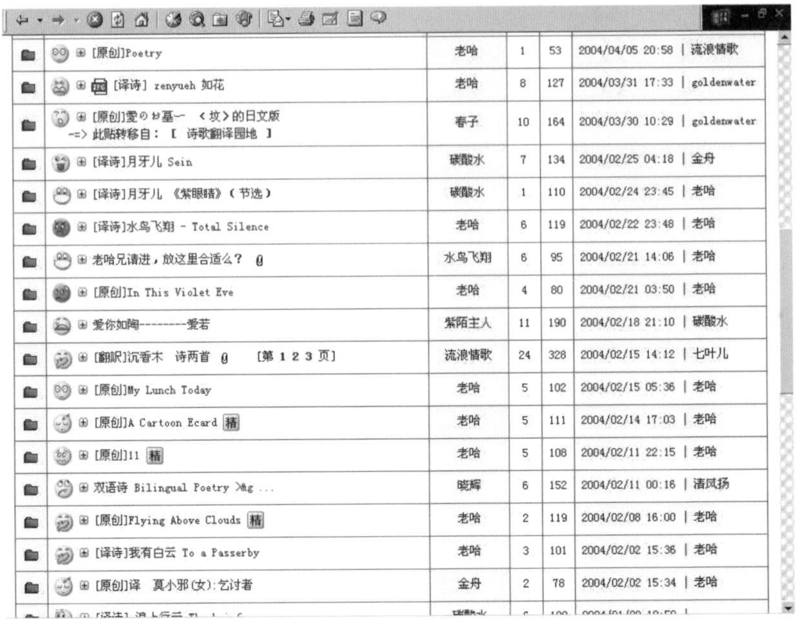

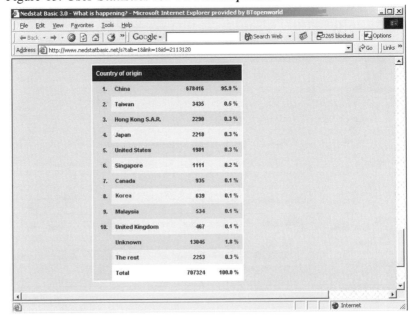

Figure 13: **User Statistics for *www.chinapoet.net***

| Country of origin | | | |
|---|---|---|---|
| 1. | China | 678416 | 95.9 % |
| 2. | Taiwan | 3435 | 0.5 % |
| 3. | Hong Kong S.A.R. | 2290 | 0.3 % |
| 4. | Japan | 2218 | 0.3 % |
| 5. | United States | 1981 | 0.3 % |
| 6. | Singapore | 1111 | 0.2 % |
| 7. | Canada | 935 | 0.1 % |
| 8. | Korea | 639 | 0.1 % |
| 9. | Malaysia | 534 | 0.1 % |
| 10. | United Kingdom | 467 | 0.1 % |
| | Unknown | 13045 | 1.8 % |
| | The rest | 2253 | 0.3 % |
| | Total | 707324 | 100.0 % |

but since the poet is a woman writing about love for a woman, it is actually much more interesting and gives the reader "food for thought" because the poet creates a "contradiction" and a "role reversal."

Unlike the US site, the PRC site has a lively forum devoted to translation. Although the forum does not limit the languages used, all translations I have seen were either from or into English (Figure 12). The forum has separate "sub-forums" for translation of famous English poems into Chinese and translation of members' poems into English. These forums naturally attract much normative discussion. The inclusion of translation and the focus on English places the Chinese site firmly in the margins of the system of world literature, whereas the total neglect of translation places the American site squarely in the centre. This mirrors the situation in print culture. The fact that, according to the site statistics, 95.9 per cent of its visitors are from China, and another 1 per cent or so from Sinophone areas such as Taiwan, Hong Kong and Singapore, shows the nature of the predicament.

## Conclusion

Online literature communities are, on the one hand, part of the print culture community, as are writing clubs, school newspapers or other communities in which aspiring writers practise, discuss and publish in the hope of finding recognition and perhaps one day becoming an acclaimed print culture author. At the same time, however, these communities foster direct interaction across vast geographical distances, coupled with publication for a potentially huge audience, a combination that print culture practices would find difficult to accommodate. The use of similar software and protocols in different cultural settings ensures that the practices of online communities all over the world have certain elements in common, such as their tendency to rely in part on statistics for recognition and the blurring of boundaries between specialized roles such as author, critic and reader, which are so crucial to the practices of print culture. Moreover, the nature of the online medium seems to favour, at least for the moment, the shorter genres such as poetry or the serialized story (or ongoing role-play), creating a more central position for genres that tend to be marginal in print culture. At the same time, cultural differences are observable and demonstrate that cyberspace is not the locus of any kind of transnational cultural expression.

In that respect, a final comment must be made about the relative status of both the US website and the PRC website in the context of internet studies and literary studies. In a provocative newspaper article entitled "Internet studies: what went wrong?" David Gauntlett uses the publication of the first edition of his edited collection *Web.Studies*[27] to criticize

27. David Gauntlett (ed.), *Web.Studies: Rewiring Media Studies for the Digital Age* (London: Arnold, 2000). (A revised edition, edited by Gauntlett and Ross Horsley, came out with the same publisher in 2004.)

other scholars of the internet for not keeping up with recent developments and for not taking their research beyond the level of description. Gauntlett writes:

The rise of the internet in the past three or four years means that its users know far more about sex, politics, hobbies, and shopping than ever before.

You would expect that internet scholars would be lapping all this up. It's a transformation of modern society, affecting many spheres of everyday life as well as broader social processes....

But no. Publishers are still churning out books called "Virtual something" and "Cyber something else." They might as well be called "Wow! Virtual communities!" and "Holy cow! In cyberspace, no-one knows who you are!" Even the journals are still publishing those articles which people were pulling out of the drawer in 1996. Has no-one changed the record? The internet might change politics. It might not. It's a global phenomenon. It's not really a global phenomenon. Something funny happened to a bunch of people in a chatroom. Give me a break.[28]

As someone interested in the relationship between internet and literature, I disagree with Gauntlett's statement. I found that what little Western scholarship on web literature exists is almost exclusively focused on the most innovative forms, especially hypertext and hypermedia.[29] It is very much up-to-date with current developments, but the majority of literary production by internet users is not considered. Some scholars even present their exclusive focus on hypertext as methodological correctness, as in the following excerpt from an article discussing questions of method in analysing internet texts:

Based on the earlier discussion of the characteristics of hypertext, it is clear that the greater the opportunities of surfing provided by the text, the greater the likelihood that readers are empowered to "write" their own texts. WWW sites that remain "close-ended" do not provide empowerment to readers and could thus be far less suitable as the starting point of the analysis. ... These texts are limited in scope and fail to use the full potential of the WWW.[30]

At the same time, I found scholarship on the Chinese internet overly concerned with the issue of censorship, while rarely addressing the enthusiasm and creativity of the majority of Chinese internet users, which is so readily observable to anyone who visits Chinese websites. There is, in other words, a tendency among Western scholars to focus on the potential of the internet to bring about a transformation of society (or literature, or culture, or politics). And there is a simultaneous tendency among Western scholars of the Chinese internet to foreground censorship issues, as if to demonstrate that lack of personal freedom will always

28. David Gauntlett, "Internet studies: what went wrong?" originally published in *Times Higher Education Supplement* in 2000, URL: http://www.newmediastudies.com/thes.htm.

29. For instance, the authoritative website for humanities research "Voice of the shuttle" (URL: http://vos.ucsb.edu/) does not have an entry for cyber literature, neither under "cyber culture" nor under "literary theory." Both categories do have entries about hypertext.

30. Ananda Mitra and Elisia Cohen, "Analyzing the Web: directions and challenges," in Steve Jones (ed.), *Doing Internet Research: Critical Issues and Methods for Examining the Net* (Thousand Oaks, London, New Delhi: Sage Publications, 1999), p. 193.

cause Chinese society (or literature, or culture, or politics) to lag behind the West when it comes to being transformative, innovative or empowering.

This article has shown that a different perspective is possible. Sure enough, there is no indication that Chinese cyber writing will radically transform Chinese society or even Chinese literature. Partly this is because the state has developed effective mechanisms to ensure that it cannot do so; partly it is because many of its practitioners lack interest in being either transformative or avant-garde or both; partly it is because literature fulfils a different function in Chinese culture. Yet although Chinese web literature is only mildly innovative, it has been the topic of intensive debate among Chinese critics and scholars of literature and it has literally made a name for itself among critics, publishers and book sellers in the larger print culture world, something that Western web literature has conspicuously failed to do.

# Urban Consumer Culture*

## Deborah Davis

ABSTRACT  Over the past decade, urban residents have experienced a consumer revolution at multiple levels. In terms of material standard of living, sustained economic growth has dramatically increased spending on discretionary consumer purchases and urbanites have enthusiastically consumed globally branded foodstuffs, pop-music videos and fashion. At the same time, however, income distribution has become increasingly unequal. Some scholars therefore emphasize the negative exclusionary and exploitative parameters of the new consumer culture seeing nothing more than a ruse of capitalism or marker of all that is negative about post-socialist city life. Building on nearly a decade of fieldwork in Shanghai, this article disputes such a linear interpretation of subordination and exclusion in favour of a more polyvalent and stratified reading that emphasizes individual narratives unfolding against memories of an impoverished personal past, and a consumer culture that simultaneously incorporates contradictory experiences of emancipation and disempowerment.

Over the decade of the 1990s urban residents experienced a consumer revolution at multiple levels. Macro economic growth doubled real incomes and almost all households substantially increased discretionary consumer purchases. Former luxuries such as refrigerators, colour televisions and washing machines became household necessities and by the turn of the century advertising for mobile phones, overseas holidays and family sedans generated substantial revenues for the state owned media.[1] Committed to full membership in the WTO, the political elite enthusiastically advanced a neo-liberal development model that identified personal consumption as a primary driver of economic growth and individual consumer choice as a spur to further efficiency and innovation.[2] Global retailers such as Carrefour, Wal-mart and Ikea invested heavily in China as the critical new consumer market of the 21st century, and by 2004 city residents had become avid – and knowledgeable – consumers of transnationally branded foodstuffs, pop-music videos and fashion.

* I thank the Council on East Asian Studies of Yale University for research grants in support of fieldwork in 1997, 2002 and 2004, and colleagues at the Shanghai Academy of Social Sciences for repeatedly extending themselves personally on my behalf.

1. In 1986, 65% of urban households owned a washing machine, 29% colour televisions and 18% refrigerators; by 1998 the percentages were 90.5%, 105% and 76%. State Statistical Bureau, *A Survey of Income and Expenditures of Urban Households in China, 1986* (Honolulu: East West Center, 1987), pp. 242–44, *Zhongguo tongji nianjian* 1999 (*China Statistical Yearbook 1999*) (Beijing: Zhongguo tongji chubanshe, 1999), p. 324.

2. "Zhengfu gongzuo baogao" ("Government work report"), *Renmin ribao* (*People's Daily*), 20 March 2003, p. 1; Li Gangqing, "Jianquan he yuanshan shehuizhuyi shichang," ("Develop and improve the socialist market"), *Renmin ribao* (*People's Daily*), 22 February 2003; Du Haishou, "Genben mudi shi gaishan shenghuo" ("The basic goal is to improve living standards"), *Renmin ribao*, 15 October 2003, p. 6.

At the same time, a newly formalized regulatory regime extended legal rights to individual consumers. In October 1993, the National People's Congress passed China's first Consumer Protection Law.[3] A month earlier, the NPC had passed the Law Against Unfair Trade and a year later China's first Advertising Law.[4] Together these three pieces of legislation established the legal framework within which consumers could seek compensation for shoddy goods, claim their rights to accurate information and organize to defend their interests.[5] Legal scholar Benjamin Liebman has demonstrated how settlements awarded under the provisions of these laws created important precedents for future class action suits.[6] Emblematic was the case where 300 Beijing residents received compensation after documenting in court that the widely promoted Mao anniversary watches that they had purchased did not contain the advertised gold and diamonds.

Article 49 of the Consumer Protection Law guaranteed cash payments worth double the sale price whenever consumers could prove that merchants had sold a fraudulent product or shoddy service. During the late 1990s, consumer activist Wang Hai popularized this principle of "double compensation" and tirelessly publicized his success via television appearances and his own website.[7] Evidence of his success even reached the pages of *Chinese Civil Affairs*, where one article explained why "hero" Wang Hai need not pay income tax on the refunds he got from merchants who had sold him counterfeit products.[8]

Since 1994, the Consumer Protection Law has also gained prominence in official publications directed at professionals. In 2003, the weekly magazine of the China Law Society identified it as one of the ten most influential laws enacted since the beginning of market reform.[9] To

3. For English translations see http://www.qis.net/chinalaw/prclaw26.htm, accessed in May 2004.

4. Copies of these laws can be found on the website of the China Consumers' Association, www.cca.org.cn, and www.lawbase.com.cn, accessed in May 2004.

5. Most relevant were the articles in the Consumer Protection Law that guaranteed consumers the right to correct information (articles 8 and 13), the right to choose and exercise supervision over commodities and services (articles 9 and 15), the right to fair trade including fair measurement (article 10), the right to receive compensation for damages (articles 11, 35, 36, 37, 38, 39 and 49), and the right to form social groups to safeguard their legitimate rights and interests (articles 12, 31 and 32). In addition, the law required the state to listen to consumer opinions when formulating laws (article 26) and the courts to simplify the procedures for consumers to file a lawsuit (article 30).

6. Benjamin Liebman, "Class action litigation in China," *Harvard Law Review*, Vol. 111 (1998), pp. 1523–41.

7. See http://www.wanghai.com/business, accessed in May 2004.

8. Chengning Ren, "Daxia yingxiong gaibugai nashui? ("For destroying fakes must a hero pay taxes"), *Zhongguo minzheng* (*Chinese Civil Affairs*), September 1996, p. 6.

9. The other nine were: the new Economic Contract Law (1981), the Constitution of 1982, the new Code of Civil Procedure (1986), a draft Law for Village Elections (1987), Administrative Litigation Law (1989), the first Company Law (1993), the first Compensation Law (1994), the new Criminal Code (1997) and the 2000 Legislative Procedure Law. "Gaizao Zhongguo de shinian dajing dianli" ("Major laws during the ten years of Chinese reforms") *Minzu yu fazhi shibao* (*Democracy and Law Times*), 12 March 2002, pp. 12–15.

illustrate the law's importance the Law Society cited surveys that showed an increase of more than 50 per cent in the number of consumers filing for damages in the first five years after passage of the law and a rising number of claims for losses under 2,000 *yuan*.[10]

However, amidst these positive trends for consumers in general, there was more sobering news on skewed distribution of income and purchasing power. Between 1985 and 1995, income inequality in China increased more quickly than in any country tracked by the World Bank since the end of the Second World War.[11] After 1995, disparities grew still larger. For example, during six years (1998–2003) when the official consumer price index for urban China barely changed, the income disparity between the richest 10 per cent and poorest 10 per cent of urban residents effectively doubled. Moreover, it was not only the very poor who fell behind. The relative share of those in the middle of the income distribution also steadily declined, dropping from 46.7 per cent in 1998 to less than a third by 2003 (see Tables 1 and 2).

In the case of Shanghai, the city that provides the empirical foundation for this article, income inequality became particularly marked as privatization intensified after 1998. By 2003 incomes in Shanghai were more skewed than in urban China as a whole, and the departures from the distributions of the recent past were stark. In 1998 the gap between the middle 20 per cent and the top 10 per cent was 8,320 *yuan*; by 2003 it exceeded 25,000 *yuan* (compare Figures 1 and 2). Clearly, analysis and interpretation of the character and trajectory of urban consumer culture must confront these income inequalities and consider if urban consumer culture is fundamentally exclusionary.

Table 1: **Changing Income Shares among Urban Households, 1998–2003 (%)**

| Income ratios | 1998 | 1999 | 2000 | 2001 | 2002 | 2003 |
|---|---|---|---|---|---|---|
| Bottom 10%: top 10% | 22.7 | 21.7 | 20.0 | 18.6 | 17.3 | 11.7 |
| Middle 20%: top 10% | 46.7 | 45.6 | 44.2 | 42.0 | 41.7 | 33.0 |

*Source:*
    *Zhongguo tongji zhaiyao 2004* (*Chinese Statistical Abstract 2004*) (Beijing: Zhongguo tongji chubanshe, 2004), p. 104.

10. "Major laws during the ten years of Chinese reforms," p. 14.
11. The literature on increased inequality is enormous. I therefore cite only a few sources from among those published since 1998: Eugene Chang, "Growing income inequality," *China Economic Review*, Vol. 11 (2002), pp. 335–340; Azizur Khan and Carl Riskin, *Inequality and Poverty in China in the Age of Globalization* (Oxford: Oxford University Press, 2001); Xueguang Zhou, "Economic transformation and income inequality in urban China," *The American Journal of Sociology*, Vol. 105 (2000), pp. 1135–74.

Table 2: **Annual Per Capita Urban Income and Expenditure, 1998–2003 (in *yuan*)**

|  | *1998* | *1999* | *2000* | *2001* | *2002* | *2003* |
|---|---|---|---|---|---|---|
| *Average incomes* |  |  |  |  |  |  |
| Bottom 10% | 2,505 | 2,646 | 2,678 | 2,834 | 3,168 | 2,762 |
| Next 10% | 3,329 | 3,518 | 3,658 | 3,888 | 4,486 | 4,209 |
| Next 20% | 4,134 | 4,391 | 4,651 | 4,983 | 5,826 | 5,705 |
| Middle 20% | 5,148 | 5,543 | 5,930 | 6,406 | 7,638 | 7,753 |
| Next 20% | 6,404 | 6,942 | 7,525 | 8,213 | 9,874 | 10,463 |
| Next 10% | 7,918 | 8,674 | 9,484 | 10,441 | 12,604 | 14,076 |
| Top 10% | 11,021 | 12,147 | 13,390 | 15,220 | 18,288 | 23,484 |
| *Annual change in consumer price index* |  |  |  |  |  |  |
|  | 99.4 | 98.7 | 100.8 | 100.7 | 99.0 | 100.9 |
| *Average expenditures* |  |  |  |  |  |  |
| Bottom 10% | 2,397 | 2,523 | 2,540 | 2,691 | 2,987 | 2,562 |
| Next 10% | 2,979 | 3,137 | 3,274 | 3,452 | 3,913 | 3,549 |
| Next 20% | 3,503 | 3,694 | 3,947 | 4,197 | 4,696 | 4,557 |
| Middle 20% | 4,179 | 4,432 | 4,794 | 5,131 | 5,846 | 5,848 |
| Next 20% | 4,980 | 5,347 | 5,894 | 6,241 | 7,155 | 7,547 |
| Next 10% | 6,003 | 6,443 | 7,102 | 7,495 | 8,701 | 9,627 |
| Top 10% | 7,594 | 8,262 | 9,250 | 9,834 | 11,224 | 14,515 |

*Source:*
  *Chinese Statistical Abstract 2004*, pp. 88 and 104.

Figure 1: **2003 Average Per Capita Incomes in All of Urban China and in Shanghai**

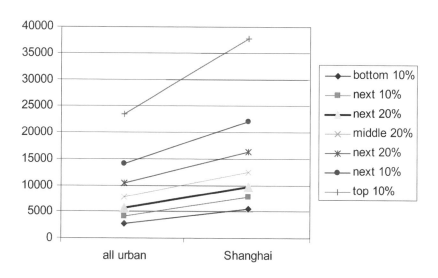

Figure 2: **Change in Shanghai Per Capita Income between 1998 and 2003**

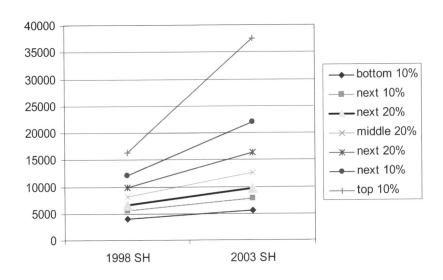

*Source:*
  *Shanghai tongji nianjian 2004 (Shanghai Statistical Yearbook 2004)* (Shanghai: Zhongguo tongji chubanshe, 2004), pp. 104 and 106; *Chinese Statistical Abstract 2004*, p. 104.

*On the Possible Illusions and Exclusions of Consumer Culture*

In her superb essay on the "phantom" of a consumer revolution Pun Ngai places the pain and injustice of exclusion at the heart of her analysis and interrogates consumer fantasy as the newest "ruse of capital."[12] Pun not only documents how the new consumer abundance lies beyond the reach of the young migrant factory workers whose labour produces the consumer cornucopia, she also argues that consumerism itself is a particularly effective form of capitalist exploitation that erodes class consciousness and offers no enchantment, emancipation or empowerment. Kevin Latham, drawing on his 1997 fieldwork in Guangzhou, also found consumption practices to function primarily as a "marker and measure of the negative aspects of economic reform."[13] Pun and Latham work within an intellectual tradition rooted in the Frankfurt school where power relations at the workplace or within systems of production are the primary sites of class formation; consumers – particularly as they participate in mass consumption – are victims with little agency. Their work also evokes Jackson Lear's and Daniel Bell's equation of consumption with hedonism and thus stands in direct contrast to more recent

12. Pun Ngai, "Subsumption or consumption?" in *Cultural Anthropology*, Vol. 18, No. 4 (2003), pp. 469–492.
13. Kevin Latham, "Rethinking Chinese consumption," in C.M. Hann (ed.), *Postsocialism* (London: Routledge, 2002), pp. 227–28.

anthropological and sociological analyses that approach consumers and the social practices of consumption as opportunities to identify and understand networks of communication or identity formation.[14] From this latter perspective, material restrictions and politics of the work place shape consumer practices, but consumers retain the possibility for fantasy, resistance and empowerment.

During more than a decade of fieldwork in Shanghai, I, like Pun and Latham, have witnessed the growing income inequalities of the 1990s and in several previous publications I have contrasted the fates of the winners and losers in the new post-socialist economy.[15] Nevertheless, when seeking to understand the character and trajectory of urban consumer culture through the experiences of city residents, I give priority to the speech of the residents themselves and do not assume the predominance of either exploitation and deception or agency and empowerment. In particular, when one approaches consumer culture as a narrative and a form of communication, the task of field research is to remain open to the multi-vocal speech of participants themselves. The structural dynamics and material inequalities of the contemporary post-socialist political economy necessarily frame these narratives, but the consumer culture that individuals create through their personal commentary and social discourse cannot *a priori* be presumed to be illusory or exploitative.

Approached through the processes of narration and dialogue, consumer cultures may be dominated by exclusion, seduction or exploitation, but they are more likely to be as polyvalent and multi-levelled as the social positions and the temporal framing of the participants.[16] Moreover, because my fieldwork focused on domestic consumption, and in particular on consuming in and for the home, my respondents emphasized the personal and private parameters of consumer culture that the publicly oriented, productionist-focused theories of the Frankfurt tradition routinely ignore or marginalize. Moreover, because furnishing urban residential space served as a primary focus of consumer desire and spending among all income groups in Shanghai during the past decade, conversations about spending for the home reveal values that are pervasive in contemporary consumer culture. In discussing their purchases for their homes my respondents recognized the injustice and pain of increasing

14. Mary Douglas, *Thought Styles* ( London: Sage, 1996); Daniel Miller, *Acknowledging Consumption* (London: Routledge, 1995), Don Slater, *Consumer Culture and Modernity* (Cambridge: Polity Press, 1997).

15. Deborah Davis, "From welfare benefit to capitalized asset," in Ray Forrest and James Lee (eds.), *Chinese Urban Housing Reform* (London: Routledge, 2003), pp. 183–196; "Inequality and insecurity among elderly in contemporary China," in Susanne Formanek and Sepp Linhart (eds.), *Asian Concepts and Experiences* (Vienna: Austrian Academy of Sciences, 1997), pp. 133–154; "Inequalities and stratification in the nineties," in *China Review 1995* (Hong Kong: Chinese University Press, 1995), pp. 1–25.

16. Erika Rappaport, *Shopping for Pleasure* (Princeton: Princeton University Press, 2000), p. 12; Maris Gillette, *Between Mecca and Beijing* (Stanford: Stanford University Press, 2000); James Watson, *Golden Arches East* (Stanford: Stanford University Press, 1997); Yunxiang Yan, "The politics of Chinese society," in Tyrene White (ed.), *China Briefing 2000* (Armonk: M.E. Sharpe, 2000), pp. 159–193.

income inequalities but they integrated this knowledge within personal memories of past political repression and material deprivation of the 1960s and 1970s. As time passes, this particular historical referent will lose its salience, the key temporal comparisons may shift to the hardships and inequalities of the post-socialist economy, and consumer culture may become more generally experienced as a ruse. However, at the turn of the 21st century, earlier experiences with subordination, dependence and politicized conformity during the Mao years decisively defined the experience of consumption for those who had come of age during the anti-consumerist culture of the 1960s and 1970s and within this temporal location they spoke of a consumer culture with visible degrees of freedom.

*Making a House a Home*

During the first 30 years in which the Chinese Communist Party monopolized political power, the national leadership defined modernity in terms of increased industrial output and the triumph of collective ownership. Within this project of economic modernization, party-state rhetoric lionized the industrial proletariat and celebrated the state's ability to meet the material needs of the masses. For urban residents, the Maoist vision of a "new" China (*xin Zhongguo*) de-commercialized city life and concentrated consumption within locations of production.[17] Ration tickets issued through places of employment controlled the sale of basic food items as well as such varied purchases as cotton cloth, coal, furniture, light bulbs and bicycles.[18] Housing became a welfare benefit that state agents distributed to the most deserving "supplicants" in a public housing queue.[19] Urban families even turned to enterprise-operated theatres or recreation centres for films and holiday celebrations.[20]

After Deng and Jiang decisively broke with this Maoist vision of de-commodified modernity, urban living standards radically improved, and consumers became key players in the official discourse of economic

---

17. Piper Gaubatz, "China's urban transformation," *Urban Studies*, Vol. 36, No. 9 (1999), pp. 1495–1521; Deborah Davis, "Social transformations of metropolitan China since 1949," in Joseph Guggler (ed.), *Cities in the Developing World* (Oxford: Oxford University Press, 1997), pp. 248–258.

18. Martin Whyte and William Parish, *Urban Life in Contemporary China* (Chicago: University of Chicago Press, 1984), pp. 85–90

19. Deborah Davis, "Urban household supplicants to the state," in Deborah Davis and Stevan Harrell (eds.), *Chinese Families in the Post-Mao Era* (Berkeley: University of California Press, 1993), pp. 50–76.

20. Gaubatz, "China's urban transformation"; Hanlong Lu, "To be relatively comfortable in an egalitarian society," in Deborah Davis (ed.), *The Consumer Revolution in Urban China* (Berkeley: University of California Press, 2000), pp. 124–144; Xiaobo Lu and Elizabeth Perry, *Danwei: The Changing Chinese Workplace* (Armonk: M.E. Sharpe, 1997); Shaoguang Wang, "The politics of private time," in Deborah Davis, Richard Kraus, Barry Naughton and Elizabeth Perry (eds.), *Urban Spaces* (Cambridge: Cambridge University Press, 1995), pp. 149–172; Whyte and Parish, *Urban Life in Contemporary China*.

development.[21] Of particular consequence for understanding domestically focused consumer culture was the unprecedented upgrading of the quality of urban homes and the privatization of nearly all residential property by 2002.[22] For permanent residents of Shanghai, extensive privatization created millions of first-time home owners, for whom decorating and furnishing a home became a preoccupation completely without precedent in the previous 40 years of city living. New condominiums were sold as concrete shells furnished only with water and sewage pipes, so that new residents needed to purchase and install every item to make a liveable space. Moving from one or two rooms with a shared toilet and kitchen to a self-contained two-bedroom apartment – the usual transition for first-time home owners – required extensive planning and comparative shopping. A home renovation industry boomed overnight, home decoration magazines (and later websites) multiplied, and international retailers rushed to gain market share. In Shanghai, even among those who had not been able to purchase a condominium, homes became a focus of consumer spending and desire. Furnishing a flat and purchasing items to improve comfort, value or distinction gained a salience unimaginable in the previous decades of *danwei* (work unit) controlled housing.

## Respondents and Field Sites

Two different groups of respondents provide the narrative material for my analysis of urban consumer culture. The first group included 41 men and women whom I first interviewed in 1987, the second group 46 men and women whom I met in 2004 through introductions by my professional colleagues. Those from the first group were "survivors" of a random sample of 100 households drawn from a residential community near one of the oldest worker settlements in Shanghai. Because the original project had been a study of parent-child job mobility after 1949, I had restricted my sample to families that included an ever-married woman born after 1925 who would have been a young adult during the 1950s and whose children would have entered the labour force after 1966. Using these gender and birth date criteria I subsequently collected the occupational histories of more than 500 family members who represented

---

21. Deborah Davis, "Introduction," *Consumer Revolution in Urban China* (Berkeley: University of California Press, 2000). The official embrace of consumers as positive agents of change can be summarized by the dramatic increase in the number of articles published in *Renmin ribao* that use the word consumer, and the very limited number of times the words consumer and waste are ever linked in one article. Not only does the basic frequency increase over time, but between 1995 and 2003 consumers became even more visible than either workers or university students The *Renmin ribao* archive that is accessible through http://willard.library reported 681 articles that included at least one reference to consumers, 504 to university students, 1,231 to workers in 1995. For 2003, the comparable frequencies were 1,126 to consumers, 1,058 to workers and 814 to students. Accessed in May 2004.

22. In 1980 less than 15% of urban residential property was owner-occupied; by 2002 80% of non-migrant residents had become home owners and almost 100% of migrants rented from private landlords. Xinhua News Agency, 9 August 2002.

the established working class and lower rungs of middle management.[23] I returned to re-interview members of these households in 1990, 1992 and 1995, and between 1997 and 2002 I returned four times to meet a subset of ten households. In spring 2004, I re-interviewed three-quarters of the households still living in the neighbourhood.[24]

In contrast to those in the neighbourhood-based sample, respondents in the second group were younger and primarily worked as municipal employees, entrepreneurs or professionals. Nine were in their late 20s and early 30s, the rest were born between 1945 and 1964. As in any snowball sample, the strength of the data is the richness and relative spontaneity of the conversation. In this analysis, I draw primarily on conversations with a subset of 37 men and women from both samples who were in their 40s and 50s. Many of these conversations took place in their homes, and a third stretched over several visits in multiple venues. As a result, the respondents often set the agenda and initiated the discussion.

All interviews, however, turned around conversations about the respondent's current living situation. Initially I had planned to orient the interviews around ownership of 20 household appliances or furnishings where I had survey results from earlier years and had also gathered comparative price estimates.[25] However, because most respondents owned 15 or more of the basic consumer durables, I found that open-ended questions about expectations for future purchases or renovations produced more sustained conversation. Before turning to the substance of these personal narratives, I briefly review the role of the decorating magazines that became extremely popular in the second half of the 1990s and provide examples of the vocabulary and grammar of urban consumer culture.

*Visualizing a Home*

From the mid-1950s until the late 1980s, municipal and enterprise housing offices distributed urban housing stock according to the size of the family and the seniority and political standing of the household head; price or ability to pay played no role.[26] In crowded Shanghai where little new residential space had been built after 1962, families rarely occupied

---

23. Only 5% of the fathers and 15% of the mothers worked outside the state sector, 24% of fathers and 66% of mothers were manual workers, 14% of fathers and 13% of mothers did routine white-collar jobs, 22% of fathers and 14% of mothers did non-routine white-collar work, 29% of fathers and 2% of mothers were middle management, and 10% of fathers and 4% of mothers were professionals.

24. Materials from occupational and housing histories collected from these families have been previously analysed in Deborah Davis, "Social class transformation," *Modern China* (July 2002), pp. 251–275; "Self-employment in Shanghai," *The China Quarterly*, No. 157 (March 1999), pp. 22–43; "Job mobility in post-Mao cities," *The China Quarterly*, No. 132 (December 1992), pp. 1062–85, "Urban households: supplicants to a socialist state."

25. The 20 items were: sofa, desk, radio, colour television, electric rice cooker, microwave oven, exhaust hood for stove, DVD/VCD, desk computer, laptop computer, fixed line phone, mobile phone, carpet, piano, hot-water heater, electric fan, air conditioner, exercise equipment, refrigerator and washing machine.

26. Davis, "Urban household: supplicants to the state," pp. 50–76.

more than two rooms; communal showers or bathrooms were the norm and kitchens were set up on the pavement, in hallways, or in alcoves built on porches and roofs. Even in the new residential area built in 1979 where my first group of respondents lived, families cooked around a window into the public corridor. If two families shared the apartment, each household piled up pans and dried foodstuffs in a locked cupboard around the single burner attached to their canister of bottled gas. In 1987, when most families had purchased a refrigerator, it stood in the inner room that served as bedroom and living room. Floors and walls were bare cement and thin curtains or bamboo shades offered a veneer of privacy.

The explosive growth of commercial housing after 1992 introduced entirely different possibilities for urban residents. New estates consisted entirely of self-contained flats, with internal walls and doors subdividing the interior space into several functionally specific enclosed spaces. After 2000, city regulations barring sales of homes with shared entrances or communal bathrooms and kitchens pushed forward further the segmentation and privatization of domestic space. In 1990, only 31.6 per cent of Shanghai households lived in self-contained flats; by the end of 2002, the percentage rose to 87.4.[27]

When I first began to collect renovation guides and decorating magazines, most new homeowners, like the respondents of my community sample, occupied two rooms totalling less than 30 square metres of interior space. Not surprisingly the magazines featured modest investments in window frames, flooring and cabinets that neighbourhood-based contractors or owners themselves could install. Magazines published in 1994 and 1995 routinely provided extensive directions on dimensions and use of each piece of hardware needed to hang a new door, install a sink or lay a wood floor.[28]

However, even as instruction focused on the mundane and immediate, a new language of style and taste as well as personal distinction rhetorically framed the practical instructions on moving walls or installing squat toilets. In one introduction, the editors promised readers who carefully planned each step of their renovation that they would experience feelings of greater openness and refinement.[29] In another, they offered to instruct readers on how to possess a cosy and harmonious family life.[30] These practically oriented magazines published in the mid-1990s also reproduced images from European and North American magazines to illustrate the importance of careful design and placement of furnishings. Thus, as

27. Hanlong Lu (ed.), *Shangahi shehui fazhan lanpi shu* (*Blue Book of Shanghai Social Development*) (Shanghai: Shanghai shekeyuan chubanshe, 2004), p. 65.

28. Li Xuan, *Shinei zhuangshi xinkuan* (*New Sincerity of Interior Decoration*) (Chengdu: Chengdu keji daxue chubanshe, 1995); He Sheng *et al.* (eds), *Jushi zhuangxiu jisu yu shili* (*Techniques and Examples for Home Renovation*) (Beijing: Zhongguowujia chubanshe, 1996); Zhen Tiegang (ed.), *Xiandai jushi de kongjian yu secai* (*Colour and Space in Today's Rooms*) (Tianjin: Tianjin daxue chubanshe, 1995); all these magazines purchased August 1997 in the bookstore of the state-owned Parkson Department Store on Huai Hai Road, Shanghai.

29. Zhen Tiegang, *Colour and Space in Today's Rooms.*

30. Li Xuan, *New Sincerity of Interior Decoration.*

they browsed magazines, Shanghai residents visualized domestic settings that connected them to global consumer practices and furnishings.[31]

By 2004 the elaborate shower fixtures, modular furniture and illuminated cabinets that had only a few years earlier been fantasies of commercial hype had become widely available throughout metropolitan Shanghai. In the age of the internet and global marketing, consumers no longer needed to purchase expensive decorating magazines or even enter a book shop. Instead, merchants distributed complimentary copies of glossy promotional materials funded by Chinese retailers who promised readers all they needed to know to create "a tasteful family and a tasteful life."[32] For the ever-growing number of consumers who surfed the world-wide web, there was hardly a Chinese or foreign product that they could not view and price online.[33] Nevertheless, thousands of city residents still spent weekend afternoons window-shopping and looking for bargains in furniture shops and department stores. And in 2004, one venue of choice was the Swedish global retailer Ikea.

*Ikea*

Ikea arrived in Shanghai in 1998 and by 2004 the Xujiahui store was the franchise's largest in Asia. In layout, size and basic goods it was identical to Ikea's 200th store that opened in New Haven, Connecticut in autumn 2004. As customers entered the signature blue and yellow big box store, they were immediately guided to the second floor where they followed a floor plan that required that they walk slowly past furniture samples for living rooms, storage units, dining rooms, kitchens, bedrooms and children's furniture. Interspersed, were complete apartments for different demographic groups.[34] In New Haven there were four household prototypes; in Shanghai there were seven. In the United States there were model apartments for a single male, a young unmarried couple, a couple with a three-year-old daughter, and a couple with two teenagers. In Shanghai, there was no prototype of a person living alone but neither was any unit as small as the one for the single American man.[35] In Shanghai

31. All the magazines cited in the footnote above were bought as I systematically viewed customers in four Shanghai bookshops in August 1997. All the magazines I bought were read or purchased during the time of my observations by people who had been reading the magazines, and the one edited by Li was particularly dog-eared.

32. "Pinwei jiating, pinwei shenghuo" cover slogan in *Deco Times*, 16 January 2004.

33. See for example advertisements accessed February 2004: www.artdeco.com for bedding; www.dulcet.com for stereo equipment; www.haier.com for all appliances; www.hangang.com.cn for high quality paint; www.hongda.com.cn for door hardware; www.hukla.de for Danish furniture; www.shjustep.com for flooring; www.shfugao.com for electronic products; www.sodun.net for luxury furnishing; as well as individual designers only some of whom were actually based in Shanghai, such as for example Tai Yun at www.taiyun.com or Rex Chan at www.xalpcc, both of whom claimed to offer sophisticated designs at economical prices.

34. Based on visits and floor plans in the two stores during February, March and December 2004.

35. The studio for the single male was 24 square metres, the smallest unit in Shanghai was 36 square metres for an elderly couple whose only son had moved out but occasionally returned to visit.

there also was no four-person household, but there was an unmarried couple introduced under the same English slogan: "moving in together." Despite these slight differences, the lay-outs of the Shanghai and US stores as well as the choices of furnishings were interchangeable.

Ikea's global promise is to provide customers "affordable solutions for better living,"[36] and in China this slogan translated into targeting households with monthly incomes of 3,350 *yuan*, or roughly US$5,000 per year.[37] In Shanghai where the average annual wage in 2003 was 30,828 *yuan*, and average household size was 2.99 with 1.55 employed persons, households in the top 60 per cent of registered (non-migrant) households qualified as Ikea's target customers even when taking into account the growing income inequality documented in Figures 1 and 2.[38] In Shanghai Ikea has, in fact, already spawned a blue and yellow imitator in the Yuexing furniture mall on the edge of the JingAn district, and Ikea prices for decorating apartments of 45 to 60 square metres of useable space fit within middle-income budgets.[39]

At least as significant for understanding the centrality of the Ikea experience for contemporary consumer culture in Shanghai are the consumer expectations associated with shopping at Ikea. Shopping at Ikea is built around imagining complete domestic interiors and then breaking down the vision into hundreds of individually sold components from screws to sofa beds. Even customers who lack a private bathroom or kitchen can purchase a wooden dish rack or assemble a cupboard and later move them to their future home. The store also has a large cafeteria strategically located on the second floor where shoppers are encouraged to review their notes, discuss their purchases, or simply socialize over Scandinavian fast food and free refills of Italian espresso or brand-name fizzy drinks. It is possible, therefore, for families or young couples to spend an entire day roaming through the cavernous store and buy nothing more than one coca-cola.

Ikea promotes a vision of an ideal ultra-modern home interior that offers sleek European designs but profits by selling the experience – if only temporary – of individualized, personal service. Thus, just as important as the price of the furnishings are the free designer service, delivery of all modular units throughout the city, and, most importantly, a guarantee of satisfaction or money-back refunds. Like much of the post-industrial consumer focused economy, Ikea profits by rationalizing

---

36. http://www.ikea.com, accessed in December 2004.

37. Alexander Brenner, based on interview with the Ikea representative in Beijing, "The Ikea-man cometh," *Institute of Current World Affairs Letter*, 20 January 2004.

38. Per capita monthly income for the middle 20% of the 2003 income distribution averaged 3,150 *yuan*, barely lower than Ikea's 3,350 *yuan* cut-off, and those in the top 40% of the income distribution all fit the Ikea profile. *Shanghai tongji nianjian 2004 (Shanghai Statistical Yearbook, 2004)* (Shanghai: Zhongguo tongji chubanshe, 2004), pp. 99, 102 and 106

39. For example, sofas which were generally the centrepiece in new living rooms cost less than 1,500 *yuan*; sofa beds were under 3,000 *yuan*. By contrast prices in a state store such as Seashore were usually 50% more expensive and, in the eyes of my colleagues, of poorer quality. For Ikea prices, I consulted http://www.ikea.com/ms/zh_CN/virtual_catalogue/main.html. Accessed in December 2004.

individuated experience and services as much as efficient production of material goods. In Shanghai these seemingly ephemeral but deliberately commodified practices systematized for profit are deeply embedded and positively valorized in the contemporary experience of urban consumer culture.

*Consumer Desire and the Life-Course*

The phrases *laosanjie* and *xinsanjie* or "old three" and "new three graduating classes" identify a specific generation with a shared history of hardship. Narrowly it defines those who graduated from junior or senior high school between 1966 and 1968 or junior high school between 1970 and 1972, and were subject to assignment to the countryside after graduation. In terms of birth year, most *laosanjie* were born between 1948 and 1953, *xinsanjie* between 1954 and 1956. Therefore, they were the first generation whose fertility was dictated – and radically restricted – by the one-child policy; they were also the first cohort of state employees to become targets of the massive industrial layoffs that began after 1992. More generally, *laosanjie* and *xinsanjie* refer to all those whose adolescence was stunted by political machinations of *jieji chengfen* (class status) during the Cultural Revolution. Throughout most of the 1980s they represented a lost generation, and much of the early "scar" literature used them as tropes for the brutality of Maoist class struggle and the crushed dreams of youth. Today, the two phrases rarely surface in the public media, but for my respondents in their 40s and 50s, *laosanjie* and *xinsanjie* resonated deeply as they reviewed their life's trajectory or their orientation towards contemporary consumer desires.

Among those who graduated from junior or senior high school between 1966 and 1968, all but two spent many years labouring in the countryside before returning to Shanghai. They delayed marriage until their late 20s or early 30s, did manual work in low wage urban collectives, and crowded into their parents' small apartments with other adult siblings. Even those who did not face rural job assignments and loss of urban *hukou* shared memories of early adulthood as a time of limited horizons and politicized shortages. Because of these experiences, conversation about contemporary purchases – especially about purchases for their homes – spontaneously invoked comparisons to a past when they "had nothing," when they slept on the street to escape summer heat, or when the fumes of the charcoal brazier used to boil drinking water created toxic fumes. Only two of my middle-aged respondents began marriage with a self-contained (*chengtao*) apartment of their own.[40] The others all shared toilets and kitchen facilities with neighbours, and a third began their married lives sharing a room with adult siblings of the wife or husband. Not surprisingly a key parameter of their current narrative of

40. In one case the husband was a PLA officer newly returned from a posting outside Shanghai; in the second, the couple were both on the faculty of a university in Tianjin.

domestic consumption emphasized the pleasures of creating a physically comfortable (*shufu*) home.

The animating consumer desires of these men and women, however, transcended desire for material comfort. Household spending during the 1960s and 1970s had necessitated hoarding coupons and frequent queuing that often resulted in purchase of shoddy goods. Thus, even when they bemoaned high prices or criticized extravagance of a recent purchase, they would spontaneously compare the situation favourably to the past when there had been no choices, when no one dared complain, and all their personal belongings fitted in one suitcase. By contrast, their every day lives of 2004, even for those who were struggling financially, included personal space in which consumer investments gave them repeated pleasure. I quote from an interview with a 50-year-old taxi driver, who had recently remarried.

When I was first divorced, I was still working as a bar tender. But it was no good for my son, so I took the test to become a taxi driver four years ago and I passed. Now I drive a second or third class car, and am off every other day. When I get home I am beat. When I first started with the taxi company, I would come home so exhausted that I would just collapse and lie there looking at the ceiling. When I come home now I want to close out the job and all the pressures, and feel comfortable and restore myself. It is important that I get rest and not drive when I am exhausted ... . [When I decided to remarry] I first knocked out the wall to the veranda, and made a small front bedroom, bought new flooring, paint and furniture. Then I made a dining area so we can all sit down together. My friends laugh at me and say I was extravagant (*tai guofen*) spending too much [for a second marriage], but I did it for myself, and I am happy ... I think back to how we first lived here [in 1979], all eight of us, or I think of my tiring job, and then I am satisfied. (Interviewee No. 23, 21 February 2004)

### Consumer Culture and the Collapse of the Danwei

The *laosanjie* and *xinsanjie* cohorts came of age within the *danwei*-dominated economy of "massified consumption."[41] They began their married lives during the 1980s when urban reforms had not radically changed the material constraints on domestic spending or increased housing choices. They moved to their first apartment – or room – of their own by rising through the housing queue at their place of employment, and only after urban housing reform accelerated did they become home-owners.

In 1992 15 per cent of non-migrant residents had purchased some form of ownership of their homes; by 2002 urban home ownership rates exceeded those in the United States.[42] All the elderly respondents in my

---

41. Hanlong Lu, "To be relatively comfortable in an egalitarian society," in Deborah Davis (ed.), *The Consumer Revolution in Urban China* (Berkeley: University of California Press, 2000), pp. 124–144.

42. Xinhua News Agency, 9 August 2002. In Shanghai 80% of non-migrant residents were homeowners. By comparison in the United States, which has one of the highest levels of home ownership, only 68% of all residential units were owner-occupied in 2003, and this percentage was the highest level in over 100 years. For US census data, see www.calvert-henderson.com/shelter2. Accessed in May 2004.

community sample had purchased their apartments during the mid-1990s when sitting tenants could purchase flats at highly discounted rates. Among the middle-aged respondents, 90 per cent were new homeowners, two-thirds since 2000. Thus at a point in the life cycle when they might have been expected to be reducing purchase of consumer durables, they were in fact focusing almost all their discretionary expenditures on their first homes. Moreover, because new apartments in China continue to be sold with no interior wiring, no floors, no finished walls, often no door frames, consuming for their homes involved extensive amounts of comparative shopping as well as extensive consumeristic conversation with friends and relatives. Again, one central theme of their consuming was the celebration of choice and individuation.

*Davis*: Can you tell me how long it took you to furnish your new apartment?

*Wife*: Months, I spent most of my lunch hour looking at advertisements, visiting showrooms and talking to my friends. After I saw what I liked I would bring my husband to see it, and then we would make a plan. As you see, the result is really ordinary.

*Davis*: I have visited many families in the past two months, and your living room is not at all ordinary. It is very special and beautiful.

*Wife*: Well I did spend a lot of time, it was really a second job and I really know how to save money.

*Husband interrupts*: And also it is important now that you individualize your home. We spent almost three months finishing the apartment, and we both came everyday after to work to inspect it. (Interviewees Nos. 74 and 75, 4 April 2004)

In shopping for every plumbing fixture, appliance and light switch, consumers were also using consumer activity to separate themselves – and their consumer practices – from their place of employment. For the two city employees quoted above, this separation was unalloyed freedom. During my visit to their home, they repeated that no one from their offices lived here, that they saw "no connection" to either of their units, and they took special pleasure in their ability to socialize with only their closest friends and relatives. Others, whose *danwei* had gone bankrupt and who were struggling to find steady employment, could hardly afford to purchase two air-conditioning units, two hot-water heaters and an Ikea model kitchen, but they could – and did – spend weeks, sometimes months shopping for supplies and one or two appliances. For example, one new bride of 30 who had lost her job in a state electronics factory and worked part-time in a private cake shop, explained with relish how she and her new husband spent every weekend for two months biking to various warehouses on the outskirts of Shanghai for floor coverings, paint and spackle. They slept in one room as they renovated the other. After several months, she said "I had the home I wanted; the renovation made us very happy (*kaixin*.)"[43]

Others I interviewed whose units had disappeared felt marooned and thrown back on their inadequate resources. The taxi driver quoted above

43. Interviewee No. 74 on 4 April 2004.

emphasized how in today's world "youth is your only capital. Now I have no capital." However, as illustrated in the quotation above, when asked to talk about what he had purchased recently for his home, he became expansive, and spoke about his acquisitions and improvements with pleasure. Pun Ngai is correct to see stratification, frustration and envy in the acts of consumption. She is also correct that the neo-liberal spin on consumer freedom has served the interest of capital more than labour. Where the conversations with these Shanghai residents refute Pun's equation of consumption with capital's ruse is in their articulation of equally authentic consumer experiences that emphasize choice and personal pleasure against individual memories of political repression and meaningless sacrifice.

### Regret as the Mirror Image of Desire

Desire, choice and celebration inflected my respondents' conversations about their recent purchases and coloured subsequent use or display of the objects in their homes. But expressions of regret and disappointment also ran through their narratives. Returning home after shopping trips to furniture stores or meetings with contractors, people shared explicit regrets, and sometimes I heard a more general malaise and sense of loss that stemmed from consumer purchases that had failed to meet the original expectations. For one friend the colour of the walls did not match her image of the perfect bedroom, but the contractor refused to admit a mix-up and financially it made no sense to repaint. For another, the new floorboards were of lower quality than advertised and the stain was darker than they had imagined. However, by the time they realized the problems, they had paid the contractor and had no energy to pursue him. In 1996, a phone in the bathroom had seemed the height of sophistication. Within a year, cheap cordless models made a mockery of the purchase. On days when business was good, this respondent saw the bathroom phone as a humorous joke; on days when he saw no way to get beyond the red ink on the monthly balance sheets, it mocked his earlier ambition and his disdain for a feckless father. In 1999, other friends spent one-quarter of their renovation money on a colour television; soon after the expiration of the warranty, the picture tube failed. In 2004 watching the news on an older model taken from the bedroom stirred bitterness about the stagnant wages and insecure employment that prohibited replacement of the big-screen Sony that had previously documented their financial success and comfort.[44]

### Conclusion

Focused on the daily experience of Shenzhen factory workers, Pun Ngai describes the consumer revolution in China as the newest "ruse

---

44. From home visits to interviewees No. 20 on 3 April 2004, No. 37 on 28 March 2004, No. 27 on 27 February 1997, No. 50 on 4 March 2004.

of capital … whereby the extraction of surplus value of labor is … suppressed by the overvaluation of consumption and its neoliberal ideologies of self-transformation."[45] For Pun consumption is neither the economist's essential twin of production nor a neutral information system.[46] Rather it is a "new mode of governmentality" that manipulates and exploits individual desire in the service of domination by capital and an alliance of party-state officials and private business owners against the interests of manual labour. My fieldwork in Shanghai confirms the stratified character of consumption practices. However, as I listened to how my respondents placed contemporary home-centred consumption into their longer life histories, I discovered a more reflexive and critical narrative that signified agency and individuation more than manipulation and domination. As Elisabeth Croll observed during the conference, Chinese citizens who for decades subordinated individual preference and desires to conform with the party-state's priorities are particularly likely to understand expanded consumer choices within a larger "re-exercise of agency."

When reporters in *Renmin ribao* (*People's Daily*) praised consumer autonomy, they wrote in the banal rhetoric of marketers and official endorsements of private entrepreneurship and neo-liberal economics. When, however, one listens to consumers themselves reflect on purchases as part of a larger conversation about their leisure time or expectations for the future, the sociological terrain becomes a complex performance space with observable degrees of freedom. Unequal distributions of wealth and income restrict the ability to purchase desired consumer goods and services, and my poorest respondents were explicit about the disappointment – even anger – that they felt when the newest consumer offerings were beyond their reach. For example, the taxi driver who had remarried also noted: "Now in Shanghai we can see everything, but we also know that we can not have it. So in comparison to before we know there is a lot out there, but we can't have it."

Among my interviewees, skilled technical workers in foreign multinationals and white-collar professionals and managers more easily realized the freedoms of consumer choice than wage workers or self-employed service workers. However, it would be a mistake to use unequal access to consumer goods to conclude that consumer culture is nothing more than a ruse or manipulation. Among this cohort of middle-aged Shanghai men and women visited in their homes during the early spring of 2004, personal memories of the exploitative use of class struggle by Maoist elites informed their reaction to contemporary inequalities and emotional investments in consumer culture. Viewing their

45. Pun, "Subsumption or consumption?" p. 469.
46. Mike Featherstone, "Life style and consumer culture," *Theory, Culture and Society*, No.4 (1987), pp. 55–70; Gillette, *Between Mecca and Beijing*; Nicola Green, "How everyday life became virtual," *Journal of Consumer Culture*, Vol. 1 No. 1 (2001), pp. 73–92; Michele Lamont and Virag Molnar, "How blacks use consumption to shape their collective identity," *Journal of Consumer Culture,* Vol. 1 No. 1 (2001), pp. 31–45

current consumer choices against a past of shortage, crowding and bureaucratic controls, respondents of different income levels discussed recent purchases as representing expanded autonomy, even freedom. As a result, even as they openly criticized growing income inequalities, they commented on their consumer activities with pride. These conversations with Shanghai residents therefore illustrate the complexity of consumer culture at the level of individual practice. Consuming for their homes these urban residents have created an intimate sphere through which they make sense of their own life trajectories as well as make claims for a personal realm beyond the reach of the party-state. As Jing Wang has argued in her earlier work on expanded leisure activities in Beijing, urban consumer culture simultaneously incorporates contradictory experiences of emancipation and disempowerment.[47]

47. Jing Wang, "Culture as leisure and culture as capital," *Positions*, Vol. 9, No. 1 (2001), pp. 69–104.

# Glossary of Chinese Terms

The following is a glossary of Chinese terms used in the main text of all articles and research reports. All characters have been supplied by authors.

| Romanization | English equivalent | Chinese characters |
| --- | --- | --- |
| Aidekang | | 爱德康 |
| *Asipilin* | *Aspirin* | 阿司匹林 |
| "Baozha" | "Explode" | 爆炸 |
| Bei Dao | | 北岛 |
| *Beijing wanbao* | *Beijing Evening News* | 北京晚报 |
| biaoxian | expressive | 表现 |
| bobo | bobo | 波 波 |
| boximiya | Bohemia | 波西米亚 |
| bubo | bobo | 布波 |
| bubo jueshi | Sir Bobo | 布波爵士 |
| buerqiaoya | bourgeois | 布尔乔亚 |
| "Bufen tudou jincheng" | "Some potatoes go to the city" | 部分土豆进成 |
| bulaji | frock | 布拉吉 |
| Jackie Chan | | 成龙 |
| Chaoji shichang | Supermarket | 超级市场 |
| Che Qianzi | | 车前子 |
| Chen Cun | | 陈村 |
| Chen Hongxia | | 陈红霞 |
| Chen Kaige | | 陈凯歌 |
| Chen Suojian | | 陈硕坚 |
| chengshi minge | urban folk | 城市民歌 |
| chengtao | self-contained apartment | 成套 |
| chenlie yishu | the art of exhibition | 陈列艺术 |
| chiren de shehui | cannibalistic society | 吃人的社会 |
| *chizi zhi xin* | utter innocence | 赤子之心 |
| Jay Chou (Zhou Jie) | | 周杰伦 |
| Chow Sing-chi (Zhou Xingchi) | Stephen Chow | 周星驰 |

| | | |
|---|---|---|
| chukou | export | 出口 |
| Cui Jian | | 崔建 |
| Dai Jinhua | | 戴锦华 |
| "Daibiao" | "Representative(s)" | 代表 |
| daibiao zuo | "representative work" | 代表作 |
| dakou | | 打口 |
| danwei | work unit | 单位 |
| Daolang | Dolan | 刀郎 |
| dawan'r | high-level managers | 大腕儿 |
| *Dawan'r* | *Big Shot's Funeral* | 大腕 |
| Deng Zhongxia | | 邓仲夏 |
| *Denglimei shizhuang* | *Denglimei Fashion* | 登丽美时装 |
| dianzi yinyue | electronic music | 电子音乐 |
| dixia yinyue | underground sound | 地下音乐 |
| Donghua | | 东华 |
| Dou Wei | | 窦唯 |
| du | | 度 |
| duomeiti jingxiang | multi-media scene box | 多媒体景箱 |
| Erdaoqiao | Döng Kövrük | 二道桥 |
| *Erzi* | *Sons* | 儿子 |
| falun gong | falun gong | 法轮功 |
| fei guanfang | "unofficial" | 非官方 |
| *Feidegao de niao bu luo zai paobukuai de niu de beishan* | *A High-flying Bird Won't Land on the Back of a Slow-moving Cow"* | 飞的高的鸟不落在跑不快的牛的背上 |
| Feng Gong | | 冯巩 |
| Feng Ling | | 枫翎 |
| Feng Xiaogang. | | 冯小刚 |
| fengshui | geomancy | 风水 |
| Fu Chung | | 付狆 |
| Fushun | | 抚顺 |
| ganranli | influence | 感染力 |
| Ge You | | 葛优 |
| Gong Li | | 巩俐 |

| | | |
|---|---|---|
| Gu Cheng | | 顾城 |
| Gu Long | | 古龙 |
| guanfang | "official" | 官方 |
| Gui Xinghua | | 桂兴华 |
| guoying | national | 国营 |
| *Guxiang* | *Hometown* | 故乡 |
| haipai | Shanghai set | 海派 |
| Haizhan bowuguan | Naval War Museum | 海战博物馆 |
| Haizi | | 海子 |
| Han Feng | | 韩枫 |
| "Hao meng yiri you" | "The Day Trip of Your Dreams" | 好梦一日游 |
| *Haojile* | *Very Good* | 好极了 |
| He Yong | | 何勇 |
| Hei Bao | | 黑豹 |
| Hei Dachun | | 黑大春 |
| hesuipian | New Year's film | 贺岁片 |
| Hong Xiuquan | | 洪秀全 |
| Hongdu | | 红都 |
| Hongyan | | 红岩 |
| "hongyang xianlie jingshen, xianshen sihua shiye" | "keep alive the spirit of the former martyrs, devote yourself to the four modernizations enterprise" | 弘扬先烈精神，献身四化事业 |
| Hu Mage | | 胡吗个 |
| Huai'an | | 淮安 |
| Huangpu | | 黄埔 |
| Huayi | | 华谊 |
| Hui lang | Grey Wolf | 灰狼 |
| Humen | | 虎门 |
| *Jiafang yifang* | *Dream Factory* (lit. "Party A, Party B") | 甲方乙方 |
| jian yi shan yi | If we see one, we delete one | 见一删一 |
| Jiang He | | 江河 |
| Jiang Jinrui | | 蒋金锐 |

| | | |
|---|---|---|
| Jiang Yinmei | | 蒋银妹 |
| jianshe | construction | 建设 |
| jieceng | class | 阶层 |
| jieji | class | 阶级 |
| jieji chengfen | class status | 阶级成分 |
| *jietou shizhuang* | street fashion | 街头时装 |
| jingpai | Beijing set | 京派 |
| jinkou | import | 进口 |
| *Jintian* | *Today* | 今天 |
| kaixin | happy | 开心 |
| Kekou kele | Coca Cola | 可口可乐 |
| Kexiao kele | Crazy Cola | 可笑可乐 |
| *Koudai* | | 口袋 |
| kouli | inside the mouth (of the Gansu corridor) | 口里 |
| Kuangren jinianguan | Madman Memorial Hall | 狂人纪念馆 |
| Kwan Chi-Lam | Rosamund Kwan | 关之琳 |
| "Lang zhi he" | "The river of wolves" | 狼之河 |
| laosanjie | "old three" graduating class | 老三届 |
| Laozi | | 老子 |
| Lehaha | | 乐哈哈 |
| Lei Feng | | 雷锋 |
| "Lei Feng de yi tian" | "A day in the life of Lei Feng" | 雷锋的一天 |
| Li Chunling | | 李 春 玲 |
| Li Geng | | 李耕 |
| Li Keyu | | 李克瑜 |
| Li Lianjie | Jet Li | 李连杰 |
| Li Yanping | | 李艳萍 |
| Liangjiang | | 两江 |
| Liang Xiaobin | | 梁小斌 |
| Liao Yiwu | | 廖亦武 |
| Lin Zexu | | 林则徐 |
| Liu Ping | | 刘平 |

| | | |
|---|---|---|
| Liu Xiaogang | | 刘晓刚 |
| Liu Yang | | 刘洋 |
| liumang | hooligan | 流氓 |
| *Liuxing se* | *Fashion Colour* | 流行色 |
| Lo, Vincent Hong Sui | | 罗康瑞 |
| Longhua | | 龙华 |
| Longjing | | 龙井 |
| Lü Bo | | 吕玻 |
| Lu Xun | | 鲁迅 |
| Lü Yan | | 吕燕 |
| Lü Yue | | 吕越 |
| *Lücha* | *Green tea* | 绿茶 |
| luntan | discussion forums, "bulletin boards" (BBS) | 论坛 |
| Luo Yihe | | 骆一禾 |
| Luzhen | | 鲁镇 |
| Ma Jiajue | | 马家爵 |
| Ma Ling | | 马羚 |
| Mang Ke | | 芒克 |
| Mao Dun | | 矛盾 |
| Meng Huan | | 孟欢 |
| menglong shi | Obscure poetry | 朦胧诗 |
| Mi Jiashan | | 米家山 |
| minge | folk song | 民歌 |
| minge yaogun | folk rock | 民歌摇滚 |
| minjian | "popular" | 民间 |
| *Minjing gushi* | *On the Beat* | 民警故事 |
| minyao | folk song | 民谣 |
| minying | private industry | 民营 |
| minzu hun | soul of the people | 民族魂 |
| Momo | | 默默 |
| *Moyang* | *The Look* | 模样 |
| Ning Ying | | 宁瀛 |

| | | |
|---|---|---|
| Niu Qun | | 牛群 |
| nongcun | villages | 农村 |
| nongmin | peasants | 农民 |
| nongye | agriculture | 农业 |
| pailou | memorial arch | 牌楼 |
| Pan Shiyi | | 潘石屹 |
| Peng Li | | 彭莉 |
| personal manifestos | *geren xuanyan* | 个人宣言 |
| Ping Fang | | 平房 |
| pipa | Chinese lute | 琵琶 |
| pizi wenxue | "hoodlum literature" | 痞子文学 |
| Pu Shu | | 朴树 |
| Qi Kang | | 齐康 |
| Qian Kang | | 钱康 |
| Qingxing | Sober | 清醒 |
| qipao | cheongsam | 旗袍 |
| re | fever | 热 |
| *Renren dou you ge xiao bandeng, wo de bu dairu ershiyi shiji* | *Everyone has a Little Wooden Stool, Won't Take Mine to the 21st Century"* | 人人都有个小板凳，我的不带入二十一世纪 |
| Renyu | Half Man Half Fish | 人鱼 |
| "Rongshu xia" | Under the Banyan Tree | 榕树下 |
| ruanxing guanggao | "soft advertisement" (product placement) | 软性广告 |
| sajiao pai | Coquetry School | 撒娇派 |
| san nong | three rural problems | 三农 |
| Shang Du | | 尚都 |
| *Shanghai fushi* | *Shanghai Style* | 上海服饰 |
| *Shanghai shizhuang bao* | *Shanghai Fashion Times* | 上海时装报 |
| shangji | marketing opportunities | 商机 |
| Shaoshan | | 韶山 |
| Shaoxing | | 绍兴 |
| shehui gongzheng | social justice | 社会公正 |
| Shen Haobo | | 沈浩波 |

| | | |
|---|---|---|
| Shen Lihui | | 沈黎晖 |
| Shetou | Tongue | 舌头 |
| Shi Lin | | 史林 |
| *shige luntan* | poetry forums | 诗歌论坛 |
| *Shijie shizhuang zhi yuan* | *Elle* | 世界时装之苑 |
| shikumen | | 石窟门 |
| shimao yuedui | "fashionable bands" | 时髦乐队 |
| *Shimian maifu* | *House of Flying Daggers* | 十面埋伏 |
| *Shizhuang* | *Fashion* | 时装 |
| *Shouji* | *Cell Phone* | 手机 |
| Shu Ting | | 舒婷 |
| shufu | comfortable | 舒服 |
| Shui On | | 瑞安 |
| siban | "dead" exhibitions | 死板 |
| Su Donghai | | 苏东海 |
| suipai | Guangzhou set | 穗派 |
| tai guofen | extravagant | 太过分 |
| Taihe | | 泰和 |
| "Tamen laile" | "They are coming" | 他们来了 |
| Tang chao | Tang Dynasty | 唐朝 |
| Tianma | | 天馬 |
| *Tianxia wuzei* | *A World without Thieves* | 天下无贼 |
| *tiezi* | post | 帖子 |
| tifa | discourse | 提法 |
| tongqian | copper coin | 铜钱 |
| Tsui Hark | | 徐克 |
| tuoli le duiwu | "divorces itself from the [revolutionary] ranks" | 脱离了队伍 |
| Wahaha | | 瓦哈哈 |
| Wan Xia | | 万夏 |
| wan'r | play around | 玩儿 |
| Wang Aiping | | 王爱萍 |
| Wang Di | | 王迪 |

| | | |
|---|---|---|
| Wang Hongjun | | 王宏钧 |
| Louis Wang | | 路易-王 |
| Wang Hai | | 王海 |
| Wang Luobin | | 王洛宾 |
| Wang Shuo | | 王朔 |
| Wangfujing | | 王府井 |
| *wangkan* | web journals | 网刊 |
| *wangluo wenxue* | web literature | 网络文学 |
| *Wanzhu* | *The Troubleshooters* | 玩主 |
| wei zhexue | pseudo-philosophy | 伪哲学 |
| Weihai | | 威海 |
| Weiyuan | | 威远 |
| Wen Hui | | 文慧 |
| wen yi zai dao | literature to convey the Way | 文以载道 |
| wenhua jingji | cultural economy | 文化经济 |
| wenhua re | culture fever | 文化热 |
| Faye Wong (Wang Fei) | | 王菲 |
| Wu Ershan | | 乌尔善 |
| Wu Haiyan | | 吴海燕 |
| Wu Wenguang | | 吴文光 |
| Wuming gaodi | "Nameless highland" | 无名高地 |
| *Wuqi* | *Weapon* | 武器 |
| Xi Chuan | | 西川 |
| xiabanshen | Lower Body | 下半身 |
| xiaceng minzhong | lower level people | 下层民众 |
| xiahai | plunge into the ocean (engage in business) | 下海 |
| *Xiandai fuzhuang* | *Modern Dress* | 现代服装 |
| Xianglin Sao | | 祥林嫂 |
| Xiao He | | 小河 |
| xiaofei zhongchan | consumer middle class | 消费中产 |
| *Xiaoji chuke* | *Chicken coming out of an Egg* | 小鸡出壳 |
| xiaokang | comparatively well-to-do | 小康 |

| | | |
|---|---|---|
| Xiaolong | Little Dragon | 小龙 |
| xiaozi | petty bourgeoisie | 小资 |
| *Xiari nuanyangyang* | *I Love Beijing* | 夏日暖洋洋 |
| Xibaipo | | 西柏坡 |
| Xici hutong | | 西祠胡同 |
| Xie Ye | | 谢烨 |
| *xieshou* | author | 写手 |
| xin chengshi dianying | New Urban Cinema | 新城市电影 |
| xin gongye jinshu | new industrial metal | 新工业金属 |
| xin xin renlei | neo-neo-tribe | 新新人类 |
| xin Zhongguo | new China | 新中国 |
| *Xingfu shiguang* | *Happy times* | 幸福时光 |
| xinsanjie | "new three" graduating class | 新三届 |
| Xintiandi | New Universe | 新天地 |
| xiyinli | attractiveness | 吸引力 |
| *Xiyouji di yibailingyi hui zhi yueguang baohe* | *A Chinese Odyssey* | 西游记第101回之月光宝盒 |
| Xujiahui | | 徐家汇 |
| xungen wenxue | "root-seeking literature" | 寻根文学 |
| Yan Jun | | 颜峻 |
| Yang Li | | 杨黎 |
| Yang Lian | | 杨炼 |
| Yang Zhong | | 杨重 |
| Yao Yuan | | 姚远 |
| Ye Shanghai | | 夜上海 |
| Ye Ying | | 叶滢 |
| *Yecao* | *Wild Grass* | 野草 |
| Yi Sha | | 伊沙 |
| Yili Tequ | | 伊力特曲 |
| Yin Lichuan | | 尹丽川 |
| Ying Da | | 英达 |
| *Yingxiong* | *Hero* | 英雄 |

| Yining | Ghulja | 伊宁 |
|---|---|---|
| You Dali | | 游大力 |
| Yoyo | | 优优 |
| Yu Guan | | 于观 |
| Yu Jian | | 于坚 |
| *Yu mingong yiqi wudao* | *Dancing with Migrant Workers* | 与民工一起舞蹈 |
| yu shijie jiegui | "link up with the tracks of the world" | 与世界接轨 |
| Yuanyang tiandi | Ocean Paradise | 远洋天地 |
| Yuanyang yishu zhongxin | Eastern Modern Art Center | 远洋艺术中心 |
| Yuexing | | 月星 |
| Yuhuatai | | 雨花台 |
| Yun Daiying | | 恽代英 |
| *zaiti* | medium | 载体 |
| zaixian | representational | 再现 |
| Zang Tianshuo | | 臧天朔 |
| Zhai Yongming | | 翟永明 |
| Zhang Chu | | 张楚 |
| Zhang Guoli | | 张国立 |
| Zhang Weiping | | 张伟平 |
| Zhang Xianliang | | 张贤亮 |
| Zhang Xin | | 张欣 |
| Zhang Yimou | | 张艺谋 |
| Zhang Youdai | | 张有待 |
| Zhang Yuan | | 张元 |
| Zhang Zhaoda | Mark Cheung | 张肇达 |
| Zhang Ziyi | | 章子怡 |
| Zhao Ke | | 赵可 |
| *Zhao le* | *For Fun* | 找乐 |
| zhengzhi shuqing shi | political lyricism | 政治抒情诗 |
| zhenshigan | sense of reality | 真实感 |
| zhiguanxing | directly through the senses | 直观性 |
| Zhiqing | sent-down youth | 知青 |

| | | |
|---|---|---|
| zhishifenzi | "intellectual" | 知识分子 |
| zhiye zhongchan | middle class by profession | 职业中产 |
| Zhong Ming | | 钟鸣 |
| Zhongguo bowuguan xiehui | Chinese Museum Association | 中国博物馆协会 |
| *Zhongguo fuzhuang* | *China Garments* | 中国服装 |
| *Zhongguo mingpai shizhuang* | *Chinese Popular Brand Fashion* | 中国名牌时装 |
| Zhongnanhai | | 中南海 |
| Zhongtumen | | 中图门 |
| Zhou Guoping | | 周国屏 |
| Zhou Haiying | | 周海婴 |
| Zhu Tong | | 朱彤 |
| zhuti gongyuan | theme park | 主题公园 |
| ziji dongshou, fengyi zushi | "if you work hard, you will not want for food and clothing" | 自己动手，丰衣足食 |
| *Ziye* | *Midnight* | 子夜 |
| zongtong fu | Presidential Palace | 总统府 |
| *Zoushi de zhuren* | *Missing Master* | 走失的主人 |
| zu | tribe (neo-tribe) | 族 |
| Zu Zhou | | 祖咒 |
| zuguo | motherland | 祖国 |
| *Zuoxiao Zu Zhou zai Di'anmen* | *Zuoxiao Zu Zhou at Di'anmen* | 左小祖咒在地安门 |
| zuqun | tribe (neo-tribe) | 族群 |

# Index